In this prophetic and vital "mu ... [barcode] ... thoroughly shows the eternal an ... has no hope, BUT lament has HOPE from its intrinsic trust and affirmation of God's pervasive sovereignty, and one's faith in HIS creative, ultimate justice. As we rest in Jesus, we know that hope NOW.

Tom Phillips
Billy Graham Evangelistic Association
Vice President, Donor Ministries

Like repentance, the gift and power of lamentation is a topic that needs to surface as soon as possible to begin to activate the body of Christ to prepare for His soon return as our Bridegroom. Pastors and priests, all church leaders especially, will be blessed by reading this solid, passionate plea for lamentation. Judgment begins in the house of God. We are called to bear fruit worthy of repentance to begin to restore the lukewarmness in our churches today. May our Teacher, the Holy Spirit, not only comfort us but also convict us of sin: our worldliness, our shallowness, our attraction to the self, to the flesh, to other idols such as our families and work; our lack of worship songs of lamentation; our fixation with pleasures of this world. The storms are with us; more are coming; it is time to use lament to search through the debris after the storm.

Pastor Jeffrey Daly
National Day of Repentance

Small has captured what God is speaking to prayer movements around the globe that the time has come for the church to lament, weep, wail, and travail in prayer. Every pastor, seminary professor, prayer leader, church worker, and intercessor needs to read this book and make it available to their members and students.

Rev. Sandra Kay Williams
Pastor of Prayer & Women's Ministries
North Cleveland Church of God
& International Prayer Center

This book is a rich treasure for all of us who wish to "go deeper" in the life of prayer. Drawing upon – and honoring – the travail of our sisters in Africa, Doug has researched the depths of Scripture to point us to the need, and the blessing, of offering travailing prayers. This volume is so well-researched and documented. A real "treasure" for those of us who are "ploughing deeply" into the fields of harvest. Each chapter concludes with a thought-provoking Discussion Guide, which is a terrific resource for personal or group reflection.

Sara Ballenger
Capitol Hill Prayer Partners

My understanding about lamenting prayer has been broadened. The scholarly approach for the subject is carefully woven into a readable story. Doug's assessment about the U.S. church being a celebratory gathering is accurate. We have often neglected the second portion of Romans 12:15 *"Rejoice with those who rejoice; mourn with those who mourn."* Thank you, Dr. Doug Small, for bringing perspective into the life of those who follow Jesus.

Dr. Lou Shirey
Director of Clergy Development/WIN Prayer Ministry
International Pentecostal Holiness Church

LAMENT: WHEN PRAYER BECOMES TEARS

P. Douglas Small

Lament: When Prayer Becomes Tears

ISBN: 978-0-9986034-9-0

©Copyright 2019 by P. Douglas Small

Published by Alive Publications
a division of
Alive Ministries: PROJECT PRAY
PO Box 1245
Kannapolis, NC 28082

www.alivepublications.org
www.projectpray.org

This content, in part, was published previously in similar form in
The Praying Church Handbook, Volume IV, by Alive Publications.

Cover Images:
© www.123rf.com/profile_shotsstudio
© www.123rf.com/profile_nata7777

DEDICATION

To the 'Wailing Women' and their peers.

These African immigrants have taken on the burden of intercessory lament, for the United States, of praying for revival and spiritual awakening for the nation. They have been engaged, for some season, through a relatively small group, in 24-7 prayer, often connecting virtually by conference call.

They are truly the forerunners of a movement of passionate, tearful intercessory prayer. It is ironic, perhaps, that God would give America such a gift from Africa and its women. They are travailing for a new nation – a godly nation, a spiritually awakened nation.

May God bless them, keep them, smile upon them and hear their prayers for a spiritual awakening in the nation.

CONTENTS

1. Lament as Prayer...11

Section One: An Old Testament Perspective

2. Finding a Theological Trajectory 29

3. The Voice of Creation 49

4. Restoring Order..67

5. The Nature and Character of Lament.......................85

6. Bold Lament: Brokenness – Standing Up to Oppression........103

7. Lament and Job: Creation's Strange Resolve...........111

Section Two: A New Testament Perspective

8. Lament in the New Testament 127

9. Lament Answered with Resurrection.......................143

10. Modern Western Resistance to Lament 161

11. Intercessory Lament – God's Call Upon the Church Today....179

12. Breaking the Silence...199

13. Grounding Lament in God's Sovereignty 215

Appendix

Appendix 1 – Examples of Lament in Scripture 241

Appendix 2 – A Caution Against Mysticism.................247

FOREWORD

This is a serious book on scriptural prayer with power before God – with the emotion and heart on full display. Many examples spring to life in the passages referenced. Personally I am challenged by the intimacy that I know will come by applying the interactive lament with our heavenly Father. Yet, why do we stuff our thoughts and fear such depth in our prayers? There are some places that can only be expressed through tears – where words are not enough. Are we letting our 'keep it together and fast paced culture' keep us from such honest depth and total forthrightness of lamenting before the LORD? Whether the passion of joy, anguish or pain, take time for the moment rather than rushing past such heights and depths missing the ministry the LORD has hoped for us to absorb. Let's allow ourselves authentic real, true, and pure lament before our Maker – *often*. Here we will find new levels of revelation, hope, power, peace and fulfillment through the greater zeal as we fully express ourselves and receive the Lord's heart in all matters.

Lisa Crump
Vice-President Volunteer Mobilization
and Liaison to Prayer Ministries
National Day of Prayer Task Force

1

Lament as Prayer

In the early 1990s, when Rwanda erupted into tribal warfare between the Hutu and Tutsi peoples, two hundred Tutsis fled to a convent only two-hundred meters from the United Nations peace compound. So close to sanctuary, and yet so far away, they were discovered by the Hutus, rounded up, hacked to death, beheaded, and their bodies tossed into a large pit unceremoniously.

A few years after the national tragedy, spouses, siblings and friends of those who died so ruthlessly returned to the convent and unearthed the remains of their loved ones. As best they could, they identified family members and friends, mostly from fabric remnants of their clothing. They washed the bones and reconfigured the bodies. Then they placed each set of remains in its own coffin which they draped in white and marked with a purple cross. They sought to give these loved ones the dignity that their lives deserved, dignity denied them at their ruthless death.

As they worked at the morbid multi-day task, they prayed and cried, sang and laughed. At the close of each day, they gathered to share memories of their loved ones, talk of their own future lives without those they loved, about the necessity of moving on and letting go, and the critical necessity of forgiveness.

These conversations constituted the emotional burial of their loved ones; it allowed them to bring closure to the way the horrid national nightmare had touched them so personally, and yet, spared them. The memories, the tears, the mutual prayer and sharing sustained them. In the end, they gave a proper burial to those they loved and walked away with new friends and an ongoing conversation of their common painful history. Their sharing of suffering and sorrow, topped by joy and peace, is the essence of *theologia gloria,* a theology of glory.[1]

Why Aren't We Weeping?

We read and sing the psalms and simultaneously ignore them. We might say that we selectively read and sing the psalter. The dominant genre in the collection of Old Testament songs and poems, the writings and litanies is lament. But that is not reflected in either our public or private worship. When we do weep, it is rarely before God as prayer. Hermann Gunkel, who first called attention to the Lament Psalms, called them a critical subcategory in the corporate prayer and hymnbook of Israel, and subsequently, the hymnbook and literature of the church. Why do we avoid these songs of lament used in both the temple and subsequently in the synagogues, as well as the apostolic church? Those psalms are so numerous, so prevalent in the Old Testament songbook that they can hardly be ignored. Yet, they are set aside in favor of more positive faith language, particularly in our contemporary Evangelical-Pentecostal traditions.

While we publicly banish these psalms from corporate worship, we quickly turn to them when we are confused or disappointed. In them, we find ourselves, our life situations, and emotions. From them, we draw language to express our anger, our grief, and our pain. We resonate with these psalms emotionally and spiritually. When we are numb and speechless, we feel with them and use their language to pray through our pain.[2] These laments are not, however, intended only for private personal use. Gunkel[3] proposed two primary categories for the Lament Psalms – individual/personal[4] and communal.[5]

Their form, individual and communal, is basically the same. Personal laments are more divergent; they have greater individuality and a wider range of passions. Among them are confessional laments, judgement laments – imprecations, penitent laments, messianic-royal laments. Personal laments are often very intense, but our wounds are not all personal. They affect families, churches, cities, and at times, nations. Corporate grieving and loss must be processed together – lamenting is both a personal and community prayer practice in scripture.

In the past, funerals were well attended and they provided an opportunity for families, with their friends, to weep over the loss of a loved one. Today, though it is only one measure of our denial, funerals are not as well attended. Increasingly, no funeral takes place. There is no formal grieving process. No transitional ritual. No celebration of life, and more rarely, no contemplation over a life riddled with bad choices – that is really a moment for lament. In today's funeral, everyone goes to heaven! There is no cause to weep – except for momentary loss.

> The violets in the mountains are breaking the rocks.[25]

We have cultivated a worship mood in Evangelical-Pentecostal churches that is triumphal. To sustain this positive, life-on-top-of-the-world corporate worship mood, we only allow a victorious, celebratory worship narrative. Even if lament is appropriate – in light of ongoing war and terrorism, global economic and political changes, challenges that engulf whole nations, issues that threaten our way of life – the one-sided narrative still dominates. The absence of our lament doesn't change reality – it only encourages the stuffing of our pain. It requires that we almost always process lament personally, often alone, and that narrows the corporate worship experience, wrenching it free from the reality of our experience in life. It tends to make worship pseudo, superficial, and fake. It splits it – denying whole and balanced worship. We then worship with our public self, not our private and personal self. Denial only aids avoidance. "Do we imagine," Ron Guengerich asked caustically, "that the church's happy hour on Sunday morning is really a balm in Gilead for those worshippers who live with brokenness and isolation?"[6] Having narrowed worship, we are in danger of missing the opportunity, and responsibility, of ministering more wholly and fully to those who are the victims of the cultural fallout, who come to church wounded or don't come at all.

Buoyant faith is now so highly valued, that, as Guengerich puts it, we cannot seem to admit "limping faith to the circle of champions." In Scripture, faith comes in a variety of conditions – great faith, little faith, increasing faith, weak faith, faith as the grain of a mustard seed, and faith that can move mountains. But, in whatever condition or quantity, it is still faith – and those who show up to worship are the faithful, even if they come to the house of the Lord with a hole in their soul and in tears.

> *A questioning faith is still faith. It is honest, but still hanging on. Such faith needs a place to be confessed and nurtured.*

Our churches are full of people in the midst of pain and loss, but they know with all the hip music and praise dancers that weeping will not be honored. Is the church no longer a place that admits those who weep and mourn? Isn't there a blessing for the mourner promised by Jesus, himself, a word for those who need comfort? (Mt. 5:4) Indeed, it is the first blessing among the beatitudes! At some point in worship, a voice should rise that recognizes those in pain, gives language to their heartache, to which they can say, "Amen!"

One scholar maintains that the idea and practice of lament is foreign, particularly to Pentecostals. In this generation, that is generally true, at least in the West. Here, Pentecostalism, which first flourished among the poor and socially disenfranchised, has experienced, what the late Peter Wagner called, "redemption and lift." A century ago, perhaps as recently as fifty years ago, travail was as common in Pentecostal congregations as were corporate prayer sessions. There were times in which an entire congregation tarried before God in prayer and wept. In such a season, groaning in the Spirit still was a common practice. Travailing prayer was still heard as a part of the Pentecostal tradition and as a shared experience in the Spirit.[7] Often destitute, powerless, in financial deprivation, not a part of the privileged social class – Pentecostals were deeply dependent on God. Prosperity – "redemption and the lift" – has elevated the educational profile of Pentecostal pastors and leaders, as well as laity. In turn, their social status and cultural acceptance has appreciated. With that has come blessing and provision. We now rarely lament. That does not mean that all those among us are without a reason to weep. Where lament is not admitted:

> This leads to dishonesty in peoples' relationship with God. Instead of giving utterance to their negative emotions and experiences with intensity, Pentecostals [as do other believers] try to hide their feelings of rage, pain, suffering, anxiety, fear and revenge from God, thereby putting on a veil of hypocrisy with which they think we are pleasing God.[8]

Laments represent raw honest prayer. We now seem to prefer polished, pretty prayer, which is sadly, also powerless prayer.

In churches of other traditions, typically liturgical, and not dominated by positive praise, the posture of the worshipper is too often stoic. Those churches also foster a form of denial with regard to some untimely death, abuse, divorce, tragedy, or loss. It is as if Western worship, no matter the tradition, has been cut-off from reality. "For the most part," Ron Guengerich charges, "we in the established, privileged church have not learned how to name and grieve the injustice, oppression, and suffering in our midst, in our communities, and in the wider world."[9]

History of Scholarship

Hermann Gunkel, in 1933, called attention to the Biblical genre of lament in the theological community. Lament as a literary genre extends beyond the holy scriptures to include not only the Ancient Near East, but also to Greco-Roman cultures. Gunkel's ground-breaking work pointed out the preponderance of lament in Scripture. This work has been followed by others, but the idea still has not broken through to the mainstream church. It has not been embraced either personally or liturgically. Its theological importance, particularly in Evangelical movements, remains minimal. In a church that pays far too little attention to prayer and has also narrowed it, lament surely seems odd and foreign.

Over one third of the Psalms contain laments.

Some scholars now suggest more than half. These often appear as complaints against God, coupled with a plea for His help – where else can one turn? In times of trouble and loss, disappointment and despair, we turn to the God of salvation, the God who promises to save, who has saved us in the past, and we appeal to his character – save us! Baffled as to why a certain thing happened, confused, perhaps angry, even at God, we pray!

The components in Biblical laments are not static, but they are consistent enough to suggest that "these writers were following an accepted literary convention, as poets frequently do" in culture.[10] Laments are more than mere emotional outbursts of personal pain.

They are not simply spontaneous expressions of bewilderment, puzzlement or a confused complaint formed into a prayer. Often they are well-constructed songs that allow a solitary soul or a community to sing through its pain. The literary construction shows deliberation.[11] Used as a part of an ancient worship liturgy, in each case, they are prayers for God's intervention. Scholars refer to the concept of 'framing' in art, drama and literature. Pictures are 'framed.' Theatrical productions are 'framed' by a stage. Literary works and genres are 'framed' by some distinctive structure that serves to present the vital information – the form of poetry or prose, biography or history, historical fiction or a novel, story or technical journals, dictionaries or encyclopedias, pictorials or guides. Each genre is 'framed' differently. The structure itself implies information, apart from the explicit text.

"Ritualism and sacramentalism, as worship goals, are dead-end roads, but the church still needs rituals and sacraments that enable it to retain continuity with its past history."[12] The position of the reformers was that ritual and sacrament rose from scripture, from the Word. They are a means of proclaiming, of engaging individuals and the church gathered, in the Word.

Dietrich Bonhoeffer asserted that prayer was distinct from all other forms of speech.

We may hope and wish, sigh and generally lament, rejoice and shout, but none may qualify precisely as prayer. They are all natural expressions of the human heart. Praying, however, demands a human-divine interface. In prayer, we speak to God and wait for

His answer. If we sigh, to be a prayer it must be a sigh to God, a groan aimed at heaven. Prayer does have a cathartic dimension, but the heart of prayer is not catharsis, it is communion, and explicitly, communication with God. This God-directed speech is not meant for men. Though others may hear it, such speech is more than a form of self-talk.[13] Spurgeon would say, "One sigh of the soul has more power in it than half an hour's recitation of pretty pious words. Oh for a sob from the soul, or a tear from the heart."[14]

The core elements in individual laments are:

1. An introduction – *the problem* is presented to God.
2. Often with a theme that indicates *the mood* of the petitioner (request, complaint, perhaps thankfulness).
3. And then, the issue at hand, *the cause* of the lament is noted.
4. And finally, there is usually resolve – thanks to God for the hearing or *an expression of confidence* that an answer will come, or a word of praise may be given, and at times, a vow.[15]
5. There is always an *I-Thou-them triad.* "Thou, O Lord," and "'my' – 'enemies.'"
6. The *complaint is* before God, about some issue or problem, some person or people, but it may also be against God.

In lament, we seek justice from God and by God. He alone is Judge. Lament is a buffer against our desire for vengeance. We may feel grossly wronged, criminally violated, a victim of brutal injustice, but rather than act in revenge, in lament, we take the case to heaven. The lamenter does not take vengeance into his own hands. Lament, not violence or revenge, becomes the emotional, psychological outlet. However, the lamenter does envision a God who cares about justice (cf. Psalm 94). The case is brought to God, who cares about his covenant and takes the issue of justice and righteousness seriously. The lament then turns to joy on the anticipation of God's intervention (cf. Psalm 52:6-7).

What is a Lament?

Each lament is unique, but with common elements. Yet, all the common elements do not always appear in every lament, and if they do, the order may vary. Laments are dynamic. The initial address is often truncated, brief, as if formality is cast aside given the urgency. Lament psalms go directly to the point, "O Lord, have mercy!" In doing so, they assume the immediacy of God, even if it seems from the complaint that He is unengaged and distant. The complaint is a charge, a report or a question that engages God, "How long will you hide your face? Why? Will your anger burn forever?" (Psalm 89:46)

Claus Westermann summarizes the structure:

1. Address/Thou ——→ May be Against God
2. The Complaint/Lament ——→ I/We Complain, Confess Guilt Plead Innocence!?
   They/The Enemy did...
3. Reflection – the Past/A Review. Expressions of Trust/Affirmation of Faith in God
4. Petition/Request/Plea for Action and Intervention
5. Motive – Praise is Promised; Help is only in 'You', etc.
6. The Double Wish (Deliver us; Punish them)
7. The Divine Response
8. Vow to Praise[16]

Craig Broyles observes:

A lament psalm relates an experience, so it conveys a narrative. It presents this within a metrical structure, so it is poetry. It asks for something from God, so it is prayer. It pleads a case, so it is argument. It expresses faith, so it is theology. This list is but the beginning.[17]

Scholarship is by nature precise and exacting – and sometimes, as a result, it is rigid and non-emotional. It is blatantly objective. However, the most important aspect of lament is the subjective element. With lament, "it is the mood, purpose, and situation that dictate its presence."[18] The Old Testament lament was not meant to be a static literary device, but a form to convey something very alive and dynamic. Hermann Gunkel, the theological pioneer in the area of lament as prayer, called it "direct address to the Lord about distress."[19] The form is the frame, the lament is the fire – the message.

A Biblical lament is *more* than emotion translated to words. It is more than grief. It may involve a complaint, but it goes beyond that. It is *prayer to God* about the distress, at times laying out the particulars, identifying enemies, though with a rare exception leaving them unnamed (God knows), and then, at times, charging God with inaction – and finally turning to Him in hope. Lament is a legal act, a formal petition, offered in the courtroom of heaven. Its direction is toward God, not an identified enemy, not the evil that is of great concern, not the pain or the problem. It concerns itself with those things, but the face of lament is heavenward. It is a recognition that the world is on its head in some way, order has been toppled, something is amiss, and God must act to right it, because He alone knows what is right and what reorientation looks like.[20] So lament is a petition, it makes a request of God.

Laments seem to be full of doubt, angst, at times rage, even against God. But laments are not *God-denying* language. On the contrary, they are *God-affirming* language revealing *radical* faith.[21] To whom can we turn? Others may have abandoned their faith. Some may have walked away. We have all heard the rationale, "How can I believe in God in a world of senseless suffering?" At times, there are attempts to defend God, to present a reasoned argument in the face of such charges. Lament joins in, not denying, not avoiding, but in full view of the senselessness of it all, and it engages God – authentically, passionately, with throbbing questions, and expectant faith, even if such faith is faint. Lament often comes at the point of desperation when so many questions have overpowered answers. Instead of walking away, denying God and abandoning faith, the faithful turn to lament – it keeps us engaged. It keeps us hanging on to hope.

As we have noted before, the heart of prayer is communion with God. That prayerful, devotional, love relationship, which wants nothing but Him, grants us the right of legal petition and the responsibility of intercession, all wrapped in thanksgiving. Lament is an extension of petition. In a first person posture, the lamenter personally engages God. Some issue has driven him to heaven's courtroom for a personal hearing before God. Such matters cannot be dealt with by proxy or by the power of attorney – the wounded must testify, the disappointment must be told in person, the situation must be described to God by an eyewitness. More impor-

> *Rouse yourself! Why do you sleep, O Lord?...Why do you forget our affliction? (Ps 44:23-24).*

tantly, communion with God, love, provides the context for the lament. It is not a complaint raised from a distance, but heartfelt doubts and confusion voiced from inside the relationship.

A lament brings forward the fragile and vulnerable state of humanity. We feel alone when we cannot see the evident hand of God in our lives. In prosperity, God can be forgotten and self-reliance can triumph. But in some painful, pulsating moment, the human condition is seen for what it really is – dependent, even for its breath, on God. In a lament, the pain is physical. It is measurable and felt – the body thirsts, the bones ache, and the joints are loosened. At times, the lament is combined with an imprecation, desiring not only God's salvation, but also the destruction of some ruthless enemy. This is the "double wish"[22] to which Westermann refers. It is a plea for focused, incisive action by God to deal with some malevolent person or group, who would, given their nature, continue to oppose God's people and purposes if God did not act to stop them and their actions. Interestingly enough, these persons are rarely identified by name – God knows. That allows the lament, as literature, to be more transferable. In any situation, God already knows the names.

Imprecatory prayer seems so foreign to us, as it should. We have been called to love our enemies, and indeed, that is to be the grace-empowered norm. It is the expected posture for New Testament Christians. However, there are times when a person or people have become so toxic, so effective against retarding the spread of the gospel, as an example, of persecuting the church or of capturing the hearts of the next generation and enslaving them, that God must be urged to act for His own purposes. An imprecatory lament, imploring the "double wish," desires God's salvation, but also the destruction of some ruthless enemy. An imprecation is not personal revenge; it is tied to a higher purpose.

> The core of spirituality is prayer![27]

Action is left in the hands of God. At times, the imprecatory prayer is that God would award the enemy with the consequences of their own destructive acts. What they intended, let that be turned back onto them.

Human calamity, in animism and other pagan traditions, is attributed to evil powers, demons, and dark spirits. Surprisingly, and for many a baffling idea, is that in Scripture, the cause of calamity is often assigned to God. This is done to emphasize His sovereignty.

Laments are not directed to the darkness – we do not pray to Satan or his imps. We address our complaints to God.

In this way, lament and praise, complaint and thanks, though they appear at different ends of the continuum, are bound together. God is ultimately responsible; there is nothing outside His control. No dark force qualifies as His peer. None have veto power or the ability to intrude on His determinations. That doesn't mean that there are no complicating factors that presently *appear*, from earth's limited perspective, to challenge His kingship or His will. Sin does that, as does Satan and the spirit of the world, but the Scripture emphasizes the ultimate triumph of God's sovereignty.

Sitz im Leben is a theological term meaning "the setting in life." It speaks of the need to contextualize our faith and worship. Out of what setting in life does this or that threat arise, and to what setting in life should the lament apply? Laments are not the psalms of daily life – they are employed in life-threatening situations (illness, misfortune, conflict, the emergence of some personal enemy or nemesis). At times, a lament is a plea of innocence. As such, it is a query from a sincerely righteous person. In the face of God's sovereignty, it cries out – "Why?" (Psalms 5; 7; 17; 26). Then, there are confessional laments (51; 130). Psalms 78, 81, and 106, express lament as national penitence (as do prayer movements in Ezra 9:9-15; Nehemiah 9:9-38; Daniel 9:4-19). Here you discover the acute language and throbbing mindfulness of sin against God and its consequences. There is repentance and an appeal for forgiveness and grace. There are also edgy laments with curses and requests for God's retribution on enemies (109). And there are laments that resolve in trust and faith (4, 11, 16, 23, 27:1-6, 62, and 131). Psalm 125 is a national song of trust. These faith and trust psalms, Gunkel says, "reformulate the lament psalms and shift their focus to an expression of trust and confidence, so much so, that often the complaint, petition, and certainty of hearing are displaced."[23] The worshipper is distressed, but suddenly and confidently overwhelmed with God's grace, so as to mute the complaint. The declaration of trust is the affirmation that God has heard and will intervene.

When a lament does not resolve, it is often combined with an imprecation which urges divine radical action. Intervention is urgently needed because the situation is overwhelming. God is petitioned to act decisively to remove the supernaturally empowered darkness that has entrenched itself in the land. For some, there is no place in their theology for an imprecatory (judgement) lament to a God of love. But, God's love in Scripture never eclipses or blinds his commitment to justice and righteousness, nor should it in us. There is a legitimate, righteous anger, rising appropriately out of God's holiness, which we seem unwilling to acknowledge. That righteous anger yearns for oppression to cease and for righteousness and justice to flourish, whatever the costs. It refuses the naïve assumption that we can kill all evil with kindness. There are incorrigible hearts. Not every war can be averted by a peace treaty. Not every soul will convert in view of the cross – some rebels will march to hell unchanged. Our reluctance to make use of prayerful imprecations is legitimately rooted in this fact – God alone has the purity to act on such matters. The Hebrew term *naham* is often translated as "vengeance." It means, essentially, to get even or repay in kind. That too easily translates into an eye-for-an-eye judicial system *(lex talionis)*. To avoid that, we lament. The lament embraces the need for justice, for judgement, but commits the matter to the courtroom of heaven. As C. S. Lewis said, "The hardness of God is kinder than the softness of men, and His compulsion is our liberation."[24]

Lament without a call to action by God leaves us without resolve, buried in uncertainty and a sea of negative emotion. Imprecations, that is, calls to God for action, even if they involve some form of judgement, first, must be left with God. Only His heart is pure enough to take such action. As Lewis said, His 'hardness' is kinder than our 'softness.' Second, to ask God for intervention without lament, without tears, reveals a hardness in our hearts. We want balance. One extreme leaves us absorbing the effect of the negative world in which we live, without the prospect of heaven's intervention – and that leads to despair and hopelessness. The other extreme urges God's punitive action too lightly, without compassion, without tears – that leads to vengeance, to callous hearts.

Neither extreme is acceptable – thus, we lament.

Discussion Guide

1. Why aren't we weeping?
2. Discuss the worship style and mood of the Church in light of the idea of lament.
3. Review the core elements of individual laments.
4. Review the relationship between lament and justice.
5. How is lament, with its doubt and anger, a prayer of faith?
6. Define an imprecatory lament.
7. Review the connection between an imprecatory lament and vengeance. Talk about God's role; about justice and mercy; about ultimate authority.

SECTION 1

An Old Testament Perspective

2

Finding a Theological Trajectory

Psalms is a book, a carefully constructed composition. It is not merely a random collection. In fact, the psalms are not one book, but five books. Each, in some way, finds an anchor in the five books of the Pentateuch.[1] The books are different in nature and the differences correspond to one another. The Psalms appear to be a set of companion song books, tied to the synagogue reading and study of each of the first five books of the Bible. The psalms are constructed from Creation through Israel's deliverance, to King David, and to the restoration of the nation following the return from Babylon after the 70 years of captivity. And finally, they offer a forward look toward the Millennial Kingdom.

The first psalm in each of the five books sets the trajectory for the division. The last is a doxology or hymn of praise. The collection is an ideological journey. They point to Christ. "There are more verses quoted in the New Testament from the book of Psalms which contain prophecies about Christ than from any other book of the Old Testament."[2]

- Book 1 contains Psalms 1-41. Most are the compositions of David. They reflect his life and understanding of God. At points, they reach back to Genesis (Psalm 8, 19, 29).
- Book 2 contains Psalms 42-72, written for worship, used in

the tabernacle era and subsequently the temple. They also contain psalms of deliverance, reflecting the book of Exodus.

- Book 3 is comprised of Psalms 73-89, mostly written by Asaph. These were the psalms sung by the temple choirs, liturgical psalms, pointing to God's holiness, calling for reverence, relating to Leviticus. *"Truly God is good to Israel"* (73:1), they begin.

- Book 4 are Psalms 90-106, most of them anonymous, except for Psalm 90 by Moses, and Psalms 101 and 103, by David. These relate to Numbers, Israel in relation to its neighbors.

- Psalms 107-150 constitute Book 5. Fifteen of these psalms are ascribed to David, the 127th to Solomon. These are primarily psalms of praise to God for His Word, reflections in light of Deuteronomy. Thanksgiving is the major theme. Here the perfect sacrifice is faithfulness and obedience to His revealed word and will.

The Jews partnered each section of the psalms with another five book collection, called the *Megillot*, which relates not only to the five divisions in the Psalms, but also to the seasons of the year and the Jewish festivals. This was the backbone of a reading schedule for the temple and synagogue. It guaranteed an annual review by the Jewish people, not only of the Pentateuch and the Psalms, but also of Israel's history.

- The Song of Songs was tied to Genesis and Psalms, Book 1.
- Ruth was tied to Exodus and Psalms, Book 2.
- Lamentations was tied to Leviticus and Psalms, Book 3.
- Ecclesiastes was tied to Numbers and Psalms, Book 4.
- Then Esther was tied to Psalms, Book 5, and to Deuteronomy.

The Psalms were also keyed to the festivals.

- The Passover used Psalms Book 1, the creation, springtime, and the birth of the nation.

- The season of Pentecost was related to Psalms Book 2, new beginnings in the Exodus as well as the first fruit harvest (Ruth).
- The anniversary of the destruction of the first temple at thetime of the Babylonian captivity reached to Psalms Book 3 and was utilized during the Feast of Trumpets and the Day of Atonement. It was related to Lamentations.
- During the Feast of Tabernacles, Psalms Book 4 and Ecclesiastes were used.
- And finally, Psalms, Book 5, was related to redemption in the time of Esther and the Feast of Purim.

The psalms may appear to be a random collection, but they are far from it. They have an order about them, a progression, a certain unity. James Mays asserts that the unifying theme of the psalms is *"Yahweh Malak" – the Lord reigns.*[3] The kingship of Israel's God not only shapes their worship and their praise, but their prayers and laments as well. He is the king above all other kings, the God above all gods. Interestingly enough, laments appear in every section. The point? Our journey dances with opportunities for tears; lament, no matter the season, is never far from us. But lament is not our destination.

> *We may stop for tears, for reorientation and fresh direction, but only momentarily. Lament is not the whole story – despite the tears, the journey continues toward the King. That is the story.*

The Key Psalms

Psalm 1 – Clear, Crisp Categories

Psalm 1 is regarded not only as the first among other psalms, but as the keynote and essential psalm, a kind of prelude to all others. It is a psalm about "the way of the righteous." It is a reflection on two types of persons – one righteous and one wicked. It is, in this sense, the decision psalm. Its inference is covenantal and behavioral – the righteous [one] is blessed (v. 1) and prospers (v. 3). Conversely, as we would expect, the wicked do not prosper (v. 4-5) and have no right to the blessing of the righteous (v. 5). The categories are stark, clearly black and white, with no gray.

In Psalm 1, God is sovereign, in control, and there are clear consequences for disobedience and blessings for those who are godly. God *"watches over the way of the righteous"* (v. 6). This is a Torah psalm, a call to live one's life according to godly revelation. It is not explicitly a Torah psalm as 'law', but implicitly as 'instruction.'[4] Under Yahweh's rule there is a specific way of living, and with the embrace of those rules of life comes blessing. Psalm 1 "is life with Yahweh as king."[5]

The psalm is simple, straightforward, idealistic, black-and-white. How does it then relate to lament? The psalm does not directly address lament, but it is the psalm that sets up all the lament that follows in the psalms. As the first psalm, it stands behind every lament. What should be, is not! The righteous are not always so clearly prosperous (1:3) and the wicked are not always so clearly blown away like the chaff or on an evident path to ruin (1:4, 6). Sometimes it doesn't seem that God is doing as He decreed, 'watching over the way of the righteous' (1:6). So, we lament. Things are not as they should be.

> We live in a world that is beyond our control, and life is in a constant flux of change. So we have a decision to make: keep trying to control a storm that is not going to go away or start learning how to live within the rain.[9]

When things do not go as Psalm 1 so neatly promises, truth becomes muddled and seems bent. Lament then expresses the pain. Doubt has entered. Trust is at times ruptured. The relationship has been disrupted. The blessings promised do not materialize. The wicked seem to be blessed more than the righteous. The lament is the objection, the 'but you said, you promised, we're confused!' (Job 21:7; Psalm 10:13; Jeremiah 12:1; Habakkuk 1:13).

Its intensity is not a mere rousing response to the pain – that would be a mere emotional, cultural, time-and-space-bound response. Lament's intensity is experienced when the petitioner appears *before* God, and weeps, in part, *because* of God. The lament is because of God's inaction, His unfulfilled promises, His character of love and grace contrasted with some overwhelming and mystifying merciless incident, His history of intervention in the face of the present silence.

> **It is a hopeful protest, and yet, a faith-filled plea, through tears, to the one who is our only hope.**

Spurgeon reminds us, "He who prays without fervency does not pray at all."[6]

Psalm 2 – The Raging Nations: War Without

Psalm 2 offers a corporate perspective of lament. It is unmistakably a royal, kingship psalm. Psalm 1 speaks to the individual, setting forth the clean, crisp categories for the righteous and the wicked with resultant consequences. In Psalm 2, we are confronted not only with a wicked individual, but with wicked nations – angry kings and rulers are aligned against God. There, *"the nations rage"* and gather in a global conspiracy against God and His anointed one – the earthly king, David, but also eschatologically, against Christ. What is in view is a

global culture of wickedness that is adversarial to God and righteousness. It can be found in families and businesses, in cities and frater-
nities, in people groups and networks, in corporations and nations.

God has enthroned and installed a human king on the holy hill
of Zion (v. 6). But, the kings of the earth object to both God and
His earthly regent – to His intrusion onto the earth. They gather to
conspire against God's kingdom and His Anointed (v. 2). For us,
caught in the vortex of these God-haters, the force of their animosity
is threatening, severe and intimidating. In contrast, God laughs (v.
4). He declares, in messianic tones, *"You are my son; today I have become your father"* (v. 7). This is not casual. In the face of such opposition, there is an assuring affirmation of the father-child relationship.
This is a huge promise. A true father does not, will not abandon his
son, even in the midst of such international upheaval. The 'child'
may have doubts, so the father, even in the midst of war, pauses to
say with assurance, "You are my son [child]."

Then, there is a statement of the international mission, *"Ask me,"*
pray, *"and I will make the nations your inheritance, the ends of the earth
your possession"* (v. 8). In the face of adversarial threats by kings, God
asserts, *"You will break them with a rod of iron; you will dash them to
pieces like pottery"* (v. 9). And to the pagan kings of the earth, God advises, *"Therefore, you kings, be wise; be warned, you rulers of the earth.
Serve the Lord with fear and celebrate his rule with trembling"* (v. 11).

God will triumph. His purposes will prevail. But in the midst
of the time-space confusion, God wants his kids to be assured that
the relationship is what matters. This messianic psalm, in line with
David's kingship, is the psalm which the early church prayed in Acts
4. When they first experienced persecution by the same powers that
had crucified Christ, they recognized that the oppression they faced
was against something bigger than them. It was against the larger

purposes of God. So they lamented about the threats and persecution and realistically, about their possible death. Christ had been crucified, and for the same global mission they might be required to give their lives. So they prayed out of this personal, yet cosmic framework, asking God to note the opposition and give them greater boldness, and also to manifest Christ with signs following.

You spoke by the Holy Spirit through the mouth of your servant, our father David: "Why do the nations rage and the peoples plot in vain? The kings of the earth rise up and the rulers band together against the Lord and against his anointed one (Acts 4:25-26).

They contextualized the psalm, making it applicable to them, *"Indeed, Herod and Pontius Pilate met together with the Gentiles and the people of Israel in this city to conspire against your holy servant Jesus, whom you anointed"* (v. 27) – not against David, but against Christ. They were living history – what happened then was happening again. What happened there, to David, was happening here and now, in Jerusalem – let God be God. Notice their appeal to sovereignty, *"They [Herod and Pontius Pilate, the Gentiles (nations) and Israel with the residents of Jerusalem] did what your power and will had decided beforehand should happen"* (v. 28).

In their prayer, they doubled down on persistence and tenacity. They would not be intimidated. This is not lament tied to helplessness as it often was in the Old Testament; but to power, to a bouyant boldness, *"Now, Lord, consider their threats and enable your servants to speak your word with great boldness. Stretch out your hand to heal and perform signs and wonders through the name of your holy servant Jesus"* (vv. 29-30). Crucifixion and intensified persecution were possibilities, but so was resurrection. They had witnessed the greatest miracle of all time – and they were emboldened. *"After they prayed, the place where they were meeting was shaken. And they were all filled with the Holy Spirit and spoke the word of God boldly"* (v. 31).

They refused to interpret their pain in a narrow, personal sense. This psalm provides a clue for us to interpret our lives in this larger context, in light of the global mission given to us by Christ and the certain resistance of the world and its governments. The presuppositions here are that nations and kings are predisposed to wickedness. Kings act capriciously and conveniently, and as a result, the nations they lead then come under the influence of evil powers that negate righteousness and persecute the righteous followers of Christ. They stand against even the Lord's anointed. Here, the church, borrowing language from Psalm 2, will not be intimidated. With the resurrection freshly impressed on them, they pray for boldness in the face of ungodly authority.

In Psalm 1, there was the appeal to walk in righteousness – indirectly invoking the principles of the Torah. In Psalm 2, Israel's king, David, was introduced. Thus, you have the authority of Scripture (the Torah) and then of godly office (the king). Wicked men reject the law of God; and wicked kings rail against God's representative throne on the earth. Among the nations, neither the Torah nor the divine Throne were popular. Behind them, stood Yahweh. He had given the law (Mt. Sinai) and also declared, *"I have consecrated My King on Zion, My holy mountain"* (2:6). Psalm 2 is a regal psalm. It infers the revealed law, the way of righteousness; what God gave Israel when they emerged from Egypt. He had not given them

> Let not a libation of tears be the only offering at the shrine of Jesus; let us also rejoice with joy unspeakable. If we have need to lament our sin, how much more to rejoice at our pardon![10]

an earthly king, but rather, first, He gave the law as king. This is the principle that gave rise to our American form of government – the law as king, thus, it is often said, "We are a nation of laws." Every nation *has* laws, but every nation is not "a nation *of* laws." Standing behind our laws was the law of God. This was the model God gave Israel. Later, God reluctantly allowed them to have a king. Unfortunately, their kings were not loyal to the divinely given law. They did not respect the law as the first and rightful king, itself a surrogate for God, and as a result, the nation eventually perished. And in that sense, Psalm 2 is an extension of Psalm 1. David's rule, as the rule of every king, rose out of the covenant, *"So now, kings, be wise; receive instruction, you judges of the earth. Serve the Lord with reverential awe..."* (2:10-11).

So, in Israel, the law was the first king – *Lex Rex*. The earthly king was subject to the divine law, as were all other citizens. He did not, as in other nations, write the laws – that was a prerogative of God. The culture of Israel was not *Rex Lex* – the king or whatever he said was law. Rather, it was God, and in His stead, His law *(Lex)* was king *(Rex)*. The founders of the United States had in view – a nation of law, led by a President, himself subject to law, and a congress that from time to time clarified law, yet, always based on the Constitution and Bill of Rights, on existing law; and finally, a court that ruled when disputes arose, but did not create new law. Note the order again. First, we have Psalm 1, the law, principles of righteousness; then, Psalm 2, Kings, the establishment of authority in office.

In Christ, the 'word' (law) becomes flesh, and the 'glory' of God is revealed (John 1:1, 14; Hebrews 1:1-3; 9:11-15). In Christ, the authority of law and the office of the king came together. He is the righteous King of kings.

So we lament when kings arise and do not lead by righteous principles. We weep when governments oppose God. International agitators see righteousness as chains and rebel to be free from godly restraints. In the face of the global rejection of God and His kingdom and of Christ, we too lament. In the international chaos that results from national rebellion, plots, conspirators, unbridled violence and evil – we lament (Psalm 2:1-3).

Psalm 3

In Psalm 3, David, the king, is fleeing from the wicked conspirator, Absalom, his own son, who has treacherously claimed his kingdom.

Lord, how are they increased that trouble me! Many are they that rise up against me. Many there be who say of my soul, there is no help for him in God (3:1-2).

King David is written off as finished. He is surrounded by traitors, enemies on the inside of his family and supposed friends. The devout doubt that even God can reverse the situation. The glory days of the Davidic kingdom are passed, they conclude. But David prays, *"You, O Lord, are a shield for me; my glory, and the lifter up of my head"* (v. 3). His head is bowed, not merely in reverence, but in shame. He has been humiliated by the attempted coup, from inside his own family and royal administration. Only God can cause him to lift his head again, reversing the shame and restoring honor. And that can only happen out of prayer, *"I cried unto the LORD with my voice, and he heard me out of his holy hill"* (v. 4). The plea is made. The prayer is sent heavenward. The lament is offered, and now, all he can do is trust, *"I laid me down and slept; I awaked; for the Lord sustained me"* (v. 5).

Here, resolution finds its way to peace and trust in God. *"I will not be afraid of ten thousands of people, that have set themselves against me round about"* (v. 6). He is emboldened by prayer. At peace in the middle of a national rebellion and cultural, political chaos, he is confident.

Arise, O Lord; save me, O my God: for you have smitten all my enemies upon the cheek bone; you have broken the teeth of the ungodly. Salvation belongs unto the Lord: your blessing is upon your people (v. 7-8).

"Families," someone has said, "are like fudge – mostly sweet with a few nuts." Absalom lost his head and wrecked his father's kingdom.

Once in a while, right in the middle of an ordinary life, love gives us a fairy tale. David reaped a nightmare. His personal pain was a cause to lament, as family pain is for us.

Psalms 1-3 – Perspective

In Psalm 1, there are crisp categories and consequences – blessing on the righteous; and punishment for the wicked, based on compliance with God's law. In Psalm 2, it is clear that the pagan nations will object, both to the reign of David and even of Yahweh. War is inevitable. There is a battle between good and evil, the righteous and the wicked, over the whole planet. And that obscures the crisp categories in Psalm 1. But in Psalm 3, that battle comes home. It divides Israel, indeed, it divides David's own house, he and his son. These three psalms set the trajectory for the remainder of the psalter – crisp principles of Psalm 1, God's king and kingdom against the objecting outsiders (Psalm 2), and finally, objecting insiders, a war with the wicked within the king's own house (Psalm 3).

> **In Psalms 2 and 3, the crisp edges and the simple formula of Psalm 1 become frazzled.**

The simplicity of linear action and the forthright concept in Psalm 1, 'Obedience equals blessing,' is blurred. Life isn't simple. Yet, Psalm 2 doesn't negate the principle of Psalm 1. It does, however, reveal the challenge to such neat categories by the contesting wicked. Nations are aligned against God and His Kingdom. Earthly kings nonchalantly ignore God and at times seem to roar against the righteous. The dissonance is even felt in our own families with members not committed to the same values (Psalm 3). This is the backdrop of lament. In Psalm 2, there is still a clear them-us, we-they distinction. But in Psalm 3, the enemy is from within, one of our own, and the co-conspirators are brothers. This is when life really gets messy and tears come very easily.

These psalms are keys to the whole psalter. God is present, guiding, blessing, in Psalm 1. In Psalm 2, he is challenged, but unshaken, unmoved. Instead of being seriously threatened by the kings of the earth with all their power and bluster, God is amused. He is seen laughing, unaffected by such human challenges. Then He speaks (v. 5) and the sound of His voice causes dismay and terror. He decrees an affirmation of His Son (v. 7). Mere men will perish, not by great wrath, but by his "little" anger (v. 12).

In Psalm 3, we meet a more difficult challenge, threats to righteousness from within. At first, God appears to be absent, not acting in a saving manner. David implores God to "arise," to become engaged in resolving the crisis (3:7). This is the real world of the psalms and it is our world, where life is not black and white. It is life without crisp and clean edges. It is the world of our lament. The clear principles don't go away, but they are obscured by the messy layers of life. Lament is the search through the debris after some storm. It appeals to God that the lines of right and wrong, good and evil, must not be subsumed by the chaos of life.

Psalms 87-89 – The Kingship Trio

Psalms 87, 88, and 89 are kingship psalms. Psalm 88, the center psalm in this trio, is an individual lament of David, *"O, Lord, God of my salvation, I have cried out day and night before You"* (88:1). David's soul was *"full of trouble"* and he felt that he was near death (88:2). He reminded God of his daily prayers for intervention (88:9, 13). The tone of the psalm is desperate, personal and final, dark and hopeless. It is a dance with death (vv. 3-5, 10-12).

Here again is contrast, as you find between the ideal of Psalm 1, and the raging nations of Psalm 2, and the familial treachery of Psalm 3. The disparity between them is the cause for lament. The idealism of Psalm 1 is juxtaposed against the violence in nations (2) and the family (3). Similarly, the two ideal points of Psalms 87 and 89, are like mountain peaks on either side of the valley of lament in Psalm 88.

Psalm 87

Psalm 87 is bright – a psalm of the city of God, *"His foundation is in the holy mountains,"* and He *"loves the gates of Zion more than all the other dwelling places of Jacob."* He continues, *"Glorious things are spoken of you, O city of God"* (87:1-2). The psalm is poetic, exalting Jerusalem as beloved of God. It is a royal, kingly psalm. The contrast between the settled mood of Psalm 87 and the challenge to Zion's earthly king, David, in Psalm 88, seem worlds apart. But, in the construction of the psalms, they are purposely partnered. Here is the point. What seems settled, indeed, what should be settled, is in this world unsettled, challenged and apparently, at times, unhinged. But that is only the tangled view from 'underneath'. It is not the finished, final word on the matter as seen from heaven.

Psalm 89

Psalm 89 is also a lofty psalm. In it, the mercy of God is to be an everlasting song sung by his people to all generations (89:1).

> ### O, that we would fulfill this call – this is our destiny.

Jerusalem, and now by extension, the church, is to be the singing, exalted nation (people) of God among the nations. God's faithfulness is established in the heavens; his covenant (law, Torah) is with David, whose seed and throne will be established forever (vv. 2-4). The psalm is cosmic, *"The heavens will praise Your wonders, O Lord,"* and also earthy, *"also in the assembly of the holy ones"* (vv. 5-6). God is to be reverenced by all realms. He is incomparable, awesome (v. 7-8). He rules nature and nations (vv. 9-10). Heaven and earth are under His power – as ruler and creator (vv. 11-12). He is omnipotent – His arm is strong, His hand is mighty and exalted (v. 13). Yet, His rule is tempered by mercy and guided by truth (v. 14). His people are blessed – they joyfully walk in the light of his smile (vv. 15-16). God is their strength (v. 17). He favors them and protects them (v. 18).

"I have granted help to a warrior; I have exalted one chosen from the people. I have found David My servant," the psalm declares (89:19-20). He has been *"anointed with sacred oil"* (89:20) and can always expect God's hand to be with him, God's arm to strengthen him, no enemy to afflict him (89:21-22). God will *"love"* and *"exalt"* him, extending his kingdom to the sea. David will call God *"my Father… the rock of my salvation"* and he will become the *"greatest of the kings of the earth"* (89:23-27).

In the end, after all the glowing optimism, the psalm becomes dark.

You [God] have spurned and rejected him [David]; You have become enraged with Your anointed. You have repudiated the covenant… completely dishonored his crown…broken down all his walls…reduced his fortified cities to ruins…made all his enemies rejoice…not let him stand in battle…

And then the lament comes, *"How long, Lord? Will You hide Yourself forever?"* (89:38-46, HCSB).

Psalm 88 – the Messianic Lament Between the Ideals

Between Psalm 87, the great and glorious city, Jerusalem, and Psalm 89, the great king, David, (with the ending of lament) is the despairing Psalm 88, like a valley between two towering mountain peaks. At one level, Psalm 88 is about transparent reality – the other side, the private side of David. But, it points beyond both Jerusalem (87) and David as King (89).

Psalm 89:1-29 is an extraordinary, triumphant, almost utopian psalm, that gives us an idyllic view of David's dynasty, while Psalm 87 presents the unmovable Zion. Between them, you find the incredible and painful lament of Psalm 88. This contrast of calamity and uncertainty; this vision of the incontrovertible ideal and the unstable present reality – this is the disparity that births and drives lament.

> Lord...I cry out before You day and night...my life is near Sheol, I am...
> going down to the Pit...without strength, abandoned among the dead.
> I am like the slain lying in the grave, whom You no longer remember...
> cut off...from Your care...in the darkest places, in the depths. Your
> wrath weighs heavily on me; You have overwhelmed me...distanced my
> friends from me...I am shut in...worn out from crying...Lord, why do
> You reject me?...hide Your face from me? (Psalm 88:1-14).

This is messianic – it is the battle of Christ at Golgotha. He is fighting with the sin of mankind and with death in order to reclaim Jerusalem (Psalm 87) as God's city in the earth and with it the kingly throne (Psalm 89). He will triumph, not David (Psalm 89:39-46). The vision of the coming community is now tied to an unfailing godly king, not David or his seed who failed in covenant keeping, but rather, to the Son of David,

> I have found David My servant [Jesus, the Christ]; with My holy oil I
> have anointed him, with whom My hand will be established; My arm
> also will strengthen him. The enemy will not deceive him, nor the son of
> wickedness afflict him. But I shall crush his adversaries before him, and
> strike those who hate him (89:19-23).

Upon the shoulders of the Son of David, the Messiah, Jesus, the Christ, the government is established for a new community of God-followers. *"He will cry to Me, 'You are my Father, My God, and the rock of my salvation.' I also shall make him My firstborn, the highest of the kings of the earth"* (89:26-27). In him, the covenant is established (89:28). In Christ, the seed of David, David's throne and kingdom finds an extension, and a glorious new regal status, as Christ reigns in exile, from the throne in heaven (89:29). David's descendants, with Gentile believers, are invited to know an altogether different kingdom dynamic from this heavenly throne and this son of David (89:29). The psalm then turns back to the historical David – and in view of the failure of the earthly kingdom (89:46-51), there is a lament, *"How long…will You hide Yourself forever? Will Your wrath burn like fire?"* (89:46). How long will the period of time be between the collapse of David's dynasty, and the resurrection of his line in Christ?

Psalm 89 continues with a testimony of ongoing prayer and dependence on God, but with the end of abandonment, *"I have called upon You every day, O Lord…"* (v. 9). And then comes the teasing question, *"Will You perform wonders for the dead?"* – of course, the messianic answer is, "Yes!" *"Will the departed spirits rise and praise You?"* – again, the answer is, "Yes," but not yet. Not until the resurrection of Christ, and not again, until the second resurrection. And in between, we lament whenever the cross touches our lives.

> We whine about things we have little control over; we lament what we believe ought to be changed.[11]

Our hope is not in Jerusalem below (Psalm 87), but the Jerusalem above (Galatians 4:26). Our hope is not in David, but in the son of David. *"Will Your lovingkindness be declared in the grave, Your faithfulness in Abaddon?"* (88:11) – yes, he preached there to the captives.

"Will Your wonders be made known in the darkness?" (88:12a) – yes, he triumphed over the powers, making a show of them openly. *"And Your righteousness in the land of forgetfulness?"* (88:12b) – yes, God did not leave his soul in hell. He knew no sin and rose from the dead.

Yet, for a brief moment in time, Christ too, felt abandoned, *"I, O Lord, have cried out to You for help, and in the morning my prayer comes before You. O Lord, why do You reject my soul? Why do You hide Your face from me?"* (88:13-14). *"Your burning anger has passed over me"* – He tasted the wrath of God on sin, our sin, and as a result, he tasted the fruit of sin – death.

> **We have a new city, Jerusalem above, and a new king, Jesus – the Christ – and to him we cry when things in the valley go awry.**

We remember, the earth is not a place of righteousness and justice. Cities become corrupt and kings fail – so we lament, we cry out for God's intervention. And we hang our hopes on Christ, God, who came to earth and died in the troubled city of Jerusalem because he cares about us and our world. Lament here, tied to Christ, is not about mere personal pain. It is a struggle for the restoration of God's kingdom and His throne on the earth.

Psalm 90

Psalm 90, which begins the fourth book of psalms, reaches back to Moses. In fact, it is the only psalm of Moses in the psalter. It begins, *"How long?"* continuing the question of Psalm 89:46. *"Lord, You [not Jerusalem] have been our dwelling place in all generations"* (90:1). Before Jerusalem. Before David. Yes, *"before the mountains were born or You gave birth to the earth and the world, even from everlasting to everlasting, You are God"* (v. 2). Here is the call to go back, not only to the pre-monarchial context (David), or to the liberation from Egypt and the sojourn in the wilderness (Moses), but past Creation – to the eternal God. Institutions disappoint. Men fail. Covenants break down. People err and communities grow godless, but there is a God, beyond all and behind all. Go to God, even when He seems to have abandoned you (Psalm 88). In truth, He is never nearer than during your crucible moments. *"Do return, O Lord; how long will it be?...* *O satisfy us in the morning with Your lovingkindness, that we may sing* *for joy and be glad all our days"* (vv. 13-15). Until Jerusalem becomes the joy of the whole earth and Jesus, not merely David, is King – we pray, "Thy kingdom come." Until then, we lament, living in the valley between the unmovable hills of God's certainties.

Summary

The bottom line is this – we praise because *God* reigns. Not David. Not Jerusalem, but Yahweh. "Yahweh's supreme, creation-grounded, nation-transcendent, kingship over all," is the ground of praise.[7]

Psalm 1 is, by implication, a Torah psalm. Yahweh and His law reign. In Psalm 2, we see the global challenge to God's kingship by pagan rulers. In Psalm 3, we are shocked by the internal upheaval of David's household visited on the nation. The goal, however, is not perfect Torah keeping or the establishment by our efforts of a geo-political kingdom (Psalm 2; 87, 89), or yet, a perfectly ordered family or church structure (Psalm 3). Nor is it that we abdicate our role as salt and light, as cultural change agents; or yet, that we dismiss our obligation to cultivate a godly culture in our homes and produce Christ-honoring children. In the midst of our attempts to live out the implications of our faith, we are never to cease praise to God, according to Bruggemann, because "He reigns!" Above the lack of clarity, the fuzziness of life, the international and domestic disorder of our lives – "He reigns!"

Obedience to God's law and its principles are important, but that is not precisely our goal (Mt. 5; 19:17; John 14:15). Rather, it is worship![8] The Father is seeking worshipers (John 4:23; Mt. 22:37). In the world (Psalm 2), and in our homes (Psalm 3), things are not always in the neat categories of righteous and wicked (Psalm 1), obedient and blessed, disobedient and worthy of judgement.

The challenge to righteousness and obedience are fought on dual fronts. We struggle with global tyranny, the macro, and with family dysfunction, the micro. We lament over the global chaos and the 'Absalom' in our family – and that is appropriate, but then, we dry our eyes and we worship. From our worshipful encounters with a holy God, we recalibrate righteousness in our lives. We nurture fractured faith. We are reassured of God's love. We see His glory through our tears.

Discussion Guide

1. Review the idea that the psalms are not one book, but five.
2. How are the five books of Psalms related to the Pentateuch, the historical books and the feasts of Israel?
3. Review Psalm and its ideas – its clear commands, promises and warnings, its crisp categories.
4. Review the global dynamics in Psalm 2, against the background of Psalm 1. What are the implications?
5. Review Psalm 3 against the backdrop of Psalm 1. Again, what are the implications?
6. Consider the primary ideas of Psalm 1-3 in contrast to one another. What is the message?
7. Review the trio of kingship psalms. Again look at their meaning in contrast to one another. What is their message to us?

3

The Voice of Creation

We have seen nations raging against God and frazzled warring families (Psalm 2, 3), both challenges to the clear order between the righteous and the wicked (Psalm 1). We have seen the glory of Jerusalem (Psalm 87), and God's intent that David's throne be established forever (Psalm 89), and in the midst of those ideals the tragic failure of David's dynasty (89:38-45; cf. 30-27), and followed by the messianic hope of restoration (Psalm 87-89).

Psalms 8 and 19 testify to the majesty of God.

Nature, it turns out, is not a passive backdrop for this drama, unaffected by all the dissension.

In both psalms, Creation praises God. In other psalms and in prophetic literature, the land mourns. Creation laments. We quickly reduce this to metaphorical language. In Christian liturgies, the voice of Creation is like a faint choir in the background, if we hear it all.

On an African safari, Barbara and I were camped in a tent by the Zambezi River at the border of Zambia and Zimbabwe. Into the night and early in the morning, the sounds of the jungle, the river, birds and animals melted together. We began to relate the sounds to various instruments in a symphony – the deep tuba-like sounds of the hippos, the flute-like songs of the birds, the trumpeting-trombone blast of a distant elephant, the sounds of frogs and crickets, the rustling of leaves, drums in the distance, the soft flow of the river's current – nature's symphony.

God's Life in Creation

We have considered the earth an 'it,' as inanimate matter, neutral, deaf and dumb, its worth determined only by what we can extract, minerals and jewels, gold and silver, diamonds and sapphires, gas and oil. Even its beauty is often reduced to a backdrop for the human drama. We have seen it as dead, not alive, as non-personal, and yet, as wild and needing to be tamed. In part, that is due to our proper resistance to animism, to nature religions.

Note the views. First, there is the worship of nature and with that, the belief that the earth is our mother, Gaia, the source of our life, apart from the Biblical God. That, we may easily dismiss. Second, in contrast, is the rather stoic view of nature that many Christians now hold, viewing nature as an 'it,' as a mere stage for the human story, but not an actor in that drama. Third, there is another view, the biblical view. Through the eyes of scripture, we discover the earth to be quite alive. We came from it,

> Crying is like a thundershower for the soul. The air feels so wonderful after the rain. Don't think too much. Breathe. Don't be harsh or demanding on yourself. Just experience your feelings and know that your tears are announcing change in your life. Change is coming; like a summer rain – to wash away your pain. Have faith that things are getting better.[1]

and we will return to it (Gen. 3:19). Though, in the truest sense, we are neither from it or headed back to it. The elements of nature that comprise our bodies are from the lively materials on which God left His fingerprints in Creation. On this matter, God impressed a measure of divine life, imprinted His image, and animated mankind with His own breath. We come from Him and, redeemed, we will return to Him. And yet, in man, nature and divinity dance together. The first human, Adam, is from the ground, *adamah*. The creatures, too, are made from *adamah* as is the flora. There is a unity in creation's order, yet, what we hear is a dissonance that is the result of sin. There are bad musicians in the symphony. There are instruments badly out of tune. The discordant music illustrates the struggle of life and death, between merely surviving and thriving.

While the Bible sees nature as alive, nature is not an appropriate object of our worship. Of admiration and inspiration? Yes. Of adoration? No. Rather, as stunning as we find nature in its glory – the sunset or a rainbow; Niagara and Victoria Falls; Alaska and the Alps; the Grand Canyon and the Amazon River basin; New Zealand and the green hills of Scotland; the Rainbow Mountains of China and the Redwoods of California – its beauty in comparison to God is trivial, negligible, minor. So nature, in Scripture, far from competing for our worship, longs to join us in worship to the Creator. Its worship is now repressed, but the day is coming when the earth's muzzle will be removed and *"the mountains and hills will burst in singing"* a song to God, *"the trees of the field will clap their hands"* (Isa. 55:12). The rivers will clap as the mountains sing together for joy (Psa. 98:8). Praise is demanded, and so is testimony.

Were there to be no voice at all, pointing to God as Creator, Jesus said, *"the rocks would cry out"* (Luke 19:40). This is a clear call to neither ignore nature, nor see it as neutral, as Evangelical-Pentecostal praise theology often does.

Cosmic Disorder and Destiny in Creation

While God is distinct from creation, He is not detached from it. Man bears God's image, but nature carries His fingerprints. The impact of the fall of man on creation is reflected in Psalm 93, a royal psalm, where cosmic disorder is seen, *"The Lord reigns, he is robed in majesty... armed with strength"* and we are assured, and need to be assured that *"the world is established, firm and secure"* because God's *"throne was established long ago...from all eternity"* (93:1-2). Nevertheless, *"The seas have lifted up, Lord, the seas have lifted up their voice; the seas have lifted up their pounding waves"* (v. 3). They are misbehaving and out of order. They are violent, pounding the coastlines where men dwell. Ah, but *"mightier than the thunder of the great waters, mightier than the breakers of the sea – the Lord on high is mighty"* (v. 4). Creation has gone mad, and its power is raw and untamable – by men. Here is the disorder of nature, the terrible turbulence in our natural environment. Nature appears conflicted by the sin in its bosom.

Things are not as they were, and they are not as they were intended to be. Psalm 96:11-12, declares, *"Let the heavens rejoice, let the earth be glad; let the sea resound, and all that is in it. Let the fields be jubilant, and everything in them; let all the trees of the forest sing for joy."* And Psalm 19:1 asserts that even now, *"The heavens declare the glory of God; the skies proclaim the work of his hands."* Paul pointed to the witness in nature, despite man's sin and his fall, and the effect on nature. He declares in Romans 1:20,

> For since the creation of the world God's invisible qualities – his eternal power and divine nature – have been clearly seen, being understood from what has been made, so that people are without excuse.

What is nature saying? Psalm 33:5 says, *"...the earth is full of his unfailing love."* When Israel's faithfulness was being disputed, God spoke through Isaiah, declaring, *"The wild animals honor me, the jackals and the owls, because I provide water in the wilderness and streams in the wasteland…"* (43:20). When Israel failed to give God honor, 'wild animals' still honored Him, and when we too fail, in some strange way, the same thing happens.

A dirge (response to death — a funeral) and a lament are not synonymous. A funeral dirge is consumed with grief; a lament turns grief into a hopeful prayer. A funeral dirge can be the occasion of lament, laced with hope — indeed, it should be. A lament always has three characters — the one who laments, God, and others, usually those causing pain.[2] Additional elements often include the questioning of God, "Why?," "How long?" While a lament rehearses some situation, it is more than a rambling account of a problem. It is a prayer, a plea for intervention. In the Old Testament, it is often a distressful complaint/question/appeal directed toward God (a prayer) in order to work change for a real or perceived problem. "Biblical lament is prayer; secular complaint collapses into the meaningless."[3] Lament is the transition out of pain toward promise.

God and the Creatures of Creation

In Genesis, God commanded Noah to build an ark, but strangely not to round up animals and fill it. He was only to bring the animals into it (Gen. 6:19). The animals apparently came, as if on some cue from God Himself, and *"went into the ark to Noah"* (Gen. 7:9). When Elijah was in hiding from the wicked king, Ahab, God commanded ravens to bring him food (1 Kings 17:4-6). Does God talk to animals? He certainly cares about them (Matthew 10:29-31). He feeds sparrows, and when one falls, if no one else notices, He takes note. When judgement was lifted from Nineveh, despite the reluctant obedience of Jonah, 120,000 people were spared, and also, *"many animals"* (Jonah 4:11). The revival spared not only the city, saving human lives, but it prevented the death of animals as well.

When a prophet named Balaam went mad after financial gain and resisted God's arrest, He used the prophet's donkey to speak to him (Numbers 22:28). The dumb ass in the narrative is not only more perceptive than a prophet, but more obedient, more sensitive to God, more accurately articulate – what a message! Balaam was willing to prophesy a lie; the donkey would only tell the truth. Driving his donkey onward to be complicit in his rebellion, the beast "turned aside," seeing an angel. What a fascinating suggestion! Here, an animal perceived angelic presence when a prophet was blind to it. The idea of greater human insensitivity to God than that of animals remains beyond intriguing. It is suggestive of nature's awareness of God and of the spiritual dimension when men are blind to it. In the story of Jonah, another dissonant prophet, the sinful sailors submissively prayed, the wind and waves obeyed, and the 'big fish' became an obedient servant of God sent to swallow the disobedient Jonah and deliver him live to the shore, eventually to obey. Everyone – nature, sinners, and the big fish – obeyed. Only the prophet was in rebellion (Jonah 2:10).

At the birth of Jesus, we imagine animals as present, though the text does not mention them. Since Jesus, the infant, was laid in a feeding trough and thought to be born in a place where animals were kept – we surmise his birth to be attended by animals. Angels certainly sang to shepherds in the fields (Luke 2:8) who were watching sheep. Creation and incarnation connect the animal world to God. In Genesis, we see God creating the animal world, parading them before Adam, who names them. Around the throne, in heaven, are four living creatures, strangely different and yet strangely like earth's creatures – an eagle, an ox, a lion, and a man. They sing and praise, and seem attached to the throne (Rev. 5:14; 19:4). God has a connection with nature's creatures. And they are represented around His throne.

The Death of Innocence

It has been suggested that animals have a kind of neutrality, an innocence about them, left vulnerable to man's justice. Our sin affects them. They were under the dominion of Adam, and when his regime collapsed, they were made victims.

When God revealed the tabernacle in heaven to Moses and ordered a replica built on the earth, he then instructed Moses to institute the sacrificial system. That mandated the sacrifice of animals at the occurrence of any human sin, as well as the collective, corporate sin of the nation. It pointed, of course, prophetically, to our killing, by our sin, the innocent Lamb of God, Jesus, the Christ. It also pointed out, quite graphically, how human sin negatively affects the creatures, who under our dominion, should be under our protection. Sin is not private – somehow, in a mysterious way we cannot understand, it affects the whole of our ecosystem, as well as the animal kingdom and it does so more directly than we realize. Innocent animals suffered with and because of the sin of men in the sacrificial system.

Hosea lamented, *"Cursing, lying, murder, stealing, and adultery are rampant; one act of bloodshed follows another. For this reason, the land mourns..."* Creation laments – when such sin is committed by the race of men, *"and everyone who lives in it languishes, along with the wild animals and the birds of the sky; even the fish of the sea disappear"* (Hosea 4:2-3).

The word mourn means to 'cause lamentation.' The effect is that everyone and everything languishes – *amal,* meaning to be weak, to fail, to decay, to fade, to wither. Sin's affect is pervasive. We rarely connect nature's failings to sin, but the Bible frequently does. Jeremiah laments, not merely over the sin of the nation, but also over its effect on nature.

> *I will weep and mourn for the grasslands on the mountains, I will sing a mournful song for the pastures in the wilderness because they are so scorched no one travels through them. The sound of livestock is no longer heard there. Even the birds in the sky and the wild animals in the fields have fled and are gone* (9:10 NET).

Our modern world rarely sees that sin impacts creation, the land and its animals. We allow no such connection having been desensitized by our naturalism and rationalism in a spiritually stripped-down world.

In Jeremiah 11, the lamenting prophet is told that tears and lament will not abate the coming judgement. *"A conspiracy...among the men of Judah and among the inhabitants of Jerusalem"* have turned the nation *"back to the iniquities of their ancestors...they have gone after other gods"* and the covenant is broken (Jeremiah 11:9-10). Disaster is coming, and lament will not save the city or the nation. A metaphor of the coming judgement follows. It will be like a noisy fire on a beautiful green olive tree (v. 16), made worthless. The plots against the innocent prophet, Jeremiah, are *"like a gentle lamb led to the slaughter,"* the destruction of *"the tree with its fruit"* (vv. 18-19). Here, in the imagery, the violent sin aimed at the innocent man affects trees and animals.

The Languishing and Lamenting Land

God not only cares about us, he also cares about His creation, also about the land itself.

He protects it – from sin. His commitment to the land is so unmistakable that He exiled His sinful and rebellious people from the land. He had merely loaned it to them, and He had declared it sacred, which demanded that they live in congruence with its sacred nature. When their sins accumulated, He protected the land by exiling sinful humanity. He did so, according to the Biblical record, to allow the defiled land to rest. Israel was not practicing an appropriate and sacred stewardship of the land, so God heard the land mourning, and He acted to protect it.

In the ancient world, man labored, tilling the soil, and the soil labored as well, yielding fruit. In God's scheme, both man and the land needed periodic rest, so he designed a calendar that called for an agricultural vacation every seven years (Lev. 25). Man would rest and renew his relationship with God, and the land would be allowed to rest. Nature and man, worship and renewal are conjoined here with domesticated and wild animals. When Israel refused to care for their own souls, when they relentlessly plowed and planted to fill up their barns and they abused Creation, specifically, the land, God ordered the rest needed by the land. He collected the debt of Israel's neglected Sabbath years during the exile, "...*the land will rest and enjoy its Sabbaths*" (Lev. 26:34; 2 Chron. 36:21).

Don't miss the point. In Scripture, Creation is endowed with a kind of consciousness, a sacredness, a desire to glorify God and to host a holy, worshipping people. According to the prophets, the response of the land when its inhabitants sin is to mourn, to grieve and to languish (Hosea 4:3; Joel 1:10; Isaiah 39:9). When people repent and return to God, the land, wounded by sin, is healed (2 Chron. 7:14).

Sin is not merely personal. It has ecological consequences. Redemption is not narrowly personal either. It is restorative, even to nature. In Joshua 14:15, when the wars of the tribal conquest were over, "...*the land had rest from war.*" A godly people had settled on the land, idolatry and pagan practices would soon be banished – so the land rested. Idolatry and murder are not mere social disturbances; they are spiritual and moral, incongruent, so they wake up nature's wrath. They unsettle the planet. The land mourns. The lament of nature is a message to which we are essentially deaf. Even in conservative Christian circles, the idea of God's voice, of the earth's rumbling discontent with its unrighteous residents, is ignored.

Corporate Laments

Biblical laments were not merely individuals struggling with their faith or some life crisis. These were psalms in the hymnbook of God's people, designed to be sung corporately.[4]

Paul Wayne Ferris identifies the following Psalms as communal laments in his study of the genre: Psalms 31, 35, 42-44, 56, 59, 60, 69, 74, 77, 79-80, 83, 85, 89, 94, 102, 109, 137, 142.[5] Anderson identifies communal laments as 12, 14, 58, 60, 74, 79-80, 83, 85, 90, 94, 123, 126, 129.[6] Bellinger also identifies 44, 53, 106, 108.[7] Of these, there is a general consensus, as Bouzard argues, that the following are clearly communal laments: Psalms 44, 60, 74, 79, 80, 83, 85, 89.[8]

Taking these lists together, potential communal laments include: 12, 14, 31, 35, 42-44, 53, 56, 58, 59, 60, 69, 74, 77, 79-80, 83, 85, 89, 90, 94, 102, 106, 108, 109, 123, 126, 129, 137, 142. This is a massive amount of worship material, virtually overlooked. This should inform our worship, but it does not.

The God Who Hides

In Psalm 104, God is seen wrapped up with the sky as an umbrella, taking a walk through his world. He rides on the clouds and walks on the wind. Lightning is a messenger for him (vv. 1-4). He is the Creator and sustainer of life (v. 5) and He continues to speak to the waters and as He does, they flee (v. 7). The mountains rise and fall at the sound of his voice (v. 8). He checks on the mountain springs and creeks (v. 10) and waters, both wild and domesticated animals (v. 11). He notices the birds that are using the springs and nesting in the nearby foliage (v. 12). This is His 'labor' (v. 13). The Creator is still a blue-collar God, doing maintenance work in the earth, watering the mountains and causing grass to grow for the cattle. The Hebrew terms here show the direct action of God (v. 14).

Man may plow and plant, but God produces the food. The nests of birds and the homes of the goats in the high mountains are on His conservation route (vv. 17-18). The moon and sun are within His reach (vv. 18-19). He works during the day and the night shift when the animals stir (vv. 20-21). He watches men rise and go to work (v. 23). The sea is full, *"teeming with creatures beyond number,"* large and small, that He made. They, not only man, are 'His creatures' (vv. 24-25). All the sea creatures *"wait"* for God *"to give them their food at the right time… they gather it,"* eating from the open hand of God (v. 28). When God hides, *"they are terrified"* (v. 29).

Here again, we meet greater sensitivity in nature than we do in man. Nature notices God's hiddenness. Nature and its creatures wait for God and depend on Him. They feed from His hand. His desire is not to be hidden or cause terror, rather, it is for Creation to *"rejoice in His works"* (v. 31). His glory is awesome. He merely looks *"at the earth, and it trembles; He touches the mountains, and they pour out smoke"* (v. 32).

The penultimate place for which man was created is praise.

"I will sing to the Lord all my life; I will sing praise to my God while I live...I will rejoice in the Lord" (vv. 33-34). The problem is that appropriate praise is being prevented by sin. Both the condition of sin itself and a people disposed to sin, compromised by it, find praise muffled in their hearts. The consequence is the hiddenness of God. Not only does sin obscure our view of God, deaden our capacity to sense and know him, but it offends God. It places tension in the relationship and disrupts it. But here, another consequence is seen and it is compelling. Sin affects creation; it diminishes creation's worship, whereas praise reflects and magnifies God's order. The prayer that follows is an imprecation: *"May sinners vanish from the earth and wicked people be no more"* (v. 35). It is the only means to restore order. Until sin vanishes, nature mourns.

Man was given dominion over every living thing at creation (Gen. 1:26). It was a stewardship role, a partnership with God, who retained sovereignty over all (Col. 1:16; Rom. 11:36; Heb. 2:10). After the flood, from which God saved animals along with humans, He reiterated man's stewardship role. Here is the triangle again – God, man, Creation (land and creatures). We split off Creation. We ignore it, disregarding either our obligation to nature or its connection to God. After the fall and the flood, the span of a human life on the earth became fleeting, short, brief. *"A generation comes and a generation goes, but the earth remains the same through the ages"* (Ecc. 1:4).

Creation continues, man comes and goes, but the earth, the land, provides a home for the generations. In some strange way, nature seems to also witness our seasons of apostasy and renewal. It suffers and rejoices, languishes and then experiences renewal with us.

Creation's Legal Claim Against Sinful Man

Creation, according to Scripture, has a legal claim against us before heaven – for the crimes we have committed and the deadly consequences, the damages they have done to nature as a result. Because of these sins and crimes, *"...people must bear their guilt"* (Isa. 24:6). Creation, the land, the creatures under Adam's dominion, and subsequently, under the dominion of fallen mankind were all innocent. The legal claim has not yet been settled. The matter is still pending in God's courtroom. In the interim, as God calls men to repentance, He cares for creation, He does what man should have done – He is a God of mercy who will not allow the innocent to suffer maliciously. This is one of the key complaints in a lament, the suffering of the innocent.

While man charges God with negligence, God does man's chores and feeds the animals, serving as nature's maintenance man. But God will, at some point in time, enforce a fine against humanity for its sins against nature, *"Therefore earth's inhabitants are burned up, and very few are left"* (Isa. 24:4-6).

In John's Revelation of Christ and last day's events (11:18), one verse is often overlooked. It is the moment of God's wrath, *"The nations were angry, and your wrath has come"* – this reaches back to Psalm 2. It is God's answer to the persistent global conspiracy of kings. It is His answer to the absence of corporate repentance. Not individual remorse, but the national-global consciousness of offending God and the refusal to change. Nations are accountable to God, not only for their own souls, but for the moral trajectory of those they lead. It is a 'time for judging and rewarding.'

Those who revere the Lord's name and serve Him are rewarded. The time has also come – notice the line *"...for destroying those who destroy the earth."* The earth is neither to be mistreated, ignored, nor yet, worshipped. It longs to join the worship. This becomes the background of Paul's note, that *"creation groans"* because it too is enslaved by corruption due to sin. Thus, Creation not only praises, it also laments:

> ...*creation itself also will be set free from its slavery to corruption into the freedom of the glory of the children of God. For we know that the whole creation groans and suffers the pains of childbirth together until now* (Romans 8:22-23).

Creation – Mentoring Lamenters

Creation and its creatures rarely make it into any discussion on lament. We'll consider Job, the book so given to the lament of one man later, but for a moment, let's look at how the lament of Job is resolved. At the end of Job's lament, God conducts a guided tour of creation and of earth's creatures to help Job resolve his own lament. God instructs Job,

> *Ask the animals, and they will teach you, or the birds in the sky, and they will tell you; or speak to the earth, and it will teach you, or let the fish in the sea inform you"* (Job 12:7-8). *"They all know...* (v. 9).

The answer and resolve to Job's lament comes with this parade of earth's creatures. It is reminiscent of God parading the animals before Adam to test his discernment, to see what he would name them (Gen 2:19). The animals know what Job and other humans do not know. Creation groans, with the Spirit, for redemption – but man is silent (Rom 8:22). Job's answer is not in a theology or philosophy lesson. Insight is seen in the simple way God helps animals, provides for them, watches over them, despite their creaturely limitations. *"Brace yourself...I have some questions for you,"* God challenges Job. *"You have been asking me, now you must answer"* (38:3). In Job, the resolve to lament is not in questioning God, but the openness to discovery in the revelation of the God in nature.

God Points Job Back to Creation

As you read Job 38-40, you will find yourself gripped with a stunning survey of the earth and the universe, in poetic form – the foundations (38:4), the stars (v. 7), and the sea (v. 8). God reveals the larger order in the midst of micro chaos, the bigger picture against which Job's personal catastrophe is minuscule. Despite evil, order still remains. The cosmic God cannot be measured by His presence or absence in some personal life situation at some fleeting moment – there is a bigger picture.

In our faith in the sovereignty of God, we find rest and resolve to our laments – and that is attached to our theology of creation. God is in control when things seem otherwise. In Job 40, He claims a sovereign connection over the sphere of the animal kingdom – wild goats and deer, the wild donkeys and the ox. Each creature is characterized by strengths and weaknesses, and the lesson is: so is man. And yet, God delights in them all. He watches over and cares for them all.

When Job sees God's hand in nature, in care and provision, for animals who would otherwise perish, he repents before God's sovereignty (Job 42:6). The care and attention of God to the magnificent and the mighty, as well as the disdained and the devalued is so obvious, and yet obscured by Job's own hurt and pain. Here he is being re-centered. One of the reasons the view of nature is so helpful in re-centering us is that before it, we seem small and powerless. Who can fight off a lion or survive an encounter with a hippo? Who wants to swim with Leviathan? Who can stay on his feet in the swirling whirlwind? God rides His chariot through the fierce storm. Nature humbles us; and if creation humbles us, how much more should we exhibit humility before the Creator?

God Calls Job to Humility

The process of Job's re-centering begins in his humility before creation and its creatures, but the final re-centering is before the Sovereign God, the Creator and Sustainer of all life, Himself. Notice Job's resolve in humility, *"It is I – and I was talking about things I knew nothing about, things far too wonderful for me"* (v. 3). He confesses, *"I*

*had only heard about you before, but now I have seen you with my own
eyes. I take back everything I said, and I sit in dust and ashes to show my
repentance"* (vv. 5-6).

> **In the end, his lament turns to praise, as
> does every healthy lament. And then it moves
> to intercession and reconciliation (Job 42:10f).**

Creation Worshipping

One of the features of animals is that they play – and their play
is instructive to us. God formed Leviathan *"to play"* in the sea (Psalm
104:26). Animals play – dogs and cats, calves and colts, squirrels
and dolphins. As children, we play and laugh; but as adults, we lose
our capacity for play. Interestingly, the same Hebrew word for play
that describes Leviathan is used of David, when the ark was being
returned to Jerusalem (2 Samuel 6:21). It can mean – *ecstatic.* David
playfully worshipped. He didn't play at worship, but he worshipped
with joy! He was ecstatic that the ark was finally in Jerusalem. Watching our children enjoy animals is also a clue that God, our Father,
enjoys them as well. And he enjoys us. The Westminster Catechism
says, "The chief end of man is to glorify God by enjoying Him forever." Worship is never to be rote or regimental and without joy.
Lament cannot be allowed to drown worship and put out the fire of
joy. We lament, Westermann says, to return to praise.

> **We lament that we are not praising God
> as we should, that life has so overwhelmed us
> and that it has diminished our praise.**

In Psalm 148, everything is to praise the Lord – the creatures of
the sea, beasts and cattle, birds and creepy-crawly things – everything

(vv. 7, 10). The climax is, *"Let everything that has breath praise the Lord. Praise the Lord!"* (Ps. 150:6). Lament is not a narrow personal thing. It is the gateway, not only to restoration, but to the restoration of all things – to nature and animals and mankind joining in one glorious symphony of praise to God. Creation is groaning – lamenting. But it is also rejoicing through its tears, marching through its seasons, continuing to 'play' and glorifying God in the midst of chaos.

Discussion Guide

1. Wrestle with the idea of creation as alive unto God.

2. How do we admit the idea of nature as alive and not cross the threshold into animism?

3. What is the evidence that creation, despite the fall, continues its relationship with the Creator?

4. Is it possible that Creation be more aware of the sin of man, than man himself?

5. Review the abundance of corporate laments. Have we under-emphasized lament? What is the implication of such a large volume of prayer materials?

6. How have you experienced the hiddenness of God?

7. How does Creation have a legal claim against humanity? How can it mentor us in lament?

4

Restoring Order

P salm 22, messianic in nature, contains the cry of dereliction, *"My God, my God, why have You forsaken me? Why are You so far from my deliverance and from my words of groaning?"* This is the lament of God-forsakenness used by Jesus on the cross. It is his lament. Surprisingly, the psalm is also filled with beastly metaphors. Here is nature again, metaphorically, at the cross, *"Many bulls surround me; strong ones...encircle me"* (v. 13). It is as if, with the angry men that encircled Christ, nature too, was incited against him. Lions are said to be mauling him and roaring with open mouths against him (v. 13). The bulls surround and gore, the lions roar and maul and pull his bones apart (v. 14), and finally the *"dogs have surrounded"* him. His hands and feet are pierced, and his garments divided (vv. 15-18). Creation then, Psalm 22 claims, was present at the cross – not merely Jewish leaders and Roman soldiers. At Golgotha, Jesus died, not only for mankind, but to redeem Creation from its curse and to ultimately restore order to the earth itself.

There is a note that does not appear in all translations at the beginning of Psalm 22, a note for the choir director. The psalm is to be sung *"according to 'The Deer of the Dawn.'"* The meaning of that note is a mystery. Some say the meaning is that Psalm 22 is to be played at *"the strength of the morning,"* at dawn, when the deer stir and seek water and food. Isaiah 14 may contain a clue. It is a proverb against the King of Babylon (v. 4). *"The whole earth is at rest, and is quiet: they [the trees] break forth into singing"* (v. 7). The Chaldeans had little regard for land or nature. They stripped the lands they conquered bare, cutting down trees in a forest wholesale, not with a purposeful use in mind, but as a senseless act of devastation. The Persians had more respect for nature. With the change of empires from Chaldean to Persian rule, the trees were said to rejoice. Babylon's demise meant they would not be spared an ecological disaster, *"…the fir trees rejoice at thee, and the cedars of Lebanon, saying, 'Since thou art laid down, no feller is come up against us'"* (v. 8). God has acted and 'laid down' the king of Babylon, and as a result, the trees will not be 'laid down.' 'No feller' of trees will destroy them, so nature rejoices. Nature is not neutral, not unaware of the degree of malevolence in the heart of its conquerors. What a fascinating idea!

So, if we understand the mysterious note to the choir director, the tune of Psalm 22 is one of redemption, of the changing of the guards, of the fall of Babylon, of the sparing not only of the souls of men, but an ecological redemptive act as well. *"The wolf will live with the lamb, the leopard will lie down with the goat, the calf and the lion and the yearling together; and a little child will lead them"* (Isa 11:6).

Nature is now groaning, living in an atmosphere of aggression, the survival of the fittest, but that does not reflect the peace of creation's original order. It wants to be free, again, from the curse. In intercession, there is a sense in which we join nature. In praise, we express its joy and exuberance. In faith, we see it, as well, rejoicing and free.

Psalm 29 – Another Creation Motif

Psalm 29 is another Creation motif, describing the troubled waters on the earth (vv. 3, 10). Notice God's way of dealing with the dissonance.

*The voice of the Lord is over the waters; the God of glory thunders...
over the mighty waters. The voice of the Lord is powerful...majestic...
breaking the cedars...making the hills of Lebanon leap...The voice of
the Lord strikes with flashes of lightning...shaking the desert...stripping
the forests bare (29:3-9).*

Penitential Laments

There are seven penitential laments (6, 32, 38, 51, 102, 130, 143). These are sometimes combined with Psalms 5, 7, 39, and 44. There are individual and corporate laments, differing pastoral theologies of "lament" by Christian commentators. The dictum is often quoted, "tell me how you lament, and I will tell you who you are." In lament, with the mask removed, one is more deeply revealed.[1]

St. Basil the Great urged, "Weep over your sin: it is a spiritual ailment; it is death to your immortal soul; it deserves ceaseless, unending weeping and crying; let all tears flow for it, and sighing come forth without ceasing from the depths of your heart."[2] The great leader confessed that he wept for his sins, "voluntary and involuntary, conscious and unconscious, covert and overt, great and little, committed by word and deed, in thought and intention, day and night, at every hour and minute of my life."[3] This is life lived in the mode of reset, of repentance, about the insidious sins of pride, ambition, self-preoccupation. These individual laments, C. A. Vos says, "are rightly known as the backbone of the Psalter."[4]

God is not silent. He is speaking. His voice is 'over the waters.' This is God's interaction with creation at another level. Here we find an affirmation of 'His Word.' His voice is revealed as sovereign, as powerful and majestic, in the middle of primordial chaos. It is more powerful than the natural storm. It is more important than a momentary, miraculous, but narrow fix.

That means that God's 'peace be still,' uttered through Christ over the stormy waters was not an erratic exception. God continues to speak into the stormy chaos. Though we often fail to hear His voice, nature hears and obeys. Thus we are to, *"Ascribe to the Lord the glory due his name...worship the Lord in the splendor of his holiness...And in his temple all cry, 'Glory!'"* (vv. 2, 9b). There may be a flood, disorder, seeming chaos, a reason to lament and fear, but the assurance comes, *"The Lord sits enthroned over the flood...enthroned as King forever"* (v. 10), and though He may not make a given storm disappear, *"The Lord gives strength to his people; the Lord blesses his people with peace"* (v. 11), even in the midst of some storm. Thus, we cry, in the temple, in our gatherings, "Glory!" Christoph Blumhardt asserted, "God can well hear the sighs of everyone, even the foolish; yet, in reality, only those can pray who listen to God."[5] Lament may begin with our concern that God hear us, but it must find its resolve in our willingness to hear Him.

We lament in the face of Creation gone mad – tsunamis, hurricanes, tornadoes, floods and droughts, pestilence and disease. Something in us revolts at the sight of disorder and disaster. We display passion in the face of earth's victims after a ravaging episode of nature's wrath. In such moments, the denial of God is common, "If there was a God, why this?" Or, "How can I believe in a God who would..." At times, we hint at faith, "Our prayers are with you," which today, sadly means little more than a wish for better times. We believe and disbelieve. We want to pray, but how can we? To whom do we pray, when God allowed all this?

On one hand God is excused – He is not responsible. Certainly He did not do 'this' – whatever the nature of the tragedy. Having released Him from culpability, we simultaneously de-God Him, stripping Him of sovereignty. We argue, "God did not do 'this.' He could not stop it. He too, at the cross, is a victim." On the other hand, we attribute the incident directly to Him, without introducing the mediating problem of sin and its consequences that have made nature schizophrenic. There is now a wild card in nature's deck, an alien dynamic, a foreign essence, a malevolent traitor. We want God to assert His sovereignty – to stop the chaos, to evict the traitor, and yet do so without calling us back to live in the categories of Psalm 1 – without demanding righteousness by His standards and obedience. It is an impossible and untenable demand we make of God.

Lament stands between the order of creation, the current chaos of nature and the promise of a new creation. It weeps for the victims of the disorder, who are angry at God and confused. It weeps with Creation, travailing for the consummation of redemption. It wonders, "How long?"

Lament Over Social Injustice

In Psalm 10, we find a lament based on social injustice. The disorder in nations and families is connected to an unhealthy ethos in the culture of society. The crisp categories of Psalm 1 are again turned on their head.

Here, the wicked man hunts down the vulnerable and the weak. He devises entrapping schemes (10:2). He is a proud, boastful man whose evil appetites seem forever satiated (v. 3). He gets what he craves, with little resistance to his wicked ways, while reviling the Lord and enriching himself and his evil comrades. He has created a life without room for God (v. 4). He prospers, rejecting righteousness. No one who challenges him is taken seriously. He is intoxicated on selfishness, utterly insensitive and without values. "Nothing will ever shake me," the wicked confess. "No one will ever do me harm."

He feels invincible. His success and lack of accountability embolden him. He is a habitual and conniving liar, leveraging deception with intimidation (v. 7). Lies and deceptive practices perpetrated on victims have escalated to the murder of the innocent – he is a serial killer (v. 8). He is wicked *par excellence.* He has developed wickedness into a skill. He is a persistent, patient, cool, and detached predator: *"...from ambush he murders the innocent. His eyes watch in secret for his victims"* (v. 8). He has become ruthless, beastly, less than human, *"...like a lion in cover he lies in wait...to catch the helpless...His victims are crushed; they collapse; they fall under his strength"* (vv. 9-10). He moves from pride to prosperity, then to predator, increasingly unaware of his darkening character. He is growing blind and becoming viciously insensitive.

The power of the wicked described here is stunning, almost breathtaking. It is the opposite of Psalm 1 and so it provokes the lament – where is God? Indeed, this wicked predator *"says to himself, 'God will never notice; he covers his face and never sees'"* (v. 11). The lament is a protest against God's inactivity and a plea for His intervention: *"Arise, Lord! Lift up your hand, O God. Do not forget the helpless"* (v. 12).

Then comes the puzzlement, *"Why does the wicked man revile God? Why does he say to himself, 'He won't call me to account?'"* (v. 13). The question is dual. It not only asks why does the wicked do this or that, but why does God allow him do it? *"But you, God, see the trouble of the afflicted; you consider their grief and take it in hand. The victims commit themselves to you; you are the helper of the fatherless"* (v. 14).

Prayer, lament, is the prayerful intervening legal protest that urges God to act in behalf of the innocent. An imprecation follows: *"Break the arm of the wicked man; call the evildoer to account for his wickedness that would not otherwise be found out"* (v. 15). 'God, act! Stop this wicked man in his tracks. Stop the stealing and the plundering, the intimidation and the bloodshed – stop it, God, whatever action is required.' What right does God have to do this?

> 'The Lord is King for ever and ever,' and in such a place where the wicked triumph and there is no justice, where the human king or leader is derelict and judges are jaded, God must judge – He must. He must assert his Kingship, here and now. Indeed, 'the nations will perish from his land' (v. 16).

This is an imprecatory and desperate lamentation that says, "Enough with the unrestrained wicked – act, God, whatever the consequences." It is also an appeal to God's character,

> You, Lord, hear the desire of the afflicted; you encourage them, and you listen to their cry, defending the fatherless and the oppressed, so that mere earthly mortals will never again strike terror (vv. 17-18).

The lament emerges when, in the face of such ruthless evil, God appears inactive, restrained. *"Why, Lord, do you stand far off? Why do you hide yourself in times of trouble?"* (v. 1). Lament urges God to show up, to come 'out of hiding,' and reveal Himself, not only to the righteous, but also to the wicked. It calls for the intervention of God on behalf of the powerless victim.

> *The people of God miss a glorious opportunity in evangelism when they fail to show compassion in the face of social injustice.*

Our first movement should be a display of empathy out of love – not the assignment of guilt, out of truth. The lead issue with evangelicals is often right or wrong, truth. Innocence or guilt. Instead, it should first be identification with and compassion for pain and suffering, deprivation and want, violence and bloodshed. The first movement in evangelism is the incarnational, establishing a bond, affinity. It weeps and prays. And then, having built a bridge of trust, truth can travel more easily on that relational bridge. It can be transmitted over the chasm, where there had been a relationship vacuum. For this to happen, love must lead. Too often, we lead with truth, becoming confronting prophets before we are relating priests. The result is an increasing divide between the culture and the church, between the hurting world and the people of God. We hold a sword of truth, but we fight with feet shod with the preparation of the gospel of peace, as agents of reconciliation. Our aim is not war, but peace.

The Messianic Lament – A Cry of Dereliction

Now we return to Psalm 22. We visited that psalm earlier in connection with the overview of Creation psalms. Psalm 22 is in one sense the ultimate lament, perhaps, *the* messianic lament because in it we meet the "cry of dereliction," *"My God, my God, why have you forsaken me?"*

This cry is also found in Lamentations 5:20. There it is communal and associated with the destruction of the temple. Lamentations is an entire book devoted to lament, written by Jeremiah. The laments there occur over the rise of Babylon, the destruction of Jerusalem and the temple. The fall of Jerusalem and the rise of Babylon is a prophetic parody of the coming war of the nations against Jerusalem and the global alliance against both Jews and Christians, the people of 'the Book.'

Psalm 22 pleads with God, *"Why do you continue to forget us? Why have you abandoned us for so long?"* (NLT). Of course, we remember this language from the cross. *"And at three in the afternoon Jesus cried out in a loud voice, 'Eloi, Eloi, lema sabachthani?' (which means) 'My God, my God, why have you forsaken me?'"* (Mark 15:34). It is the personal lament of Jesus. Prophetically, it is also the lament of the last day's church, the persecuted church, the bride of Christ. In this sense, Jesus takes up our cry, he begins, even in the garden of Gethsemane, his intercessory ministry that is now continuing in heaven. He laments, as we should. He enters the pit. He suffers persecution. He experiences the physical symptoms of distress related to deep intercession. God seems, as in other lament moments in scripture, shockingly absent.[6]

"Jesus takes on the persona – in fact, becomes the persona – of the righteous sufferer, who cries out in his physical, social, and spiritual distress, and in so doing, calls God the Father" and that identification is not only with us in our pain, but it binds us to the Christ, and the Father, in our pain.[7] This is disturbing language, upsetting our theological presuppositions. It is not merely a question of evil men triumphing or of confusion about the absence of God's blessings on the righteous and of the needed correction and restraint of evil in the midst of the dominating pagan kingdoms. Here, the unthinkable has happened. God is not merely inactive or silent. The conclusion is that He has abandoned us (or so it seems). Obviously, that is not the case. God is present – ever present. He is often the "incomprehensible obvious."[8] But perception is our reality and "to try to see God is like trying to look at your own eyes, for he is nearer to us than we are to ourselves."[9]

What happens when He *seems* absent? When every plea is met with silence? When the innocent one is slaughtered? When He does not act to rescue or save? *"My God, my God, why have you abandoned me? Why are you so far away from helping me, so far away from the words of my groaning?"* (22:1, GWT). The day and night prayers have not been answered (v. 2). The absence of God is so haunting, there is no peace, no rest, no sleep. In the past, we believe, God acted: *"Our ancestors trusted you. They trusted, and you rescued them. They cried to you and were saved. They trusted you and were never disappointed"* (vv. 4-5). We conclude that something is different now. Something has changed, demanding a lament – prayer that is desperate and beyond normal praying. What was God's evident hand is no more. It is time to weep, to wail, to lament. This, of course, is the cross, but it is not exclusively the cross of Christ. It is that cross and everyone else's cross. It is Israel's cross – the destruction of their temple and the death of their nation. It is also the crucible of every Golgotha we now face. Lament always takes us back to the cross.

In Psalm 22, it is as if all of humanity is an enemy to God, and indeed, as a messianic psalm, this is reality. We, by our sin, crucified Christ. At the cross, and in lament, we taste the consequences of sin. We feel separation from God. We are exiled from peace. We feel alone.

I am scorned by humanity and despised by people. All who see me make fun of me. Insults pour from their mouths. They shake their heads and say, 'Put yourself in the LORD's hands. Let the LORD save him! Let God rescue him since he is pleased with him!' (vv. 7-8)

At the cross, there was nothing for Jesus to do, but 'put himself' in the Lord's, the Father's hand, so that 'the Lord' would 'save' him and 'rescue' him. The place of lament, the cross, is also the place where we put ourselves in His hands. He alone can save us. Christ lamented on the cross, not only for himself, but also for us. At the cross, the highest moment of intercessory lament is introduced. Here is the model for the church. Our lament cannot be private, merely personal. In lament, we stand with Christ, between God, the Father, and a hurting world. We lament over a broken and rebellious world, tasting its pain.

As a messianic people, now forgiven, and having switched sides, we may now expect the same dynamic that Christ experienced. This is the heart of the dilemma – the faithful man trusts in God, only to feel abandoned in the hour of the trial – the cross. There is no rescue. No deliverance. No taming of the wicked. No triumph of the righteous. But the greater pain is the distance felt from God, *"Do not be so far away from me. Trouble is near, and there is no one to help"*

(v. 11). The actions of these men are beyond brutal, they are beastly, compared to a raging bull and ferocious, roaring lions. In contrast, our strength is as weak as water, as wax in a fire, as the broken pieces of a clay pot (vv. 12-14). We are speechless, with a tongue stuck to the roof of our mouths, feeling close to death – *"You lay me down in the dust of death"* (v. 15).

The messianic elements are clear – *"Gentiles [Roman soldiers] have surrounded me. A mob has encircled me. They have pierced my hands and feet...People stare. They gloat... They divide my clothes among themselves. They throw dice for my clothing"* (v. 18). Here is the lament of Jesus, the sense of abandonment he felt on the cross. As a messianic community, when we are surrounded, encircled, pierced – we are in the glorious moment in which we should intercede for others, particularly, our enemies and the enemies of God and righteousness.

In truth, the cross was the greatest moment for Christ and the great moment of redemption for all mankind. Far from being alone, abandoned, God, the Father, was with Christ at the cross, redeeming lost humanity. Jesus Christ was never, in his incarnational state, more fully in the center of God's will. We can never assume, on the basis of *our sense* of God's Presence alone, how near He might be. *"Do not be so far away, O Lord, come quickly to help me, O my strength"* (v. 19). We join our voices in the lament of Jesus, feeling alone, when we find ourselves on some crucible. In retrospect, we may discover, that God was doing His greatest work in us. Faith is not always awarded with bliss and obvious blessing. Faith is often required to endure some cross, navigate some flooding river, walk through some fiery furnace and emerge at the empty tomb.

This the ultimate triumph. The lament psalms cry out for deliverance from, relief of this or that, triumph in the natural, protection and provision, but in Christ, lament is elevated to a higher purpose. In Christ, the lament is not resolved in deliverance *from*. Rather, it delivers the believer, and Christ, the Messiah, whom we follow – to and *through* the cross. This is how lament is resolved in the New Testament. It is resolved in the cross of God's divine and cosmic, but hidden purposes, and answered in resurrection.

Additional Psalms as Laments

In the psalms, lament occurs:

1. When God seems hidden (Psalm 13, 22, 44).

2. When God is silent. God seems disengaged and inactive (44). He seems to have cast off Israel, dumped them – being the unfaithful party to the covenant. The result is that they are shamed, without a god among the nations with their visible and multiple gods.

3. When God seems inattentive. He is at times accused of sleeping (44:10; 78:6; 121:4).

4. When there are extraordinary external threats. Peace and safety are threatened by enemies (13, 22, 44, 58, 137). God has failed at his task in protecting the nation against their enemies. The enemy has triumphed.

5. When there is internal abuse, the abuse of a leader (58).

6. When death threatens, there is a cause for lament (13).

7. When anxieties are heightened. Apprehension and unrest, a state of misery, may provoke a lament (13), emotions become raw in times of stress.

8. When sin is uncovered. David's great personal lament, laced with repentance, is found in Psalm 51.

9. When there is confusion and disappointment. In Psalm 42, we meet confusion that comes in a time of disappointment and depression, *"My tears have been my food day and night, while people say to me all day long, 'Where is your God?' These things I remember as I pour out my soul: how I used to go to the house of God under the protection of the Mighty One with shouts of joy and praise among the festive throng"* (vv. 3-4).

John Calvin asserted, "…the Psalms are the mirror of the soul." At least 42 psalms are individual laments and another 16 are corporate laments.[10] Ten echo wisdom literature with roots in the Torah. R. W. L. Moberly argues,

> …the predominance of laments at the very heart of Israel's prayers means that the problems that give rise to lament are not something marginal or unusual but rather are central to the life of faith…Moreover they show that the experience of anguish and puzzlement in the life of faith is not a sign of deficient faith, something to be outgrown or put behind one, but rather is intrinsic to the very nature of faith.[11]

10. When there is an abundance of wickedness. Psalm 58 is a striking imprecatory psalm that stands against wicked men who have rebelled against God's kingdom and are intoxicated with abusive self-interests resulting in brutality and injustice.

The Disempowered and Lament

In the psalms, an amazing 18 times, the psalmist cries out to the Lord to be rescued from a pit. *"He lifted me out of the pit of despair, out of the mud and the mire. He set my feet on solid ground and steadied me as I walked along"* (Psalm 40:2, NLT).

Pits are deep and dark. And they represent powerlessness. If you are in a pit, you have either been forcibly placed in one or you have accidentally fallen into one. Chances are, you are alone in whatever pit you are in. And, you need help in getting out. In ancient times, pits were physical and real. In our times, they are most often a metaphor for the same psychologically paralyzing darkness and helplessness, as if we were in some physical pit.

Forty-three times the psalmist takes "refuge" in the LORD! *"God is our refuge and fortress, an ever-present help in times of trouble"* (Psalm 46:1). In the end, laments often take a turn toward joy and praise. Sorrow is not the last word. Trust is placed in God. Praise is offered to him. Praise language is found more than any other terminology in the Bible – it dominates. Occurring in verb form, often in the imperative, it is the anticipated mode of the true believer – to give praise to God, to point to Him, to live in ways that praise and honor him.[12] We are always moving back to praise and worship, after some distraction, some sorrow that caused lament.

Psalm 102

Psalm 102 is also a lament, an address to God (vv. 1-2). It is wrapped in a cry of distress, but laced with the anticipation of an answer (2c). Based on God's faithfulness in the past, this is an appeal to God who acts. The writer does not conceal his own pain or crisis. *"For my days consume away like smoke and my bones are burned as a firebrand"* (3). The words reveal the mental stress – time passing like wisps of smoke, with no substantive residue. Life is wasting away. He feels this down to his bones. He is so overwhelmed he describes his heart as "smitten" like the spring grass which withers before the sun on the first hot summer day. He is so traumatized, he has lost his appetite: *"I forgot to eat my bread."* Alone, at night, he cannot sleep. But the end of self is the beginning of God.

Adversity continues, *"Mine enemies reproach me all the day; and they that are mad against me are sworn against me."* In a culture where ill health was regarded as divine punishment for sins, he has found himself ostracized and persecuted. Rivals have seized the opportunity to "taunt him and misuse his name." He sees the inevitable without God's intervention – death.[13]

> *Yet lament, far from giving in to the crisis and its sorrows, is a protest against it. It cuts through the darkness. It navigates toward the light, even if it appears at the time as only a slender beam of hope.*

Lament believes for a new day (vv. 12-22). It does not look for hope in the present moment, but in the transcendent God, above time (v. 12). It appeals to His character (v. 13). It chooses to trust Him and His promises (vv. 14-16). He hears, cares and acts (vv. 17, 19-20). He acts, not merely for the moment, but with a greater destiny in mind: *"This shall be written for the generation to come"* (v. 18). God is called to act for the preservation of the next generation (v. 28).[14]

Psalm 73

In a similar way, Psalm 73 presents the disempowered as they are appealing to God, the Sovereign, for intervention. In the language of and from the posture of servants, the people appeal to the true Lord, God, the King over kings – to act, to rule, to assert Himself. In a sense, it is this idea that stands behind the prayer Jesus taught us, *"Let your kingdom come, your will be done"* (Mt. 6:10). Here, no one seems to 'hallow your holy name!' So, assert yourself, Lord.

The greater problem with unrestrained evil is its seduction, *"As for me, my feet came close to stumbling, my steps had almost slipped. I was envious of the arrogant as I saw the prosperity of the wicked"* (v. 2-3). The illusion created by God's seeming suspension of judgement, by overabundant grace and mercy, is that evil has no consequences. Not only do the evil live well, *"there are no pains in their death"* (v. 4). They seem to die so easily, and live so prosperously. Their troubles seem fewer and they appear to be above and beyond things that plague others (v. 5). Not everything about them is attractive – they are proud, and as their pride and unfettered confidence inflates, they grow increasingly insensitive, more violent (v. 6). Their center corrupts, *"The imaginations of their heart run riot,"* (v. 7), and their language reflects the change happening internally: *"They mock and wickedly speak of oppression..."* and *"set their mouth against the heavens, their tongue parades through the earth"* (vv. 8-9).

They seem unopposed, even by God. *"Surely in vain I have kept my heart pure and washed my hands in innocence"* (v. 13). On a trip into the sanctuary of God, *"I perceived their end"* (v. 17). Heaven's perspective reveals treacherous "slippery places," unstable footings and quick ends to wicked schemes. *"You cast them down to destruction. How they are destroyed in a moment! They are utterly swept away by sudden terrors!"* (vv. 18-19). Psalm 73 reaches back to Psalm 1, the implicit Torah psalm. In Psalm 73:1-14, an echo of Psalm 2, there is the disillusionment – the wicked prosper, and with that seeming reality, there is the deceptive lure: *"...in vain have I kept my heart pure."* Verse 17 is the place where one is re-centered – back in the sanctuary, being instructed, with God revealing His wisdom. What follows is the eschatological end of the wicked (vv. 18-22). The final call is for a 'Presence' orientation. Without an ongoing connection to sanctuary, and by extension, God's Presence and wisdom, we drift from truth, rationalize, become *"senseless and ignorant...like a [dumb animal] beast..."* (v. 22). The key to prevent disillusionment, by the temporary prosperity of the wicked, is to be near God, *"Nevertheless I am continually with You; You have taken hold of my right hand"* (v. 23). There is both the presence of God and the counsel of God: *"With Your counsel, You will guide me, and afterward receive me to glory"* (v. 24), *"...the nearness of God is my good"* (v. 28).

Psalm 137

In Psalm 137, lament is tied to the exile and the Jewish longing for home. Here, the sheer, unvarnished sorrow of the Jewish resettlement and the loss of their homeland after the Babylonian captivity (Psa. 137) are powerfully articulated. They had been separated from Zion and their song was gone: *"We put away our harps, hanging them on the branches of poplar trees."* Sitting by the rivers of Babylon, they wept as a result of homesickness, *"as we thought of Jerusalem."* The

Babylonians wanted to be entertained by their native music, *"Sing us one of those songs of Jerusalem!"* Coerced joy is not free. The request was tormenting. *"How can we sing the songs of the Lord in a pagan land?"* The holy and unholy could not be mixed. Their songs were not meant to entertain the godless. *"If I forget you, O Jerusalem, let my right hand forget how to play the harp."* Joy and Jerusalem were one – never to be separated. Praise and Jerusalem were joined, *"May my tongue stick to the roof of my mouth if I fail to remember you, if I don't make Jerusalem my greatest joy."* And so with us – our joy and praise are related to Christ and His kingdom. It is unseemly to sing irreverently, to praise capriciously.

Summary

In laments, you find graphic images – helpless, outstretched arms, kneeling in humility, abandonment and loneliness, lying helpless and hopeless on the ground. The body, acting with the soul and spirit, are praying. The grief has become public.[15] In the laments, we find physical affects (Psalm 22:14-15, 17; 38:3, 7-8, 10, 17; 55:17; 69:3; 77:4-10; 88:4; 137:1), social stressors and disengagement, confusion and relational disruption (22:6, 11; 38:9, 11; 41:9; 66:10; 88:8, 18), emotional raggedness (13:2; 22:1-2, 6; 38:4, 6, 9; 42:3, 5; 55:4, 5;56:8; 69:1-2, 20, 29; 73:21; 77:2, 4; 80:4-5; 88:4; 137:9; 143:4), cognitive dissonance and spiritual disorientation (13:2; 22:1; 42:11; 43:5; 55:2; 60:1, 3; 69:21-22; 77:3, 7-9; 88:5, 14), and behavioral acting out (39:12; 55:7-8; 77:4; 88:13; 126:5-6). The bottom line: Something about life is not right. Someone has paraphrased Jeremiah, saying, "God can't heal what you won't feel" (6:14). Without feeling, we allow our wound to be treated superficially.

The lament is the refusal to be silent before God. It is not, Brueggemann insists, primarily "cultural, sociological, or psychological, but it is in the end, theological."[16] And yet, it addresses the whole disenfranchised person and peoples. It is, in its resolve, holistic – physical, emotional, and spiritual[17] – with cultural, sociological and psychological implications. In lament, one "pours out" the soul in prayer, the "bones" are pulled apart, as if the body were coming unhinged (this is stress and distress). The heart, the seat of the emotions, melts. Strength, physical and psychological energy is drained.

> ### *The power of action is dried up – God alone can be the active agent that saves.*

The entirety of our being laments.[18] It is the relationship that permits, indeed, "requires a human voice that will speak out against every wrong perpetrated either on earth or by heaven."[19] This may be petition – lament out of personal pain; and it may be an intercessory lament, a personal priestly prayer in behalf of others, or a corporate lament from a church that cannot or will not be silent.

Discussion Guide

1. Review Psalm 22 as a messianic psalm.
2. How is it also a psalm of lament?
3. How do social justice and lament interface?
4. How is social injustice also a window for evangelism and compassion?
5. Why is Psalm 22 the ultimate lament? How is the cross the ultimate place of lament?
6. Review the ten reasons that lament occurs.
7. Talk about the idea of the 'pit' and God as a refuge.

5

The Nature and Character of Lament

L ament appeals to the relationship. It cries out, *"My* God." It is a pleading prayer from inside the covenant. It is the supplication of a believer, even if it is, at times, a doubting, questioning believer.

> ### *It is authenticity, a refusal to own a fake faith.*

Some extreme problem is mentioned, and often, in the same moment, God is charged with some form of neglect. At other times, the petitioner confesses sin (Psalm 25:11, 18; Psalm 51:3-5, 9, 11), which is reasoned to be a cause for the misfortune being experienced. On occasion, there is a claim of innocence (Psalms 7:3-5, 8; 26:1-8; 44), and with that, the greater wonder of 'why' bad things are happening. All of this is from inside the framework of a covenant – which not only dictates how the faithful are to behave, but also how they handle their disillusionments, their expectations of God's behavior in view of His character.

Appealing to the covenant and its promises, a lament is a complaint, based on God's revealed intent and promises, both of which seem to be failing. From inside the covenant the appeal is made for God's action, for intervention. Consistently, the appeal is tied, directly or indirectly, explicitly or implicitly, to the character of God. The situation is lamentable, precisely because it is not consistent with God's character. Where is God, in the face of some injustice, oppression, undue suffering and loss? Some laments contain imprecations–which are a call for judicial action against the enemies of justice and grace. In the end, the lament looks away from the immediate, the deadly disruption that has invaded normalcy, toward what should be, and it gives way to worship and praise. So lament, despite its depression and desperation, is always moving toward praise. The uncommon intrusion into life has disordered things, unsettled the predictable, and dampened, even quieted praise and worship. The questioning believer is in shock. Knocked to the ground breathless by some life event, as a true believer, he knows, God is due worship. So the appeal is that deliverance come, *"...that I might praise you,"*[1] that such victory would be a platform for the nations to notice the invisible God of Israel and His goodness.

> *A voice is heard in Ramah, lamentation and bitter weeping. Rachel is weeping for her children; and refuses to be comforted for her children, because they are no more* (Jer. 31:5).

Some radical change in circumstances has prompted the lament – good has turned to bad. Hope has been crushed. All may seem lost. In 2 Samuel 1:17-27 or 3:33, the *"lostness"* is expressed *"in a long series of very specific gestures and postures: one crouched on the ground, threw dust on the head, rent the clothes, donned coarse apparel, abstained from nourishment"* (Psalm 35:13-14; 69:10-12]).[2] The inward chaotic emotions are being exhibited outwardly.[3] Lamenting intercessors are at times demonstrably and disturbingly audible, with non-discernible language. Their prayers are constituted by cries of travail and anguish, as if they were in the throes of life and death, giving birth. Non-intercessors, even pastors, find their manner unnerving. They seem too emotional, too overwrought, out of control, even irrational. We, however, view them from the natural; what they are experiencing is in the realm of the spiritual. We may be in the same room with them and simultaneously in different worlds.

A number of years ago, a pastoral friend who lived near Charlotte-Douglas International Airport was awakened by the sound of a passenger jet that crashed. Choking back emotion, he described the scene of the disaster. He was surrounded by bodies and debris. What was scattered about was not indistinguishable stuff, but recognizable valuables, the human bodies and the body parts of the wounded, the dead passengers and crew, adults and children. In such a moment, it is impossible to be detached, cool and calm, reasonable.

The Old Testament emphasizes personal petitionary lament, but it serves as a backdrop for corporate intercessory lament. Intercessory lament rises above personal loss and weeps over spiritual and moral calamity, over lost people and nations, over a world that is rejecting God, over the immorality and decadence, the relational and religious chaos. Intercessory lamenters seem to have had their hearts exposed by the Spirit to some devastation of life and souls, as seen from heaven's perspective, an insight given only by the Spirit. They weep at the spiritual and moral devastation that others can't even see. What, in terms of tearful prayer, may seem abnormal to others is quite normal for them.

When overwhelming pain touches our personal lives in the natural, we weep. Intercessory lament is the greater sensitivity – it weeps over impending doom, over what cannot be seen with natural eyes. When the Twin Towers collapsed in New York on September 11, 2001, reasonable people registered panic on their faces and ran. A nation wept. All stood stunned in front of televisions. No one re-buffed the tearful anxiety of men, women, and children, who were the spouses and children of those who worked in the towers but did not make it home that night. Everyone admired the firefighters who refused to leave the scene, digging for days in the ruins at their own peril to rescue survivors. Indeed, those who did not weep, who were not moved, were the exception. Intercessory lamenters may actually be the normal ones, weeping over what we cannot see, the impend-ing peril to which we will not admit.

In the Old Testament, lament is not the perspective of a detached observer. The grief with the prayerful complaint is voiced by the one who feels abandoned and betrayed by God, wounded and disappoint-ed. The witness of a surrogate will not work in this situation.[4] This is not a mere secondhand report, it is a first personal ap-praisal from someone who is in-vested in some loss. Psalm 22:1

> How lonely sits the city that was full of people. She has become like a widow who was once great among the nations. She who was a princess among the provinces has become a forced laborer (Lamentations 1:1).

has the colloquial force of meaning, *"My God, My God, why have You forsaken Me?"* At other points in the psalms, you find, *"Let your ears be attentive!"* Or, *"Hear my cry!"*[5]

A Look Ahead – Intercessory Lament

Psalm 22 is, eschatologically, the ground on which lament shifts. It is both a personal lament and a Messianic Lament. It is a model lament for all of us, personally, as we find ourselves on some crucible or feel mysteriously disconnected from God's Presence. It is also prophetic and eschatological, since Old Testament lament moves through history toward the cross. It is understood ultimately in the suffering of Christ on the cross and it is resolved in the resurrection. Old Testament lament is in the lesser light. It can't see God suffering, God in Christ, the cross and the empty tomb, or triumph in the face of death. It is full of 'whys?' It gropes for hope and answers, peering into the darkness, questioning.

New Testament believers may lament, but since Christ, we look back to the cross through the lens of the empty tomb. Lament changes. It is answered by certain hope – the triumph of Christ. Suffering is no longer a reason to doubt God's goodness or His grace on our lives – Christ suffered. Bad things happen to good people, but *"all things work together for good"* and *"nothing can separate us from the love of God"* or destroy our victory, since *"we are more than conquerors through Christ"* (Romans 8:18, 28, 35). Such assurance allows us to lay down our own laments and now lament for others who do not have hope. Just as Christ, on the cross, became an intercessory lamenter for us, tasting our pain, bearing our sin, experiencing the abandonment of our disconnection from the Father, so we now intercede for others, for their pain, their sense of abandonment, their lack of relationship with the Father. Everything changes at the cross, and subsequently, because of the Resurrection.

In the Old Testament, lament escalates to a crucible, moving ultimately to the cross – and there, God, in Christ, tastes death. The greatest horror takes place.

> *The Messiah, the hope of Israel, the hope of the world, was rejected, killed by humanity. Then the unexpected happens – death could not contain him, the grave could not hold him.*

"He is risen!" (Mark 16:6). What then, is there to lament about after the resurrection? In view of the ascension, the enthronement of Christ, and the coming of the Holy Spirit? Christ is King, though reigning in exile, the coming kingdom is certain (Acts 2:31-33).

Our *"...present sufferings are not worth comparing with the glory that will be revealed in us"* (v. 18). The *"whole creation has been groaning as in the pains of childbirth right up to the present time"* (v. 22), but now, since the Resurrection *"we ourselves...have the firstfruits of the Spirit"* (v. 23). We continue to *"groan inwardly"* but now we do so because we know there is more. *"We wait eagerly for our [full] adoption to sonship, the redemption of our bodies,"* our own resurrection and the final victory over death (v. 23). Meanwhile, to life and all its calamities, we declare, *"If God is for us, who can be against us?"* (v. 31). The question is not, "Will someone or something be against us?" but *"Will they successfully triumph against us?"* The answer is, "No!" Not if "God is for us." That irrepressible victory, however, came through the cross, through suffering: *"He who did not spare his own Son, but gave him up for us all – how will he not also, along with him, graciously give us all things?"* This is provision out of pain. Christ died; Christ arose; Christ is enthroned, *"at the right hand of God...interceding for us"* (v. 34).

Never again should circumstances of life, as in the Old Testament, cause us to doubt God's love: *"Who shall separate us from the love of Christ? Shall trouble or hardship or persecution or famine or nakedness or danger or sword?"* (v. 35). We may feel, as did the Old Testament lamenters, that we *"face death all day long...as sheep to be slaughtered"* (v. 36), but there is now, on the other side of the suffering, beyond some cross, the Resurrection. So we say to all of life, "No," we are not victims, *"in all these things we are more than conquerors through him who loved us"* (v. 37). And we carry the conviction forward *"that neither death nor life, neither angels nor demons, neither the present nor the future, nor any powers, neither height nor depth, nor anything else in all creation, will be able to separate us from the love of God that is in Christ Jesus our Lord"* (v. 38). This is the victory, out of the empty tomb, that now allows us to weep, not only for ourselves, but also for others. Personal lament gives way to intercessory lament.

Testifying to God

In lament, the poor and oppressed, the victims and the mourners tell their own story – and the importance of that privilege is not to be overlooked.

> **Lament is a platform, offered by God, to hear the complaint of the typically disenfranchised, humans, mere mortals, who He allows to speak freely in the courtroom of heaven.**

They speak for themselves from a first-person perspective. They are in trouble, they must lament; they have been wronged, and on the earth there is no justice, so they must protest before God. Heaven is open to hear our grievances, our appeals for God's intervention, for His mercy, and if necessary, His judicial action on the agents of injustice.

Intercessors may now file a friend of the court brief, declaring an interest in the outcome of some matter, but their testimony in heaven's courtroom is from a third-person perspective. They are neither the aggrieved or the aggressor. It is the lamenter whose prayer is most relevant. Intercessors may pray, but no one can do the praying of the sufferer, the victim of injustice and distress. Intercessors pray with some degree of objective differentiation, but a testimony is needed in heaven's courtroom from someone who is in the fight. Such prayers are tearful and passionate, offered with sobs and laced with emotion.

At times, these prayers draw to silence. As the Talmud says, "The deeper the sorrow, the less tongue it has."

When the distressed, attempting to speak to God, before God, can't find the words, an intercessory voice is needed. They come alongside and give voice to the non-verbal passion. They pray in the Spirit, but also with understanding, providing Spirit-inspired, rational content that explains the raw emotion. Still, no prayerful left-brain assessment of a given situation can ever take the place of a wordless, tearful connection with God that He alone understands. This is also why the Holy Spirit has been sent to help us pray. *"In the same way, the Spirit helps us in our weakness. We do not know what we ought to pray for, but the Spirit himself intercedes for us through wordless groans"* (Romans 8:26, NIV). Or, *"We do not know how to pray as we should, but the Spirit Himself intercedes for us with groaning too deep for words"* (NAS). The NLT says, *"And the Father who knows all hearts knows what the Spirit is saying, for the Spirit pleads for us believers in harmony with God's own will"* (8:27). He knows "the mindset of the Spirit," and *"He intercedes for the saints according to God"* (Berean Literal Bible), the NAS, *"...because He intercedes for the saints according to the will of God."*

What makes Biblical lament different from mere sorrow is found in where lament lands – in its trust and affirmation of God, expressed in a prayer. What makes the lament of New Testament believers different is the cross and the resurrection. Lament, whether personal or intercessory, is tearful and unvarnished. At times, Old Testament lament is raw accusation and seemingly unbridled anger against God and others, but in the end, Biblical lament turns back to God. It affirms trust in God. It puts the right of judgement in the hands of God, and then it turns back to praise. Worship is to be the normative position of the believer. Distracted, angry, disappointed and confused, considering revenge, losing balance – in the end, we move back toward God, through lament, we discharge toxic emotions, and we move away from actions we would later regret and attitudes that are toxic, to worship.

The Purpose of Lament

Lament reveals our humanity, our frailty. It calls us to responsibility, accountability before God, even in the midst of doubt, anger with God and loss of faith. And prayer, desperate prayer, doubting prayer, is nevertheless prayer – and it is an expression of faith in God. He is there, listening. Lament takes suffering to God, as if it belongs to God, and yes, as if He were the cause of it. And in that sense, every lament looks to the cross. And the cross looks back at the fall of man, gathering up the sin of all humanity. The suffering of the cross is tied both to sin and to sickness through the stripes on the back of Jesus. Somehow, standing before the cross, Biblical prayer intuits that God understands human suffering. That He pays attention to tears. That He hears the cries of the oppressed and cares. It is a unique idea among religions, confirmed in the cross. Lament looks to the cross in another way. It pivots around sin – confessed sin, hidden sin, denied sin, the consequences of our sin and that of others. It grapples with death in a raw

> Sincerity is everything. If you can fake that, you've got it made.
> ~ George Burns

and open manner. And then it turns back to living by faith, re-centering one's life in the word, as if anticipating the resurrection.[6] Something is wrong that must be set right again. Something is dead that must live again. Righteousness has been trampled and wickedness reigns – it must not be so! Good people are suffering – indeed, the people of the earth have crucified God; bad people flourish and go unchallenged. In such a world, the meaning of Psalm 1 is now completely lost: the tree meant to stand and thrive, to bear fruit continuously without a withering leaf is now violently cut down, its fruit scattered and its leaves blown away like chaff. The wicked, who were to perish, stand. The mockers go unanswered. The world is upside down.

Erich Zengar appropriately comments about lament,

> The [lament] psalm fights for the indispensable union of religion and ethics. The truth about God that people believe or proclaim can be tested by whether it preserves its adherents from the ways of violence and impels them to a life in solidarity with the victims of violence.[7]

In lament, we protest in favor of a world that rewards righteousness and deals appropriately with the wicked. It is not merely a matter of personal pain and loss, but of justice. It is an outlet, a plea toward heaven, for justice that we do not see forthcoming here.

Lament is one of the features of prayer and biblical literature that remind us of our humanity. It is human 'reality' portrayed in scripture. Biblical characters became angry; they confessed, cried and complained, laughed and lamented, mourned and returned to mirth. In a sense, we don't originate the lament; we, in prayer, give it voice before the one who judges righteously.

Luther observed,

> What is the greatest thing in the Psalter but this earnest speaking amid the stormy winds of every kind? Where does one find finer words of joy than in the psalms of praise and thanksgiving? There you look into the hearts of all the saints...On the other hand, where do you find deeper, more sorrowful, more pitiful words of sadness than in the psalms of lamentation? There again you look into the hearts of the saints, as into death, yes, as into hell itself...When they speak of fear and hope, they use such words that no painter could so depict for your fear or hope, and no Cicero or other orator has so portrayed them. And that they speak these words to God and with

God, this I repeat, is the best thing of all. This gives the words double earnestness and life.[8]

Lament is an authentic act of truth. It groans for redemption. It longs for ultimate liberation. The sound of lament is arresting. It interrupts the superficial and creates the space to interpret pain, to point out injustice. Lament then opens the door to the prophetic – to someone who can articulate the sense of some matter, and speak God's truth into wrong or neglect, and also speak life.

> *Lament interrupts neatly packaged doxology (Exodus 2:23-25). It rocks the boat. It questions. It dares to express pain, to point out the marginalized and disempowered.*

Losing Lament in Modernism

Secularism and its worldly influence must keep its prisoners entertained and drugged to mask their pain. It cannot lament. It has taken on the philosophy of relativism – and it cannot appeal, passionately, to absolute truth. It has embraced evolutionary nihilism, and with it empty existentialism. It wallows in moral relativism, an "anything goes" philosophy of life. Lament has a basis in absolute truth, in the moral character and holiness of God, in His identity with us as Creator, and now, from the New Testament perspective, as Redeemer. Lament appeals to right and righteousness, in the face of unrighteousness, by appealing to a God of righteousness. It appeals to the sovereignty of God in the face of disorder. It appeals to the mercy of God in the face of atrocity, brutality, and barbarism. It rises out of a completely antithetical world view, as different as day and night.

We moved to secularism, but that slope is so slippery that overnight we slipped into the bog of paganism. We are now clearly a post-Christian culture, and the church, with either its Evangelical-Pentecostal happy music or its traditional liturgy, acts as if nothing has changed. The church has to live between timeless truths and timely truth, and it seems unable to do that. It must recover lament.

Lament, as a protest against God for inaction, is not merely emotional or simply personal pain poured out in prayer – it is that and more. It stands against the backdrop of Biblical ideas about justice; God's promises seem to be delayed.

Walter Brueggemann warns,

> A community of faith which negates laments soon concludes that the hard issues of justice are improper questions to pose at the throne, because the throne seems to be only a place of praise. I believe it thus follows that if justice questions are improper questions to God, they soon appear to be improper questions in public places...Justice questions disappear into civility and docility. The order of the day comes to seem absolute, beyond question, and we are left with only grim obedience and eventually despair. The point of access for serious change has been forfeited when the propriety of this speech form is denied.[9]

We may pray and we may, as do the psalms, suggest that God take a certain action, make some provision, defeat some enemy, rescue from some peril, but Stephen Crotts argues, "God has editing rights over our prayers. He will...edit them, correct them, bring them in line with His will and then hand them back to us to be resubmitted."[10]

Lament and Cultural Oppression

Lament was the way the people of God dealt with delay. "How long do we have to wait...?" Corporate weeping was a means of coping. The only alternative was to abandon faith in the face of some untenable reality. Lament was both an acknowledgment of persistent faith and simultaneously, fragile faith. "Singing is a way to keep your nerve," observes Brueggemann.[11] It was a way of believing in the face of collapsing faith, of holding onto God and holding God responsible for some outcome beyond human power.

"The African-American heritage is a culture of sorrow."[12] It is rich with lament songs, often called "negro spirituals." W.E.B. Du Bois called these "sorrow songs."[13] They nourished the soul of the African-American church. In *Performing the Psalms,* we read,

> If we use communal laments as a means to wallow in the sorrow of the human predicament so that it amounts to no more than self-pity, then we misunderstand the function of lament. Lament transforms. Lament enables perseverance. Lament empowers. Lament gives hope because embedded in the lament is an appeal that arises out of trust in the God whose love is forever. Lament is the mode by which hope is reborn.[14]

Du Bois, in *The Souls of Black Folk,* wrote, that in the "sorrow of the Sorrow Songs there breathes a hope – a faith in the ultimate justice of things."[15] He observed that the "minor cadences" were about "despair," but they "change often to triumph and calm confidence." Lament is not a place or a static posture, but a journey. It finds itself in a permanent place too painful to stay – so it moves, first to prayer. Then it moves by prayer, because, left to itself, without God's guidance, it doesn't know which way to go. Sometimes it doubts it has the faith or strength to move. The black church of America is closer to holding a lament tradition than are white evangelical churches.

Today, there is still time to lament in many black churches, embedded in poverty-stricken, high-crime neighborhoods that are collapsing socially. Yet, these same congregations are noted for their exuberant joy. Real life, New Testament life, survives because it conjoins Golgotha and Gethsemane to the empty tomb. These are incomplete alone. Lament and joy belong together. *"In this world, we have tribulation"* – lament is appropriate; but *"in Christ, we have peace"* (John 16:33) – peace in the midst of the storm. *"I have conquered the world,"* Jesus declared. Here is the triumph, the cause for joy, resurrection victory.

Poor whites, following the Civil War, were also social-economic victims in the sharecropper era. They were sometimes forced to work for a mere pittance on land they had previously owned, a veritable slave status. When the Industrial Revolution came, poor whites moved from farms into small towns and industrial villages, often controlled or financed by northerners. Paid minimal wages that kept them living at the poverty line, they were only a bit better off than their Negro counterparts. They were financially enslaved and encumbered to the company store. They also came to share a legacy of pain songs, often cast in the language of a pilgrim. They saw themselves as just passing through this earth.

> I'm just a poor wayfaring stranger
> Traveling through this world below.
> There is no sickness, no toil, nor danger
> In that bright land to which I go.[16]

For these people heaven was their only hope, and they developed a fervent eschatology and a disdain for this jaded world. In that sense, they gave up on lament as prayerful leverage before God for cultural change.

> *The world, they concluded, would not change; culture could not be redeemed. A narrow individualistic version of faith emerged, disconnected from social change and mission.*

Prayer narrowed, taking on more of the form of the Old Testament lament, a plea for God to intervene to extricate them from hurts and harms, from earthly problems. Their petitions were increasingly self-interested. Prayer, out of personal heartaches, was not a means to empathize with a world in distress – its incarnational dimension was lost in self-absorption. It did not hear the call to intercessory lament, embracing some cross in behalf of another, but holding equally to resurrection hope. Prayer became increasingly pragmatic – focused on the outcome of personal relief and betterment, not a means of identifying with a lost, hurting world. We continue to suffer from a self-interested, pragmatic, escapist prayer theology. We cling to the right of personal petition, and we hijack intercession, doubling it under as we solicit others to pray for us. We have not yet stepped into our role, our prayer destiny, as an intercessory community, confident that God will not only hear our personal pleas for assistance, but that He also will break into our time-space world for His larger kingdom purposes.

The old Negro spiritual groaned, "Sometimes I feel like a motherless child" – an orphan, in terms of this world. "A long-ways from home; there's praying everywhere." It conveyed the spirit of lament – but it had given up on the intervention of God here and now. It had succumbed to hopelessness as a means of coping, but it kept faith alive, tying hope to eternity. "O Lord, O Lord /Have mercy on me/ Trouble done bore me down."[17]

With prosperity, even the pilgrim songs have disappeared from Pentecostal congregations.

Prosperity silences lament.

Prosperity numbs cultural pain. Riches are a cultural narcotic. Hollywood is now a friend, as is every kind and style of music and entertainment. Bad is still bad, but not too bad. There is such a thing as sin, but we are no longer sure what it is. Certainly, we can't agree on it. Insulated by the blessings of God from the discomfort of this world, dry eyes characterize prayer and worship. The need for passion and desperation has passed. Repentance and holiness seem old-fashioned.

It is again time to lament.

Psalm 69:22-25 is a rare passage. It is one in which the angry righteous does not address God, appealing for Him to judge another. There, the petitioner squares off with his nemesis and straightforwardly speaks to him. The speaker is declaratively prophetic, wishing the worst on his enemy.

May your table be a trap for you, a snare for your allies. May your eyes be darkened so that you cannot see, and may your loins tremble continually. May God's indignation be poured out on you, and may God's anger overtake you. May your camp be a desolation; let no one live in your tents.

We do not need to conjecture, as some, that the speaker assumes that his words alone would fulfil the curse, that they had intrinsic power. The nature of a dark curse is its assumption that human words, like those of God, are attached to spirit-energy, and have the independent power of death. While Psalm 69 is spoken directly to the enemy, it is spoken tentatively, as a wishful curse, *'May'* this happen to you. *'May God's indignation be poured out on you, and may God's anger overtake you.'* The words themselves are not the source of the power; they require action by God.

It is important that our words and actions be vetted by heaven's judiciary process. God alone is Judge. He alone can be entrusted with righteous judgement. What distinguishes a people who live by the rule of law and those who trust vigilante justice is their commitment to the judicial process. We have been entrusted with grace and mercy – and we are, as believers, to be lavish with it. On the other hand, punitive action is surrendered to God, the Judge. It is not a right retained by us as plaintiffs.[18]

Paul urged us to, *"Bless those who persecute you; bless, do not curse them"* (Romans 12:14).

We are the people who bless. And we *"Leave room for the wrath of God; for it is written, 'Vindication is mine, I will repay,' says the Lord"* (Romans 12:19).

Discussion Guide

1. Do you think at times our modern American faith experience is too narrow? Too shallow? Less than authentic?

2. Why do we shut the deeper, passionate part of ourselves from prayer?

3. How is Psalm 22 a model lament? How has Christ and the cross created a shift in lament?

4. Why are laments sometimes called 'complaints?' This seems to be a legal concept. Discuss it.

5. Discuss the shift from personal lament to intercessory lament. What is the role of intercessory lament?

6. How is lament a protest – an act of truth? How does it interface with the prophetic?

7. How can African-Americans and the early Pentecostals mentor us in lament?

6

Bold Lament:
Brokenness - Standing Up
to Oppression

D ietrich Bonhoeffer appropriated the history of Israel's oppressive kings to Nazi Germany and used Psalm 58 as a
text. Only days after Martin Niemoller had been arrested
on July 1, 1937, Bonhoeffer lifted his voice like a trumpet against
the Nazi machine, the insanity and blindness. He spoke not only to
current injustice, but prophetically, to the coming tide of exponen-
tial mercilessness – he could see it rising. He railed against Hitler and
prayerfully implored God to act.[1]

Bonhoeffer made it clear to his own church, itself under Nazi
oppression, that boldness was essential. Yet, while this was a time for
courage, it was not a time for vengeance: [2]

It would mean much if we would learn that we must earnestly pray
to God in such distress and that whoever entrusts revenge to God
dismisses any thought of ever taking revenge himself. Whoever does
take revenge himself still does not know whom he is up against and
still wants to take charge of the cause by himself. But whoever leaves
revenge in God's hands alone has become willing to suffer and bear
it patiently – without vengeance, without a thought of one's own
revenge, without hate and without protest; such a person is meek,
peaceable, and loves his enemies. God's cause has become more
important to him than his own sufferings. He knows God will win the

victory in the end. *"Vengeance is mine, says the Lord, I will retaliate"* (Deut. 32:35) – and he will retaliate. But we are free from vengeance and retribution. Only the person who is totally free of his own desire for revenge and free of hate and who is sure not to use his prayers to satisfy his own lust for revenge-only such a person can pray with a pure heart: 'Shatter the fangs of the young lions, O Lord, break the teeth in their mouth.'

Erich Zengar offers an important perspective about Biblical lament:[3]

> In the process, [laments] very often compel us to confess that *we ourselves* are violent, and belong among the *perpetrators* of the violence lamented in these psalms. *In that way,* these psalms are God's revelation, because in them, in a certain sense, God in person confronts us with the fact that there are situations of suffering in this world of ours in which such psalms are the last things left to suffering human beings – as protest, accusation, and cry for help. It is obvious on the face of it that these psalms are contextually legitimate on the lips of victims, but a blasphemy in the mouths of the executioners, except as an expression of willingness to submit oneself, with these psalms, to God's judgement.

In classical mysticism, one escaped to the desert, disentangled oneself from the world and sought God. In that view, the "desert is a place of stripping and purifying, a place where there are no luxuries."[4] But Biblical lament, especially intercessory lament out of the cross and resurrection, is not an escape. It feels the oppression of the world, in physical and psychological ways, in a weighty spiritual way.

Lament might consider flight, but its core is fight. It doesn't flee worldliness, but seeks to square it with God's righteousness, call it into account for justice, heal it with holiness. "The gospel," Brueggemann asserts, "is a very dangerous idea."[5] It is good news, but it has an underside – judgement. The gospel does not come to judge; it comes because we are already under judgement – judged by heaven's holiness to be sinners, in the grip of evil and under the power of the Evil One. It comes because we are in a world on fire and need a Savior. Modern versions of the gospel are truncated; they are good news without the bad news; love because we are lovable, not stunning love in the face of the truth about our sin. Such preaching calls us to be *better*, not *new*. It is gospel, preached without context. It is gospel, but not 'the' gospel.

Luther spoke of prayer as "comforted despair."[6] This is the ground of lament – where despair meets comfort. Far from being disengaged or passively resigned to fate, lament asserts what is not obvious, at least in the present moment in which evil seems to be triumphant, namely, that God is in control. And it goes further, imploring Him to come out of hiding, to show up, to act and intervene. It has, to use Donald Bloesch's general terms for prayer, "an indisputably paradoxical dimension…rooted in both the experience of Godforsakeness [sic] and the sense of the presence of God."[7] It is pleading conjoined to trust and surrender.

Leaving Judgement to God

The plea for God's intervention is often connected with an imprecation – a plea for some level of judgement, and thus, it is generally labeled curse. However, there is a very important distinction. One may petition heaven and fervently argue that God deal thus-and-so in a given situation with a person or place. But in Biblical petition, the matter is left to the independent action of God. He alone has the right to judge.

In ancient times as well as contemporary times, the prayer form of a curse is different from that of petition. Imprecatory (judgement) prayers are not curses. Any petition, to be effective, must be supple, left to God's management and alteration. A curse assumes some level of spiritual power in the spoken words themselves and in the spiritual energy tied to the power of speech. Curse and imprecatory prayers differ directionally. Petition is uttered to God; curses are spoken to the person or over the place. They also differ in terms of their character. Legitimate imprecatory prayers are tied to lament. They demand tears. Any consideration of judgement without tears is less than Biblical. In the Old Testament, the tears of lament are often out of personal pain, and the plea for God's judgement is often personal, a cry for retribution, payback. However, on the resurrection side of God's redemptive activity, the imprecation, the plea for God's judgement, is connected to the larger cause of His purposes, the advance of His kingdom, the defense of His own name. Even here, offered legitimately, the imprecation is combined with lament, with tears. To invite God's judgement without tears is to reveal a hard heart. It is prayer that is out of balance, untempered by mercy. As Jesus considered the coming judgement on Jerusalem, due to its sinful past, he wept.

> O Jerusalem, Jerusalem, the city that kills the prophets and stones those who are sent to it! How often would I have gathered your children together as a hen gathers her brood under her wings, and you were not willing! See, your house is left to you desolate (Matthew 23:37-38).

The book of Jeremiah combines lament and prophetic judgement. Lament without relief, without the hope of God's intervening hand, leads only to despair. And desperate prayers for God's action, prayers resolved to see God act, even if it means judgement, without lament, only reveals us as jaded and hardened. Like the disciples, willing to call fire down on a village due to an experience of rejection, we don't know *"what manner of spirit we are of "* (Luke 9:55, KJV, paraphrased).

The petitioner posits power with God. The one who merely curses assumes residual power in themselves or power in the 'word curse' itself. When someone speaks to another the words of a curse, there are two levels of power. First, the power of the words themselves may have a psycho-social impact. Ron Guengerich says, "When the

Lament in Other Old Testament Passages

When Solomon dedicated the temple, the record is found in 2 Chronicles 6, he offered a list of causes for communal laments: loss in war (6:24-25), drought (6:26-27), natural disasters (6:28-31) and exile (36-39). Such calamities were to trigger lament in the community. When the Moabites invaded, Jehoshaphat followed the advice of Solomon, and prayed (2 Chronicles 20:6-12).

The days of lament were also days of fasting (Judges 20:26; Joel 2:15; Jeremiah 36:9; 2 Chronicles 20:3; Esther 4:3, 16). Normal patterns of life were set aside (Joel 1:14; 2:15). The people convened for corporate prayer (Judges 20:16; 1 Sam 7:5; Joel 1:14; Jeremiah 36:6, 9; 2 Chronicles 20:4, 13; Esther 4:16). They mourned, fasted (Judges 20:26; 1 Sam 7:6; Isa 22:12; Jeremiah 14:12), wore sackcloth and ashes (Isa 22:12; Isaiah 58:5; Jeremiah 6:26; 32:11; Esther 4:3), and wept (Judges 20:23, 26). Prayer was a central facet (Josh 7:6-9; 1 Sam 7:5; 2 Kings 19:14-15; 2 Chronicles 20:5; Joel 2:17).[10]

speaker curses an enemy, the powerful words of the curse begin to enact the reality expressed in the words. The speaker is unleashing the debilitating effects of the words on the person cursed."[8] Words do affect us. They have a self-fulfilling dynamic about them. Others hearing the words may accentuate their power by taking a position with the speaker against the one cursed. Second, there is not only natural energy in and around words, there is also the spiritual energy that births the material and natural – God *spoke* the world into existence. Words are powerful. God's words create. Words can also destroy. They can unify or divide. They can heal or wound. At times, they carry an anointing of either holy or dark energy. Just as

God empowers our life-giving speaking and allows His Word to ride on our words, so the Evil One replicates the process, empowering death-like curses, His energy riding on the words of a spoken curse. It is important to remember that only God's words are omnipotent. Ours, using His, are at best potent. The Evil One's words pollute and poison. They do not have the power of life. Nor do they have the power of physical death.

We are people who bless, not curse. As cursing words have the capacity to carry a dark anointing, blessing words have the intended purpose of carrying life, conveying hope, nurturing love, extending grace and forgiveness. It is possible, however, that blessing words cannot and will not be received. In such a case, the person rejecting the blessing, refusing life, ignoring the good news, has chosen to leave themselves on the dark side, vulnerable to consequences. The rejection invites judgement, confirming the previously judged in their sin and rejection of God. But, Jesus instructed his disciples, *"if the home is deserving, let your peace rest on it; if it is not, let your peace return to you"* (Mt. 10:13). The NLT says, *"If it turns out to be a worthy home, let your blessing stand; if it is not, take back the blessing."* The ISV, *"But if it isn't receptive, let your blessing of peace return to you."* It isn't wasted. It can't be wrongly used.

God's disposition is love. Luther called judgement God's "strange" or "alien" work. What a wonderful idea. It is not his "proper work," not at the center, at the core of His being – it is strange, alien to Him. Because His proper nature is love, as Luther noted, "We flee from God to God, from God's strange work of wrath and judgement to God's proper work of rescue and blessing."[9]

In some modern circles, God is not permitted to be a God of judgement. But such exclusion, such blindness, such warped theology does not affect His nature. God is Judge. And He will judge. And, at times, He enters history and judges now. In the Old Testament, when Israel entered the land, Achan wrongly took what had been set apart for destruction. His act was, on the surface, simple theft, a violation of God's moral code. It was, since he was under command, a soldier, insubordination, an act of rebellion. The appropriation of the forbidden Babylonian goods was spiritually contaminating. He died in judgement, as did his family (Joshua 7). The judgement stands at the very beginning of the conquest of the Promised Land and is a reminder that Israel cannot stay on this land if immorality, sedition and compromise are permitted. A holy land demands a holy people. After the coming of the Holy Spirit on the apostolic church, Ananias and Sapphira lied about the amount of money they had given to the church after the sale of real estate (Acts 5:1-11). Their lie was an affront to God; Peter called it a lie to the Holy Spirit and an indication that they had allowed Satan to fill their heart. Both, husband and wife died. These two episodes, one at Israel's entrance into the land, and the other in the first season of the apostolic church, are reminders that God not only judges the world, but those in the church as well. He wants integrity, purity, righteousness, earnestness, no duplicity. In Acts, God also dealt with Herod, the king (Acts 12:20-24), and with Elymas, the sorcerer (Acts 13:8-12).

> *Committing a matter of judgement to God is wise. Our hearts cannot be considered pure enough for such matters.*

God is the filter of righteousness and justice – and though, in heaven's courtroom, we may plead for more than a restraining order against some enemy or the Evil One Himself; or, we may plead for God's judicious and precise intervention to remove someone or some object – it is only a plea and not the pronouncement itself. The end result, the verdict and decree, we leave to God.

Discussion Guide

1. Review the Bonhoeffer quote at the beginning of the chapter. What ideas does he seem to be struggling to balance?

2. How does lament stand up to oppression? How is it bold?

3. How is the 'gospel' that we have today less than a biblical gospel? And how does that relate to lament?

4. We are not to curse. How then can imprecations be justified?

5. O, the power of words. Talk about language and our use of it.

6. Luther called judgement God's "strange" or "alien" work. What does that mean?

7. Does God judge? Here and now? What about Achan, Ananias, and Sapphira?

7

Lament and Job:
Creation's Strange Resolve

P robably no other character in the Bible is more identified with loss and lament than Job. By chapter 3, he has lost everything with the exception of his wife and his God. He was stripped to nothing, overnight; the shock of the multiple calamities would be the death of many. *"I have no peace, no quietness; I have no rest, but only turmoil,"* he lamented (3:26). He longs *"for death that does not come"* (3:21). He wished that he might have perished, but as we know, God had a plan. And God did not choose to inform Job of that plan, or secure his permission to play the part he was given in the drama we see unfold in scripture. So it is with us and our laments.

Not being able to die, Job wishes he had never been born (3:1). He questions God, as all do in such a crisis (7:17-21). He is angry with God (10:3-7). He issues a challenge, making demands of God, so typical in a lament (13:20-22). Maria Boulding says, "Many a prophet was not merely a failure, but a programmed failure. Only by failing could he do the Lord's work, yet his failure was no less painful for that."[1] This is the cross – the failure of Jesus himself to be accepted, to be crowned king, to win over Israel, to ride the populous wave, to convince the temple authorities of authenticity. He was programmed to succeed, through the cross.

Silencing Lament

It is such a common thing to talk instead of pray. To seek answers from humans rather than from God. Job was soon surrounded by friends, which he soon learned was worse than loneliness and his acute sense of feeling abandoned by God. The answers of his friends were of no help. They spent seven days and nights with him, as stunned by the events of his life as he was. None could find the appropriate words of comfort or insight (2:11-13). In truth, their silent presence was probably their greatest contribution to him in his suffering. Then, when Job broke his silence and began to lament, crying out to God, they censored him, attempting to silence him. And it is this tendency that remains with us today – we all attempt to smother lament with comforting, lecturing words.

Eliphaz pointed Job to God's sovereignty, to His delivering power (4:8-21). Zophar described God's sweeping and incomparable omnipotence (11:7-9). Bildad revealed God as awesome, worthy of wonder, and reverence, as having dominion over all (25:2). All of them were right. Their theology was correct, and yet, God rebuked them, *"You have not spoken the truth about me, as my servant Job has"* (25:7). Job had charged God; they had defended God, but God, to everyone's surprise, defended the honesty of Job, the raw emotion and passion, the sincere and authentic questions.

Job did not understand God, not in light of what he had experienced. They, on the other hand, had no open mind to explore the incongruity, the contradiction between Job's righteousness and such tragedy. Their answers were standard, as if memorized, canned. "The problem wasn't their theology. It was their attempt to transform facts about God into easy answers about why Job was suffering. They wanted to talk *about* God; Job was talking *to* God. They wanted to solve Job's problem, which only God could do. God wanted them to merely comfort Job with their presence, with empathy, perhaps by lamenting with him. It turns out that no matter what facts they knew about God, they didn't know God's heart and character."[2] So, they were charged with lousy practical theology, a head full of ideas about God and cold hearts.

Comfort may be provided by words, but God's great comfort to us in a world of sin was God becoming flesh, and dwelling among us in the incarnation – God present, first in Christ, and now, through the indwelling Holy Spirit, and finally in the way the Spirit helps us comfort one another. It is the art and power of presence. It is weeping with another – intercessory lament. This is what Larry Hoffman called *Beyond the Text.*[3] It is not what is said, but what is done. And this is where the book of Job goes in the end.

Job's Lament – Answered by the Creator and Creation's Animals

We ignore animals, and when we think of lament, they are nowhere on our radar screen. In the lament of Job, when the wisdom of Job's friends frustrated him and offered him no answers, there is an amazing assertion, *"Ask the animals, and they will teach you, or the birds in the sky, and they will tell you; or speak to the earth, and it will teach you, or let the fish in the sea inform you."* (Job 12:7-8). In Psalm 19, there is the revelation of Christ, and the special revelation of Scripture, and the revelation of conscience. But the most basic, not the most explicit, not the clearest or the most dependable, and yet, the simplest – is the revelation of God in Creation (Psalm 19; Romans 1:20). Nature can teach us about God and His ways, more than foolish counsel. *"Which of all these does not know that the hand of the LORD has done this? In his hand is the life of every creature and the breath of all mankind"* (Job 12:7-10).

Near the end of Job, God pointed to the animal world and His creation of specific species. The feared Behemoth and Leviathan, He revealed, were His creations (Job 40:19; 41:10). If Job was intimidated by them, as he should have been, that should have led him to recalibrate his perception of God. They were mere creatures, not the Creator. Strangely, this is the pivotal point that brings an end to Job's lament. The answer to lament comes with a kind of parade of animals and God's relationship and view of them. It is a strange lesson in theology and philosophy. The ostrich is seen flapping its wings *"joyously"* (Job 39:13). The beasts of the field are *"playing"* (40:20). The Bible says that *"the Lord answered Job from the whirlwind,"* from one of nature's fearful storms, daring him to question His wisdom (39:2). *"Brace yourself like a man, because I have some questions for you, and you must answer them"* (v. 3). The ultimate resolve in lament is not that we question God, but that His questions move us to discovery. And that discovery is not left-brain logic. It is the stuff of mystery and trust.

God resolves Job's lament by pointing back to creation, *"Where were you when I laid the foundations of the earth?"* (v. 4). He is seen as the Creator of the heavenly choirs of stars (v. 7) and the sea (v. 8). Despite the chaos that has affected Job, nature still reveals order – the sea has boundaries. There is dawn and daylight, darkness and night. *"The light disturbs the wicked and stops the arm that is raised in violence"* (v. 15); that is, the order that remains, despite the fall, restrains evil. Such order reveals God's hand, and yet, nature is still shrouded in mystery, as God and His ways remain mysterious.

We may lament and demand answers of God, but in the end, we have to lean back into the arms of faith, peer into the mystery and choose to believe. We must answer, "No," to God's searing questions. "No," we have not explored the depths of the earth's water passages, nor do we know where to find the gates of death (vv. 16-17). In the mystery of His ways, He uses snow and hail to impede war (vv. 22-23). The winds and currents of the sea are under His power, the rain and the dew, He regulates, as He does the freezing ice and the frost (v. 29). He is Sovereign over nature. His ways make water as hard as a rock (v. 30). The constellations are His design (vv. 31-32). *"Do you know,"* He asked Job, *"the laws of the universe? Can you use them to regulate the earth?"* (v. 33).

Resolving Lament in God's Pervasive Sovereignty

The answer to our laments is not where we might desire it to be – in a rational explanation of our 'whys?' Rather, it is in the sovereignty of God! Rest – He is in control, even when life seems to shout otherwise. He speaks to the clouds, and it rains (v. 34). He tilts *"the water jars of heaven when the earth is parched"* (vv. 37-38). He directs the ragged, zig-zag pattern of lightning (v. 35). He awakens the mind and heart of the human to intuit and act from instinct (v. 36).

In Job 40, God claims a sovereignty over the animal kingdom, as well as over nature generally. He knows *"when the wild goats give birth."* He has *"watched as deer are born in the wild"* (v. 1). He pays attention to them in the months that they carry their young, concerned about the yet-to-be-born goats and deer (v. 2) – what does that say about abortion and prenatal care? About the protection of the unborn? In a stunning contrast to man, God argues to Job that it is He who cares for the almost worthless wild donkey who *"hates the noise of the city"* and cannot endure the shouts of the driver. He resisted domestication, and yet, grace prevailed, and God gave the little wild donkey freedom. He untied his ropes and set him free, placing him in the wilderness, the wasteland (vv. 5-7). The message, though implicit, is still clear. 'If I care about an easily stressed, virtually useless species of wild donkeys, will I not care for you?' God's claim of sovereignty over nature and the animal kingdom is a veiled plea – 'Will you not trust me?' This is the theme Jesus echoed, when he said, *"Are not two sparrows sold for a penny? Yet not one of them will fall to the ground apart from the will of your Father. And even the very hairs of your head are all numbered. So do not be afraid; you are worth more than many sparrows"* (Matthew 10:29-31, Berean Study Bible). Lament is resolved, as Habakkuk would learn, as Paul asserted in Romans 8, in faith and trust.

Resolving Lament in Weakness and Limitation

Each creature, God argues before Job, is unique. Each has strengths and weaknesses. The stork rises from the earth by the lift capacity of its wings, but the ostrich is grounded. Flapping its wings wildly and grandly, it nevertheless can't fly (Job 39:13). The ostrich, one of the earth's largest birds, has a brain smaller than either of its eyes. It would not win an IQ award, even in the 'bird-brain' category. When a predator is near, it has the habit of spinning in a circle, as if that is a method of evasion – humans seem to do that too! Their eggs are laid on the ground and left there openly, showing no instinct to protect their yet-to-be-hatched offspring from being crushed or eaten by an animal (39:14-15). You don't want an ostrich for a mother. When their young hatch, the ostrich lacks tenderness: *"She is harsh toward her young, as if they were not her own. She doesn't care if they die"* (v. 16). And yet, God watches over and preserves the species. Who else would? She is deprived of wisdom and understanding (v. 17).

This passage is a declaration of God's care for the underprivileged and the disadvantaged. It is a revelation of the character of God, an answer in part to Job's lament. God then tells Job that He likes to see the ostrich run, *"...whenever she jumps up to run, she passes the swiftest horse with its rider"* (v. 18). Disadvantaged, intellectually limited, God finds a positive attribute in the speed of the ostrich – 'O, how the creature runs.' Here is grace, the appreciation of God for the underclass of the animal kingdom, the ability to see an asset in each creature, noble and ignoble – the horse with its strength and flowing mane, and its courage in battle: *"...it charges...it does not run from the sword"* (vv. 19-25). The horse in battle snorts in the face of fear and is not rattled by the sound of clashing swords. What we take for granted, God surveys and admires in nature – small things, like the ability of the locust to leap (v. 20) and the hawk and eagle to soar (vv. 26-27).

God cares. God notices. God does not discard, based on ability and intellect, the contribution of a species to the ecosystem – he loves them all. And therefore, it must be clear, he loves Job. In response to what Job now perceives, after this review of nature, he recants his earlier words and repents before God's sovereignty (Job 42:6).[4] His resolve is not found in the counsel of friends. What begins to re-center Job is God's disclosures on nature and animals. God has woven wonder and revelation into nature. Through its lens is seen the sovereignty of God – His omniscience and omnipotence, His power and tender, attentive care. When scripture no longer makes sense, nor do its prophets. When Christ seems silent and his revelation distant, when our hearts are confused and our consciences dull – we are drawn back to the most basic form of revelation, Creation.

Resolving Lament in Re-Centered Faith

"Then the LORD said to Job, 'Do you still want to argue with the Almighty? You are God's critic, but do you have the answers?'" (41:1, NLT). Job responds, quickly and appropriately, with humility, *"I am nothing – how could I ever find the answers?"* (v. 4). He will now end

his lament, *"I will cover my mouth with my hand. I have said too much already. I have nothing more to say"* (vv. 4b-5). But God will not allow his silence. It is not suppression God seeks. It is not silence in continued confusion and pain. God wants to ground the conversation on a different basis.

"From the whirlwind," from the swirling confusion out of which lament rises, God again challenges Job. The imagery is powerful and suggestive – God can be heard speaking out of the storms of life. Rather than silence us, and rather than the storms being indications of His silence, they are actually the megaphones of heaven. *"Then the LORD answered Job from the whirlwind: 'Brace yourself like a man, because I have some questions for you, and you must answer them'"* (41:67). Now we come to the heart of lament, the charge against God and his justice, against his character, *"Will you discredit my justice and condemn me just to prove you are right?"* (v. 8). The great danger in lament is that of stepping over the line from sincere questions and doubts to agnosticism. Lament is grappling *with* faith; agnosticism is the loss *of* faith. Lament is attempting to manage the poison, the toxic nature of failing faith; agnosticism is capitulating to it.

This is where faith is founded or flounders, where we stand or fall – on the question of God's character. Storms challenge our faith – precisely, our faith in the character of God. The disciples, in the midst of the storm on the sea of Galilee, with the boat rapidly filling with water, found God, in Christ, asleep. That is sometimes a feature of lament in the Old Testament, charging God with sleeping on the job (Psalm 44:23). The disciples asked Jesus, *"Do you not care that we are perishing?"* (Mark 4:38). This is the question in every storm – does God care? Moreover, is He, in terms of His nature, caring at all? The great challenge is never about faith in God's ability or His existence. It is a challenge to His nature and character. And that is the ultimate issue in lament and prayer generally. You will never succeed in gaining satisfying answers from a God whom you do not trust. Your faith may wobble – Will He? When? How? But, uncertain, confused faith, resolves itself in trust, even if that trust is blind. It casts its weakness on God's strength. Job is asked, *"Are you as strong as God?"* – the answer must always be, "No!" (Job 40:9 NLT). *"Can you thunder with a voice like his?"* – "No!" Here is both the force of God's sovereignty and fierceness of His speech, before our weakness and inability to even articulate our pain or problem.

Resolving Lament in Humility

What follows is a rebuke – an important corrective for lament. Sincerely meant questions, out of confusion and disappointment over what we perceive as God's lack of action are understandable. Yet, with only a slight variation, they can lead to a kind of senseless, faithless, railing against God. Faith can be lost in the multiplied questions. God warns Job here about pride. This is the unnamed nemesis that we all must slay. We have the right to pray and communicate with God in an amazingly open manner – and what a mind-bending idea that is. We, mere humans, can talk to God and ask things of Him, question Him. Yet, we must never do so without humility and respect. Even if we are passionate in our lament, frustrated, confused, asking "How long?" We must, nevertheless, remember our place – who God is and who we are. Abraham said, *"I have undertaken to speak to the Lord,"* and the sense of the passage is, *"I can't believe I am talking to God like this, so boldly, so forcefully, I who am but dust and ashes"* (Gen. 18:27, ESV). Pride stiffens lament. It corrupts it, making it a selfish tirade, not a noble inquiry in defense of God's character and honor, and in hope of His action to move forward his purposes and glorify His name.

God taunts Job, *"All right, put on your glory and splendor, your honor and majesty. Give vent to your anger"* (Job 40:10). He challenges Job to be what he cannot be – glorious and splendid, worthy of honor, majestic. Then, to direct his angry prayer words against the real enemy, knowing that the exercise will be futile. *"Let it overflow against the proud"* – in fact, God urges Job to move beyond words to action, *"...walk on the wicked where they stand. Bury them in the dust. Imprison them in the world of the dead"* (40:11b-13). Here is the hint at the 'double-wish' of the imprecatory prayer – the putting away of the wicked. Job knows he can't do this. He can't be the answer to his own prayers – that is point of prayer. And it is the point of our praying to God, who alone is our answer and resolve. The proud, and the Proud One, Lucifer, and all hell, remain unmoved by our warfare words prayerfully aimed at them. They are lost on the darkness. We pray to God, because only He cares and understands. He alone will respond with tenderness and justice. The absence of prayer is self-sufficiency; it is pride. If Job can fix his own dilemma by self-sufficiency or angry prayer tirades, God says, *"Then even I would praise you,"* why? – *"for your own strength would save you"* (v. 14). Lament is about a world that seems upside down, but the greater disorientation is a world in which there is no lament, no need of God, no God to which we can cry out. It is a nihilistic world, where people who are at the end of their rope do not pray. Even faint hope is gone. They do not ask God, "How long?" They simply give up and give in to despair. The other side of the equation is a world in which man is sufficient to himself, without God, and without a need for God. This world is upside down, and sadly, that is the affluent, elite, educated Western world. It is also the world of the typical Westernized Christian.

> *No lament. No problem we cannot solve ourselves. No need for tears. In such a world, man is to be worshipped.*

In this world, God praises and affirms us. Our own strength saves us. All is on its head.

Resolving Lament in Confession

Lament is both a declaration of weakness before some over-whelming enemy – circumstances, evil men or the devil himself – and a confession of faith and trust in God. In every case, weakness is to be cast on God. Lament finds its resolve in faith in His sovereignty. Job replies, *"I know that you can do anything, and no one can stop you"* (42:2 NLT). This is the resolution! Then Job confesses, *"You [God] asked, 'Who is this that questions my wisdom with such ignorance?'"* Our laments, though authentic, though an expression of real pain, though a gauge of our struggle for understanding of some crisis, are indications of human ignorance. Not stupidity, but ignorance – that of which we are unaware, unfamiliar, not literate in, witless about, inexperienced. *"We see through a glass darkly, we know in part"* (1 Cor. 13:12). We deal with mysteries, partial knowledge of the spiritual.

Faith does not mean that we should not lament; that we should stuff our pain and commit ourselves to silent suffering and confu-sion. Rather, lament is the journey forward, the way out – but ag-nosticism and arrogance can become lament's deadly companion, and when that happens, lament turns to depression or irrational rage against God and we lose faith.

Notice Job's resolve in humility, *"It is I – and I was talking about things I knew nothing about, things far too wonderful for me"* (42:3). What follows is a confession, *"I had only heard about you before, but now I have seen you with my own eyes. I take back everything I said, and I sit in dust and ashes to show my repentance"* (42:5-6). Humility allows the best sight-line to the throne. You must get low enough to see God. *"I dwell on a high and holy place, and also with the contrite and the lowly of spirit"* (Isaiah 57:15). In the end, Job turns back, as does every healthy lament, to praise. He sacrifices to God, building an altar, renewing his worship.

Resolving Lament in Intercessor

God rebukes Job's friends, and then says an amazing thing, *"My servant Job will pray for you, and I will accept his prayer on your behalf"* (v. 8). The weak one prays for those who have presented themselves as strong. The counselee prays for the counselors. The sick one prays for the well. Job becomes the forgiving intercessory agent for his toxic friends, *"and the Lord accepted Job's prayer"* (v. 9). Here, ministry flows from the weak, the wounded, the one branded as flawed. His credibility was gone. He was a poster child for failure. Clouds of confusion hung over him, He was the most unlikely to receive the 'spiritual leader of the year' award. And, there is more. The ideological resolve to Job's lament is first solved in his acceptance of God's sovereignty, his willingness to admit that God's strength and wisdom is beyond him. He recognized that he could not solve his own problems or defeat the wicked by himself. Yet, even with that confession, that shift in thinking, his life was not changed. His fortunes remained the same. However, *"When Job prayed for his friends, the LORD restored his fortunes. In fact, the Lord gave him twice as much as before!"* (v. 10). This is an amazing moment. Here is insight, submission to God's sovereignty. Trust – blind trust. Yet, only when personal lament is transformed into intercessory lament does the full restoration come. The result is not only relief from mental confusion, but also the immeasurable blessing of God. This is where lament moves from personal obsession with pain, through the cross and the pain of Christ, to the resurrection and to intercessory prayer. It gets better. A reconciliation follows: *"Then all his brothers, sisters, and former friends came and feasted with him in his home. And they consoled him and comforted him because of all the trials...each of them brought him a gift..."* (42:11-12). He lived for 140 years, seeing four new generations of children, grandchildren and great-grandchildren. God restored double what he had lost.

The church is still offering personal laments to God for personal problems. Its prayers are self-interested. Intercession is used to merely swap personal needs: "I will pray your problems away if you will promise to pray my problems away." While God is concerned about our needs, and we should pray about everything, our prayer focus is still far too narrow. We have failed to become an intercessory community lamenting over a lost world, praying with faith from the resurrection side of the cross. We have failed to pray for our disappointing relationships, our accusing friends. We have failed to forgive after our moments of confusion and conflict. We have failed to use the privilege of prayer for others first. Christ came to the earth to pray – to pray for us, from his own cross, for our forgiveness. And we are left on the earth, after our conversion, to serve as intercessors, for others. And when we do, our fortunes change and we experience a taste of the resurrection.

Discussion Guide

1. Job – when his name is mentioned, what is your immediate response?

2. Discuss Maria Boulding's idea of God's 'programming failure.'

3. How could Job's comforters be right – and wrong? Does that happen to us?

4. Here again, in this chapter, we meet the idea that nature honors what we do not seem to grasp. What is the message we are missing?

5. How is lament resolved in God's sovereignty?

6. What is your take-away from the parade of Creation at the end of the book of Job? What is God's message?

7. Distinguish between lament and agnosticism – the loss of faith.

8. How do we recenter our faith? What does that mean?

SECTION 2

A New Testament Perspective

8

Lament in the New Testament

The roots of early Christian worship are found in synagogue and temple worship. They adapted a Jewish worship model with a fresh Christological understanding. New Testament believers used the forms and frames of the Old Testament in their worship. Most of these early believers still considered themselves Jews, Christ-following Jews. Many Christians, still attended the temple and its festivals until its destruction in 70 AD, and they attended local synagogues across the empire. Their worship services, in homes, perhaps also in synagogues, not on the Sabbath, but Sunday, generally followed the synagogue model with fresh insights, and with a second movement added to the service which featured the Lord's Supper.[1] The psalms continued to be a primary source of the worship – there was no New Testament.[2]

They read the collected writings of the apostles and the accounts of the life of Jesus. Each church had its own collection, more or less, of the books that would eventually comprise the New Testament. In the psalms utilized by these early Christians were laments. The table of the Lord itself was a reenactment of his sufferings and in that sense, it was a joyful lament. Each week, the believers confronted the blood and brokenness of Christ, and his body; and celebrated his presence at the table with them. He was not dead, but risen. Alive.

Some scholars point to a handful of New Testament passages as lament – Matthew 2:18, 23:37-39, Luke 13:34-35, 19:41-44, and 23:27-31. There is debate about whether the passages are truly lament as a genre,[3] since they do not follow the literary form of a lament found in the Old Testament. Paul appears to make use of lament language in Romans 3:10-18, 7:7-25, and again in chapter 8, *"For your sake we face death all day long; we are considered as sheep to be slaughtered"* (Rom. 8:36 [18-39], NIV; Ps. 44:22-23). Drawing from Psalm 44, where God is charged with being asleep, with inaction, with allowing his people to needlessly suffer defeat, he signals a shift in the way believers process disappointment with God. We are not exempted from it; we triumph through it (Romans 8:31-37). Drawing from Habakkuk, he moves the church to "live by faith," not demanding proofs of God's love and mercy, as did the Old Testament laments (Hab. 2:4; Romans 1:17; Gal. 3:11; Heb. 10:38; 2 Cor. 5:7). Some have also seen lament in Romans 7:24, *"Wretched man that I am! Who will deliver me from the body of death?"* Romans 8:22 is another glimpse at lament. The groaning of Creation is to be understood as a creation lament, seen often in the Old Testament.[4] There is a lament over Babylon in Revelation 18:10, 16-17, 19.

> When Herod saw that he had been tricked by the Magi, he was enraged, and sent and slew all the male children who were in Bethlehem and all its vicinity, from two years old and under, according to the time which he had determined from the Magi. Then what had been spoken through Jeremiah the prophet was fulfilled, *"A voice was heard in Ramah, weeping, and great mourning, Rachel weeping for her children; and she refused to be comforted, because they were no more"* (Mt. 2:16-18).

Scholars assert that grief or sadness do not constitute a 'lament' – since they are not formal prayers for change. They argue, academically, that painful or tearful moments do not conform to the literary standards of true laments, because, for example, they are not accompanied by articulated prayers or because all the elements of lament's form are not present[5] – but tears are often short-hand prayers. Non-conforming New Testament laments, scholars argue, do not contain a formal plea for change. But again, such a plea is sometimes veiled in inexpressible grief and confusion. Further, such moments in the New Testament narrative stand against the backdrop of the Old Testament form, yet without the precise form – it resonates for its authenticity.

In some ways, the New Testament only gives us glimpses of the peaks of theological mountains that exist in the Old Testament. It builds on, caps and alters the contour of previous revelation. For example, we don't find a definitive worship structure in the New Testament – but we do find corrective language for worship.[6] Such language assumes an existing form (1 Cor. 11; 14; 1 Thess. 5:14-21).

> *New Testament writers, at times, appear to pull on a thread from the fabric of some Old Testament narrative, only providing for us a clue as to the textual background, as a means of calling up the whole text.*

They are not concerned about promoting an ancient literary form, but extracting its fire.[7]

In Mark 15:34 and Matthew 27:46, when both writers quote Psalm 22:1, the "cry of dereliction," it is assumed that they mean to call forth the whole psalm, by noting only the first and key verse,[8] a kind of short-hand for the entire psalm.[9] Mark understands Jesus as "the lamenter par excellence."[10] New Testament writers invoke "strands of prayers of lament" passages, that "breathe lament's spirit."[11] These are variously cited to include – the disciple's cry on the stormy sea (Mark 4:35-41, Matt. 8:23-27); Rachel's weeping (Mt. 2:17-18; cf. Jeremiah 31:5);[12] Jesus' cry on the cross, as well as his prayer in Gethsemane; his weeping over Jerusalem (Luke 19:41).

Certainly, Matthew 2:18 is not properly, in terms of form, a lament. It is a simple reference to Jeremiah 31:5, Rachel weeping for Jerusalem. Understood in the context of Herod's slaughter of the infants in Bethlehem – it strongly hints at lament. It also stands among the first frames in the life of Jesus, denoting, that when he is born there is lament. And we also know, when he dies, it is in lament. His life and ministry are therefore framed by lament. He came to the earth to weep, as God, to protest the way things are, to be the one voice from earth, agreeing with heaven, that the Kingdom of God should be fully established here on earth again and the will of God asserted, and the name of God hallowed.

In Matthew 23:37-39, paralleled by Luke 13:34-35, Jesus is seen mourning over Jerusalem. It is not the literary form of the passage that matters, but the character of the passage and the person. In Luke 19:41-44, Jesus is again weeping over the coming destruction of Jerusalem – a lament? In Luke 23:27-31, as Jesus is led away to be crucified, the women who are following begin a lament. Jesus urges them to refocus their lament, to not weep over his death, but for themselves, for their children, because of the coming judgement. He will taste God's wrath for sin, but Jerusalem will soon taste wrath as well. The nation will again perish.

Lament Refocused

In the New Testament, lament is refocused and it stands, as in Habakkuk, against the coming wrath of God. Lament in the Old Testament was often tied, as in Psalm 44, to the confusion of unfulfilled covenant promises related to personal and national obedience and disobedience, victory and defeat in battle (Leviticus 26; Deuteronomy 28). The equation had been simple – obey and be blessed (Dt. 28:1-2; Leviticus 26:3-13); disobey and experience consequences (Dt. 28:15f; Lev. 26:14-17f). The clear and crisp promise of Psalm 1 is again in view – righteous people are blessed and wicked people are punished.

However, at times, as in Psalm 44, Israel felt that they had obeyed and God had not blessed (vv. 4-5, 9-11f). They were not in rebellion or sin (vv. 17-18). They were not lying to themselves or God. Rather, Psalm 44 anticipated a theological shift. It stands behind Romans 8:32, as does Habakkuk. Paul asserts God's sovereignty, *"All things work together for good,"* not only good things, rather, all things. God's sovereignty can be seen not only when good outcomes are forthcoming, but in the face of evil's seeming triumph.

> *Faith, in the New Testament, is no longer so fragile that covenant people have to be protected, insulated from negative outcomes.*

Now, "all things" are woven into the tapestry of life and may be used to glorify God. In Psalm 44:22 we read, *"For your sake we are killed all day long; we are accounted as sheep for the slaughter."* There, in the psalms, it was a lament, a complaint to God, a "Why?" But in Romans 8:36, Paul restates this as a new way to look at life. Christians face death daily. Martyrdom stalks them. They are persecuted, as helpless as sheep, *"Yet, in all these things, more than conquerors"*

(v. 37). The victory is now assured. It is achieved not only in deliverance from, but at times, indeed often, in deliverance through. Paul, in quoting Psalm 44 in Romans 8, is setting forth a new paradigm – covenantal righteousness through Christ will not exempt believers from trouble (Psalm 1). Now, Paul asserts, believers will triumph in the midst of tribulation (8:37-39). Freedom from life's troubles is no longer a sign of blessing. And misfortunes and sufferings are not an indication of God's displeasure, as a simplistic interpretation of Psalm 1 might suggest. The suffering and battering of the world is not the final answer. God is the final answer.

We should now expect rain on the just and the unjust (Mt. 5:45). The covenant paradigm has shifted. *"What then shall we say to these things?"* (Romans 8:31) – to tribulation, distress, persecution, famine, nakedness, peril, or sword? We say, according to Paul, *"If God is for us, who can [successfully] be against us?"* (8:31). Now, we know what Job's comforters did not know, *"that all things work together for good to those who love God, to those who are the called according to His purpose"* (8:28). The goal is not a blessed life free from life's troubles; the goal is *"to be conformed to the image of His Son,"* and for this reason God has predestined the justified to victory (8:29-30) through the cross. We should not allow either the negative circumstances of life or disparaging voices who wrongly interpret such events to condemn us. *"Who shall bring a charge... God justifies; Who is he who condemns...?"* Christ himself is praying for us now (8:33-34).

> *Lament and wail, for the fierce anger of the Lord has not turned back from us (Jer. 4:8).*

In the New Testament, the old simple, cause-effect formula fades away. There are, of course, blessings for obedience and consequences for sin, but that is not at the heart of the new covenant. Our salvation is through Jesus Christ and the covenant he forged with the Father, in his own blood, by the perfect offering of himself in life and death, in the place of a sacrificial lamb. The new covenant is based not on our performance, but on his perfection – his sinless life and his perfect obedience. Unlike Israel, who had a covenant with God through the mediation of the law, we have a covenant with God through the mediation of Christ Jesus, through love and grace. We are bound to God, not by *principles,* though sacred and noble, but by our relationship though a *person.* At the cross, God judged our sin. Because of God's grace, and our grace-empowered repentance and reorientation at the cross, we enter into the covenant created between the perfect man, Christ Jesus, and the Father. This new covenant, centered in Christ, and his cross, invites something completely absent from the old, namely, that we now freely take our cross, as an act of love and follow Christ as disciples. Our life is no longer lived for ourselves. We are the people of God on a mission, commissioned to engage the globe with the gospel; commanded to love; and committed to pray everywhere, lifting holy hands, that men might be saved. We are not exempt from suffering. Indeed, the cross, our cross, now becomes a critical expression of our love and devotion in the new covenant relationship. *"If you do not carry your own cross and follow me, you cannot be my disciple"* (Luke 14:27). We carry our cross and follow, openly and publicly, and at times, we share in the sufferings of Christ. We may taste rejection by the world, stand alone, be engaged by principalities and powers, all as we carry our cross. *"Yet in all these things we are more than conquerors though Him who loved us"* (8:37).

"Lament-before-God" transcends a mere human complaint. It is not purely psychological, but a prayerful and spiritual act. In Romans 8:22, according to Paul, *"...the whole creation groans and labors with birth pangs together."* The term for groans, *sustenazó,* only

133

occurs here and implies lament. The earth's environment is in travail, not due to sulfur dioxide, carbon monoxide, or nitrogen oxides, but due, surprisingly, to sin. Creation is praying – lamenting, to be delivered from the curse of sin. It is endowed here with consciousness, in "earnest expectation," eagerly waiting for a godlier humanity to emerge, "the sons of God." Paul says *"creation was subjected to futility, not willingly, but because of Him who subjected it in hope; because the creation itself also will be delivered from the bondage of corruption into the glorious liberty of the children of God."* For that reason, it laments. It prays, as it were. It groans (Romans 8:19-22). The NIV calls Creation now "frustrated." The NLT, *"subjected to God's curse, but with eager hope."* This is "not of its own will," not due to anything Creation did – it was a victim. God hears its groans, and we do too, but we misinterpret them.

In Romans 8:26, Paul says, *"we are saved in this hope…"* of full adoption into the family of God, and the redemption of our body – a resurrection unto eternal life. For this, we persevere. We *"eagerly wait for it."* Meanwhile, we experience weakness, and at times we don't know what we should pray as we navigate life, but the Spirit has been sent to assist us, *"…the Spirit Himself makes intercession for us with groanings which cannot be uttered"* (v. 26). The NIV says, *"…the Spirit himself intercedes for us through wordless groans."* The NLT says, *"…with groanings that cannot be expressed in words,"* and the ESV, similarly, *"with groanings too deep for words"* – wordless sounds. "The more helpless you are, the better you are fitted to pray, and the more answers to prayer you will experience."[13]

Creation is groaning. And the Spirit is groaning and willing to help us pray – to lament. In fact, Paul says, *"we ourselves groan within ourselves"* (v. 23). Here is a trio of groans – Creation, the redeemed (you and I), and the Spirit. Creation *is* groaning – there is evidence of that. And *the Spirit* is groaning, but there appears to be little groaning in the Church, and little desire to have the Spirit help us offer prayerful laments. "True prayer," Spurgeon asserted, "is measured by weight...a single groan before God may have more fullness of prayer in it than a fine oration of great length."[14]

Innocence and Resurrection Power

In the Old Testament, suffering was thought to be proof of some guilt. Misery and the sorrows of life were a consequence of some misbehavior, a signal of the judgement of God. But in the New Testament, Jesus Christ himself suffered, and he suffered innocently. He suffered rejection and loneliness, misunderstanding and grief. He bore both our sin and sicknesses at the cross – innocently. He suffered, and so now do his followers (John 15:14-21; Rom. 5:1-5; 8:34-39). This forces a change in New Testament lament. We do not hear from the teachings of Jesus or the apostles lament as a protest against personal deprivation or enemies, a theme that dominates the laments in the psalms. Quite the opposite. While God promises to supply needs, momentary deprivation is seen as a part of life in a fallen, sinful world. The difference is not found in our exemption from it, but in our triumph in and over it.

Paul wrote to the Corinthians about his trouble in Asia:

> We think you ought to know, dear brothers and sisters, about the trouble we went through in the province of Asia. We were crushed and overwhelmed beyond our ability to endure, and we thought we would never live through it. In fact, we expected to die. But as a result, we stopped relying on ourselves and learned to rely only on God, who raises the dead. And he did rescue us from mortal danger, and he will rescue us again. We have placed our confidence in him, and he will continue to rescue us. And you are helping us by praying for us (2 Cor. 1:8-11a, NLT).

The NIV says, "We were under great pressure," the NAS, "burdened excessively, beyond our strength, so that we despaired even of life."

The KJV, *"we were pressed out of measure, above strength, insomuch that we despaired even of life."* God's Word Translation reads, *"It was so extreme that it was beyond our ability to endure. We even wondered if we could go on living."* The Weymouth New Testament, *"we renounced all hope even of life."* That's the cross in the context of ministry and life itself.

Paul goes on to say that the situation was so severe, he thought they might have *"received the sentence of death,"* that the lives of he and his party were over (v. 9). The NLT says, *"In fact, we expected to die."* But under the weight of the situation, he realized, *"this happened that we might not rely on ourselves but on God, who raises the dead."* The *"despairing even of life,"* and the sense of the *"sentence of death,"* the resignation, 'we're going to die,' is the substance of lament. *"The sufferings of Christ abound in us,"* Paul asserted, but, that is true *"so that our consolation also abounds through Christ"* (2 Cor. 1:5). In the new paradigm, God is the *"Father of mercies and God of all comfort, who comforts us in all our tribulation, that we may be able to comfort those who are in any trouble with the comfort with which we ourselves are comforted by God"* (vv. 3d-4). We are not extricated from the crisis, but comforted in it. As we partake of the sufferings of life, we also partake of the consolation of Christ, by the Spirit (v. 7). And we taste resurrection power. We discover the God *"who raises the dead"* (v. 9).

Paul asserts boldly, *"He has delivered us from such a deadly peril, and he will deliver us again. On him, we have set our hope that he will continue to deliver us"* (v. 10, NIV). The NLT says, *"And he did rescue us from mortal danger, and he will rescue us again."* The Berean Literal Bible, *"...who has delivered us from such a great death...in whom we have hope that also He will deliver us still."* The KJV says, *"Who delivered...and doth deliver...will yet deliver us."* The NET Bible affirms, *"We have set our hope on him that he will deliver us yet again."*

> *Now having the proof of the resurrection, we rejoice in the face of suffering. What can the world do to us? What power does the devil have over us? What can even our great nemesis, death, do? We have seen the empty tomb. We have met the resurrected Christ.*

Christ was persecuted, and therefore, we may also expect persecution. We also understand that all of our enemies are not mere mortals. We are in the crosshairs of a cosmic battle for the planet and the souls of mankind. In the great and final battle of his life, Jesus, the Christ was rejected, suffered wrongly, was crucified, and died innocently. Now, against the backdrop of the cross and global rejection, we are called to suffer with him. That suffering is something we embrace as a part of God's purifying discipline, producing character in us (Rom. 5:3-5; Jas. 1:2-3; 1 Pet. 1:7). Yet, this is not resignation to suffering. It is not a call to the cross alone, rather, it is a call to see the cross through the lens of the resurrection (2 Tim. 1:10; 1 Cor. 15:3-8). Christ rose to ascend to David's throne, not here, but in exile. We are living 'between the times.' The kingdom has come, but not fully. Christ is risen, but he has not yet been revealed as Lord of lords and King of kings.

Some devout men buried Stephen, and made loud lamentation over him (Acts 8:2).

The Old Testament laments were measured in terms of prosperity and peace, things of this world that were immediately desired. In the New Testament, our reward is not of this world. It is sometimes deferred. It is no longer primarily here and now in this world's prosperity; it is ultimately in heaven (Matthew 5:10-12; 1 Pet. 4:13). Yet, our victory is immediate, since it is a matter of our heart.

There is also the promise of the second resurrection, the consummation of all things, the eventual crowning of the rightful heir of Adam's fallen kingdom, Jesus, the Christ; and yet, we do not live with an escapist, 'by-and-by' mentality. We are convinced, that God can and will intervene here and now, not to merely minimize our pain or make our life prosperous, but to further His kingdom and use us in that process.

In the New Testament, lament is crowned with the resurrection. In the Old Testament, lament is tied to Israel's national identity, the nation among nations covenanted to God in a sea of hostile, pagan nations. National enemies abounded in the form of wicked foes, not friends.[15] In the New Testament, the dynamic changes – the people of God no longer constitute a geo-political nation. We are an *ethne,* a people group, a nation among the nations, a pilgrim people whose citizenship is in heaven. We are not at home here. We have, as a part of our mission, taken up the cross to follow Christ – suffering innocently is a part of our calling. We are *"lambs led to the slaughter,"* and yet with a buoyant, resurrection spirit. Unlike the Old Testament psalms, dominated by the lament itself, with a faint expression of hope, Christians are called to rejoice in the midst of confusion and suffering, to not lose the posture of praise, even in their pain. According to the New Testament, troubles and trials are producing something in us we cannot readily see – character (Romans 5:3-5; James 1:2-3; 1 Peter 1:7). And, in the pain and problems of life, we tap resurrection power.

Francis Bacon said, "Prosperity is the blessing of the Old Testament; adversity is the blessing of the New, which carries the greater benediction, and the clearer revelation of God's favor."[16] This adversity, the cross we carry in the face of innocence, is vindicated by resurrection moments. Lament is present, momentarily, but it is with tearful eyes fixed on an empty tomb.

The Lamenting Widow – The Church

In teaching on prayer, Jesus told a story about an oppressed widow (Luke 18:1-8) who entered a courtroom and pleaded for justice in the face of an unjust judge. It is a fascinating and somewhat contradictory story, since women had no standing in the ancient near eastern court, except through a living father or husband. This woman was widowed, so for her, there would be no justice, not even a hearing, despite an aggressive adversary that made her life miserable. However, notwithstanding multiple rebuffs, this widow refused to be turned away without her day in court. She had appropriately restrained herself from vengeance, by going to court and by refusing to take the matter of responding to her oppression into her own hands. But, she also refused to accept the injustice that had come to define her life. Living with an aggressive and relentless adversary was not acceptable to her – that had to change. In a lament, the complaint of the victim is heard. It is a first-person appearance in court. The grief comes from the aggrieved. It is the plaintiff testifying – hearsay will not work. Each person must enter their own plea. This widow had to go to court.

Initially being denied a hearing, the widow persisted and the hearing was granted (Luke 11:4-5). With the odds against her, arguing her case in front of a jaded judge (v. 2), she nevertheless recognized that only he could solve her dilemma. She won her case by persistence. This is a metaphor. The Church, the bride of Christ, is considered by the world to be a

> Prayer is life passionately wanting, wishing, desiring God's triumph. Prayer is life striving and toiling everywhere and always for that ultimate victory.
> ~ G. Campbell Morgan

widow. Our bridegroom, Jesus Christ, has been pronounced dead, crucified, and the world considers our resurrection story a myth. In earth's courts, increasingly, we will be denied justice. Our standing will be contested and we will be required to take our case before God, to make our appeal to heaven.

Like the widow, we too have a vicious adversary, the devil. There is no way to appease him or make peace with him. We must go to court – we must pray. We are not alone in the oppression; the planet itself is a victim of the tyranny of the dark prince. The church, however, is not a widow as is alleged. We are God's intercessory community in the earth. As we persist in prayer and cry out for justice, God not only grants us a hearing, but He answers our pleas for justice. When we pray in the name of Jesus, and answers come to our persistent prayers, they demonstrate that Jesus is alive, and that the Judge in heaven hears the disenfranchised, the weak and powerless of the earth. The point is clear: if a socially marginalized widow, by sheer tenacity, can move a wicked judge, *"Shall God not avenge His own elect who cry out...He will avenge them speedily!"* (vv. 7-8).

In this narrative, the answers to our prayers then become more than answers. They serve to overturn the ruling of an earthly court by heaven's supreme court. Further, they are proof to a skeptical, watching world, that our bridegroom is not dead – Jesus is alive. This is the most amazing outcome of all. Prayer then, is not primarily for our own narrow personal causes, but for kingdom purposes. Its answers are proof of a living God, a testimony that must be openly shared. We pray, in his name, for his glory, to advance his kingship – and the answer comes. And when it does, we must tell our story, to everyone, everywhere. We dare the non-believer, the skeptic, to pray: "Talk to God, and see if he does not talk back to you!" Or, begin to say to God, "If you are real, talk to me, reveal yourself, I want to know you," and see what happens.

To the believer, God's justice may seem at times slow and not forthcoming, but we have no other place to go. *"When the Son of Man comes,"* Jesus asks, *"will he find faith on earth?"* (v. 8) Will we still have the faith to pray? Will people still trust God to intervene and act justly? The survival of faith in the earth rises and falls on our confidence in God and the justice of His courtroom, where our continued pleas for intervention are heard. We "cry out," lament, "day and night" and night and day – refusing to give up on an answer from God. We are the intercessory bride, it is our calling, our destiny to pray. God will *"avenge His own elect,"* Jesus declared, *"though He bears long with them."* He will *"bring about justice for his chosen ones"* (NIV). The International Standard Version asks, *"Won't God grant his chosen people justice when they cry out to him day and night? Is he slow to help them?"* The NET, *"Will he delay long to help them?"* The Weymouth New Testament says, *"He seems slow in taking action on their behalf."* In heaven's time, Jesus says, *"He will avenge them speedily!"* Patience is required in prayer, and then, we enter a season of God's 'suddenlies.' Suddenly, the answer comes. Suddenly, he deals with an enemy. Suddenly, he opens the route in front us. Suddenly, the Spirit falls. Suddenly, the storm is calmed.

Final Note

The earth needs a voice before the throne in heaven, constantly pleading with God, for justice from our earthly adversary! "The devil is not put to flight by a courteous request. He meets us at every turn, contends for every inch, and our progress has to be registered in the heart's blood and tears."[17]

In the Old Testament, lament focused on seen, earthly enemies. Our true nemesis is sin, and by association, Satan, the tempter and the fallen angel, who along with demons and humans are willing conspirators in the continuing revolt against heaven. This is a war into which we have fallen, in which we, as humans, became complicit by the action of our flesh-father, Adam. In prayer we declare we will no longer be subject to the tyranny of Satan. We will not be willing participants in acts of sin and rebellion against the Creator. By prayer, we enter a plea, from the earth, as individuals and also as a church; as a collage of intercessory communities representing cities and states, that liberation come, that God act to consummate his redemption of the earth.

"Thy kingdom come!"

Discussion Guide

1. Review the roots of New Testament worship in the synagogue.

2. How and where is lament seen in the New Testament?

3. How is Jesus the 'lamenter par excellence?' What does that mean? To us?

4. Discuss the relationship between lament and the coming wrath of God.

5. How do triumph and lament come together?

6. How does lament shift in the post-resurrection New Testament Church?

7. How is the Church a lamenting widow? A voice before the throne?

9

Lament Answered with Resurrection

Three Resurrections

Jesus raised three people from the dead, according to Scripture. In Luke 7:11-15, Jesus and his disciples entered the village of Nain with a large crowd following. At the gate of the settlement, they met a funeral procession leaving the city. The only son of a widow had died. *"When the Lord saw her, his heart overflowed with compassion. 'Don't cry!' he said"* (v. 13, NLT). He moved toward the ensemble of people, touched the coffin and spoke to the dead, *"Young man, I say to you, get up!"* (v. 14, NLT). Immediately, he *"sat up and began to talk"* (v. 15) and was reunited with his mother. Resurrection answered lament.

The response of the crowd was reverence, fear and praise. Lament, as Claus Westermann might have noted, had rightly been reset to praise. Luke declares, *"God has visited his people today"* (v. 16, NLT). Jesus 'turned the mourning to dancing' and allowed the widow to 'throw off her sackcloth' (Psalm 30:11). *"God has come to help his people,"* the crowd responded (v. 16, NLT).

In Mark 5:38-40, we find the second resurrection by Jesus. Jairus, the ruler of the local synagogue, had come to request that Jesus heal his daughter (vv. 22-23). But, before they could reach the child, crowds pressed in on Jesus for ministry, and soon the word came that it was too late, *"Your daughter has died; why trouble the Teacher anymore?"* (v. 35, NASB). Entering the house, Jesus found it full of lament – *"a commotion, and much weeping and wailing"* (v. 39, Berean Literal Bible). He put the lamenters outside, and with the father and mother, and those with him, he entered into the room where the child was lying and spoke to her, *"Little girl, I say to you, arise! And immediately the girl arose…And immediately they were overcome with great amazement"* (vv. 41-42, BLB). Here again, resurrection answered lament.

In the third and most famous of the resurrection narratives, Jesus was summoned to the house of his friend Lazarus who was said to be dying (John 11:1-7). Strangely, learning of his sickness, he tarried, waiting two more days before making the trip to Bethany. When he arrived, he was told that Lazarus had been dead for four days (vv. 17-21). *"Your brother will rise again,"* Jesus told Martha. *"I know that he will rise again in the resurrection at the last day"* (v. 24 HCSB), she replied. Here, Jesus made the stunning claim, *"I am the resurrection and the life"* (v. 25). This is the paradigm shift – faith in Christ taps resurrection power, not only in the future, but here and now. Jesus does not merely 'do' resurrections, he 'is' the resurrection. This is not a power we control; it remains with God. And yet, resurrection power is here, now. God, at least in certain moments, asserts His sovereignty now. He intervenes. He resurrects.

This requires faith in Christ, *"The one who believes in Me, even if he dies, will live"* (v. 25, HCSB).

> *Death, hell, the grave, persecution, peril – nothing can diminish the new life available to the believer.*

This is not merely physical, it is spiritual, and yet, as here, it manifests as physical. *"Everyone who lives and believes in Me will never die – ever. Do you believe this?"* (v. 26, HCSB). This is eternal life – here and now! It is buoyant resurrection life. It is not measured by the seen and felt, not always.

Jesus called for Mary, and she came weeping, and with her came a company of lamenters. Perhaps some were family and friends, others were probably hired lamenters. *"When Jesus saw her crying, and the Jews who had come with her crying, He was angry in His spirit and deeply moved"* (v. 34 HCSB). Angry at death, angry at the pain death causes? We can only speculate.

As the way to the burial place of Lazarus is pointed out, the Scriptures say, *"Jesus wept."* Those present saw his tears as an indication of his love for Lazarus. They also hint at lament. But again, in the face of death, there is with the tears, another flash of anger. That combination – tears and anger – is classically characteristic of lament. *"Then Jesus, angry in Himself again, came to the tomb."* The cave serving as a tomb had already been sealed. *"Remove the stone,"* he ordered. He prayed (vv. 41-42), and then he cried out, *"Lazarus, come forth"* (v. 43).

> The great gift of Easter is hope - Christian hope which makes us have that confidence in God, in his ultimate triumph, and in his goodness and love, which nothing can shake.[7]

Here, for the third time in the life and ministry of Jesus, is lament against the ultimate enemy, death, met again with resurrection power.

Jesus enacts lament here and models a prayer of hope in the face of death and loss. He also exhibits the wrath of God, anger, against life's ultimate enemy, death. This is one of the features of the psalms. God is moved to action, exhibiting righteous anger and mercy together.

Here, Jesus employed resurrection power. He lamented as a friend, a human, being emotionally invested in the problem. Lazarus and the family were friends, loved ones. He interceded, standing between the helpless and death itself, squaring off with the ultimate enemy. No mere human could have done this. While he lamented as a friend, a human, he interceded as the Messianic King, the High Priest of a new order, and the ultimate prophet, seeing through the lament to eternity. In this sense, this becomes a royal lament, in the tradition of the royal lament psalms. He prays out of the office of king, albeit, a suffering king, one who weeps with us, participates in our pain, and ultimately embodies lament on the cross.

In the New Testament, on these three occasions, resurrection interrupts lament – this is the story in all the Jesus-resurrection narratives. It resets the norm to praise, but it does not displace lament or rebuke it. It does not replace normal human emotion. Rather, it ties lament to a more certain hope than the Old Testament psalms could provide.

The Passion Week has been called a choreographed lament, crowned with the resurrection.[1] As we partake of the Lord's Supper – the blood and his broken body – we lament; and we do so, until he comes, looking to the resurrection. At the table, he is present, and absent. He has been here – we hold the proof of his crucifixion. And yet, he was raised from the dead, has ascended to heaven, and is enthroned there; and is coming again. He is not here, visibly, and yet, he is present. We are in the now, and the not yet. Lament and resurrection are conjoined.

In Matthew and Mark, it is said that Jesus died *"as it was written of him,"* that is, he fulfilled his destiny on the stage of time (Matthew 26:24; Mark 14:21). He knew the cross was his fate, but not the final act. He died as the sacrificial lamb, as Isaiah's Suffering Servant, but also the Son of David, a lamenter *par excellence.*[2] He was not the triumphant militarist expected by his Jewish peers; not the leader of a political coup to restore and claim David's earthly throne, but a lamenter.

He launched a prayer revolution.

In Gethsemane, we are invited to weep with him; then, at the empty tomb, we rejoice; and in the cross, between lament and triumph, we again intercede, joining Christ in prayer, creating an intercessory community for others, bearing their burdens, lamenting for a lost world. *"Father, forgive them"* (Luke 23:34).

The Lament of Jesus

In the garden, Jesus tearfully lamented for himself, and in a sense, all of humanity, *"And being in anguish, he prayed more earnestly, and his sweat was like drops of blood falling to the ground"* (Luke 22:44). The NLT says, *"He prayed more fervently…in such agony…that his sweat fell to the ground like great drops of blood."* The Berean Bible uses the word, "anguish," praying "earnestly," perspiring. This is a fundamental element of lament. It recalls the emotional and physical state of lamenters in the psalms. They were beside themselves with what they were facing, overwhelmed, at times physically in shock due to emotional trauma. Of Jesus, Matthew writes, *"He took Peter and the two sons of Zebedee along with him, and he began to be sorrowful and troubled"* (26:37). The NLT says, *"he became anguished and distressed,"* the NASB, *"grieved."* The King James characterizes him as *"sorrowful and very heavy,"* *"deeply distressed"* (HCSB), *"grieved and troubled"* (ISV). The New Heart English Bible amplifies the mood, *"severely troubled."* The Aramaic Bible in Plain English calls him *"disheartened."*

He said to his disciples, *"My soul is overwhelmed with sorrow to the point of death"* (v. 38). And he asked them to remain near him in prayer, as he distanced himself 'a stone's throw' away. The New Living Translation reads, *"My soul is crushed with grief to the point of death."* The Berean Study Bible, *"My soul is consumed with sorrow to the point of death."* The NAS, I am *"deeply grieved,"* *"...exceeding sorrowful, even unto death"* (KJV). Stay with me, watch, he urges. *"My soul is swallowed up in sorrow"* (HCSB), he laments. And the ISV, *"I'm so deeply grieved that I feel I'm about to die."* This is lament. It is personal lament, *"My Father, if it is possible, may this cup be taken from me. Yet not as I will, but as you will"* (NIV). Here, Jesus binds his will tightly to that of the Father as we should do.

The word translated 'sorrowful' or 'grieved' is *perilupos*, meaning very sad, very sorrowful, greatly grieved. It is a compound word from *perí*, meaning, encompassing, surrounding; and *lýpē*, meaning sorrow, or being sorrowful. It carries the idea of sorrow "all-around, being engulfed in sorrow."[3] The word, *ekthambeó*, is translated variously *as deeply grieved or exceedingly sorrowful.* It is a graphic term, meaning "greatly astonished," or "awe-struck." It means, "astonished out from," out of one's senses, amazed at the level of wonder, or cast into a state of amazement or terror. It can also mean to alarm thoroughly, to terrify, to be struck with amazement, or to be astounded. This is compounded by the term *adémoneó*, to b*e distressed or troubled. This is the frazzled* emotional state, the *"I am at the end of my own strength with what I am facing,"* lament seen so often in the Old Testament. Lament has overwhelmed Jesus. He is not sure that he will humanly make it to the cross – the passionate prayer of lament is nearly killing him. The intercessory burden is crushing, draining his life. Luke 22:43 records an angel strengthening Jesus as he prayed.

In Jesus, lament finds a climax and a resolution. In the garden, he laments alone, for himself, for what he must endure – and all of us must enter that garden with him. We must 'pray through' whatever cross we must bear. At the empty tomb, lament is resolved forever.

It is not finished, but it is answered. In the Old Testament, lament found hope in some release, some escape, some temporary victory. But in the New Testament, the resolve of believers living in this unjust, unfair world is found in the empty tomb. The answer of God to lament, to the "How Longs?" are the dual resurrections – the first being that of Christ and the second being the rapture of believers and the Second Coming. In between, we tether personal laments to resurrection hope; and we embrace the ministry of lament, intercession for others who do not have hope, prayers for a world that has excluded God – and these we also tie to resurrection power.

We are not trapped in the Old Testament covenant paradigm where bad things are an indication of God's disfavor. Under the new covenant, the rain falls on the just and unjust. There is something greater at stake than personal comfort and prosperity. Jesus died on a criminal's cross, but he died a righteous and innocent man. Crosses, that of Christ, and our cross – whatever that means in the context of life – do not mean that we have failed God or that God has abandoned us. God's faithfulness is vindicated in the resurrection.

The writer of Hebrews noted, *"Christ did not take on himself the glory of becoming a high priest. But God said to him, 'You are my Son; today I have become your Father'... 'You are a priest forever, in the order of Melchizedek'"* (Hebrews 7:17). The priesthood of Christ, his intercessory ministry in heaven is based not on the covenant of law given to Moses. Nor does it rise out of Aaron's priestly line, but out of one that predated it – one that

> Clouds and darkness surround us, yet heaven is just, and the day of triumph will surely come, when justice and truth will be vindicated.[4]

is based on the son-ship of Christ. Hebrews says of Gethsemane, *"...*
he offered up prayers and petitions with fervent cries and tears to the
one who could save him from death, and he was heard because of his
reverent submission" (5:7). He was a son, but he *"learned obedience,"*
he embraced *"suffering,"* and he lamented in prayer. On the cross, he
became the perfect lamb, the perfect human, utterly obedient, and
"the source of eternal salvation for all who obey...designated by God to
be high priest in the order of Melchizedek," serving the church and all
who seek to know God, out of heaven's tabernacle (NIV).

God had heard the laments rising out of the Old Testament.
"How long?" – before a deliverer comes, before you answer the raging nations, before you provide an answer to the wicked, before you
offer assurance of salvation, *"How long?"* In the garden, God the Father heard the lament of Jesus. And that lament He answered. Christ,
himself, is the answer – his resurrection, his enthronement, his in-
stallation as the high priest of heaven, answers the Old Testament
laments. It doesn't remove lament – the natural tendency to lament
when we face some Golgotha remains: *"Father, if it is possible, let this*
cup pass." In our Gethsemane, Jesus is not sleeping there, as did his
companions, the disciples – he is praying for us. On the other side
of whatever cross we face – resurrection is certain. That changes the
character of lament. The answer has come. The answer is the resurrection. The answer is a person, not a solution to a problem. That
does not remove intercessory lament, indeed, it augments it.

> **Now, we lament, with Christ, for a world**
> **that is suffering without hope, without God,**
> **for nations that turn away from God. But we**
> **lament in hope.**

The Final Lament

Sixty years after the resurrection, the one remaining disciple had been boiled in oil – but the attempt at his martyrdom had miraculously failed. That's also a resurrection narrative. All his peers were dead, all martyred. Paul, as well, was gone. They all died in hope, but they had not seen, as they might have anticipated, the quick return of Jesus to seize the earth as a prize and establish his kingdom. Instead, wicked emperors had arisen, like a parade of horror loosed on the Jewish nation and the church – Caligula (The evil emperor who proclaimed himself a god); Nero (The mad tyrant who blamed the Christians for the burning of Rome); Titus (The emperor who destroyed the temple in Jerusalem); Domitian (The evil emperor who murdered thousands of Christians). It was Domitian who had exiled John to Patmos to die. There, in that barren, forsaken place, God opened the heavens and revealed the end of all things, the answer to the lament of righteous saints throughout the ages, the 'How long?' When will the suffering cease? When will the kingdom come?

In the Revelation, John, too, weeps. He laments. He was caught up into heaven, standing before the *"One seated on the Throne"* (4:1-2). Radiating from the throne are the colors of the rainbow and proceeding from it is lightning and thunder. Around it are twenty-four additional thrones of the elders of heaven. In the midst of it are four living creatures, full of eyes, only with a slight resemblance to anything John has seen on the earth – somewhat like a lion, an eagle, an ox and a man. The place rumbles with praise and song (vv. 3-11). Then, as the scene changes, a scroll is revealed, but sealed – the scroll of redemption. Opening it will invoke the consummation of redemption, the reclaiming of the earth and everything and everyone in it for the glory of God (5:1-11). It is the answer to the *"How long?"* However, there is a problem. No one is worthy to open the scroll and to loose the seals (v. 2), nor was anyone found in heaven, on the earth, or in the grave, under the earth, that was able to either open the scroll or examine it (v. 3). So John, contrary to the prevailing mood of praise in heaven, laments, *"I wept much"* (v. 4). The contrast is stark – singing and rejoicing, by the four living creatures and the twenty-four elders, and the weeping of John. Heaven sings, but earth's representative human, John, weeps.

His lament is silenced, *"Do not weep,"* one of the elders advises. *"Behold, the Lion of the tribe of Judah, the Root of David, has prevailed to open the scroll and to loose its seven seals"* (v. 5). The Lion is both worthy (v. 2) and able (v. 3). John turns, looking for the Lion, but there is no lion. In the midst of the throne and the twenty-four elders and the four living creatures is not a lion, but a lamb. What John sees is again contradictory – he sees a slain lamb, standing (v. 6). It is as if he "had been slain" but still stood, as indestructible. The Lamb has seven horns – perfect power; and seven eyes that *"are the seven Spirits of God sent out to all the earth."* The lamb came, acting now more like a man, and took the scroll. The response in heaven to that action was an explosion of music and song – triumph again has answered lament. This is the resurrected Lamb, the Lion who is a lamb, the victorious lamenter, Jesus, the Christ.

> *Thou art worthy to take the book, and to open the seals thereof: for thou wast slain, and hast redeemed us to God by thy blood out of every kindred, and tongue, and people, and nation; And hast made us unto our God kings and priests: and we shall reign on the earth (5:9-10 KJV).*
>
> *You are worthy to take the scroll and to open its seals because you were killed, and at the cost of your own blood you have purchased for God persons from every tribe, language, people, and nation (NET Bible).*

Now, the four living creatures, the twenty-four elders, are again singing, and they are joined by the saints. Each of the elders is seen having a harp and a golden bowl of incense, representing the prayers of the saints. These are stored up, kept, preserved, but not yet answered. They are prayers to which heaven has said, "Yes, but not yet." Now, finally, the "how long" of earth's prayers is no longer delayed; the answer is "Now!" These prayers of the saints are set to music – what an idea. For us, the sounds are groans, laments and travail, but in heaven, the sound of an intercessor's prayer is music. The incense of the prayers of the saints, stored up for so long, is released and the lyrics are set to music. Earth and heaven are now joined, singing together. 'You are worthy, and able, Lamb and Lion, the lamenter par excellence as well as the resurrection.' Suddenly, every voice in heaven is singing – ten thousand times ten thousand, and thousands of thousands of angels join in. *"Worthy is the Lamb that was slain to receive power, and riches, and wisdom, and strength, and honour, and glory, and blessing"* (5:12 KJV).

The NIV substitutes wealth for riches and praise for blessing! The NLT, ISV and the HCSB are more stark, *"Worthy is the Lamb who was slaughtered."* He died; he lives. He was not merely raised from the dead and given life, he *is* the resurrection and the life. Heaven's work is not finished in this moment of the Lamb's triumph from the terrible tragedy of the cross. It will not be silenced. Nor will it allow the earth to be silent about the Lamb. Voices are coming from every direction – from the throne, the four living creatures; from around the throne, the twenty-four elders; from every space in heaven, the angels; and now every creature in heaven and on earth, under the earth and in the sea, all are singing.

> *No one can be silent, not any longer. The repressed song is now being sung and the universe hears it. The silence is over.*

"They sang: 'Blessing and honor and glory and power belong to the one sitting on the throne and to the Lamb forever and ever'" (v. 13b NLT). The Berean Literal Bible reads:

> And I heard every creature which is in heaven, and upon the earth, and under the earth, and on the sea, and everything in them, saying: 'To the One sitting on the throne, and to the Lamb, blessing and honor and glory and might to the ages of the ages' (v. 13).

"Weep not, for the lion has prevailed..." The promised and determined redemption which John saw in the future-present has not yet manifest itself in our time-space world. We are assured by Scripture and faith, that it is certain, coming, on the way – a done deal. Meanwhile, our role as ambassadors compels us to continue to empathize with those in pain around us. We are lions – we join the worshipful roar of heaven's certain triumph; and yet, we are lambs, as Paul would remind us, at times, *"led to the slaughter."* Think of the persecuted church around the world, the high number of present day martyrs. So, we must learn to weep as we roar. We are between the times – having a kingdom that has come, that cannot be shaken, and a kingdom that has not yet fully come.

Revelation 5:5 does not end the lament. It is not a charge to dry our tears. Indeed, in Revelation 6, *"...under the altar, the souls of those who had been slain for the word of God and for the testimony which they held,"* were revealed. John sees them and hears their lament. It is the familiar, *"How long, O Lord, holy and true, until you Judge and avenge our blood on those who dwell on the earth?"* (5:9-10). Those lamenting under the altar have suffered the same fate as the slain lamb, but they will also experience the same triumphant end – resurrection. For now, they must *"rest a little while until both the number of their fellow servants and brethren, who would be killed as they were, was complete"* (v. 11). This is a pervasive call to the cross for the last-days church. The time for lamenting is not over, nor is it time to despair. Lambs will yet be led to the slaughter – but listen, from heaven, can you hear the roar – the roar of the Lion, the sound of music, the singing of angels, the certainty of triumph?

"The great day of His wrath" is coming (v. 17). Judgement has been held back by mercy, but there is coming a day, when the earth itself will burst forth with its final lament, its great groan.

> *There was a great earthquake. The sun turned black like sackcloth made of goat hair, the whole moon turned blood red, and the stars in the sky fell to earth, as figs drop from a fig tree when shaken by a strong wind. The heavens receded like a scroll being rolled up, and every mountain and island was removed from its place (6:12-14).*

The NLT says, *"the stars of the sky fell to the earth like green figs falling from a tree shaken by a strong wind."* And the *"kings of the earth, the princes, the generals, the rich, the mighty, and everyone else, both slave and free, hid in caves and among the rocks of the mountains. They called to the mountains and the rocks,"* as if they were alive, as if the nature-gods could intervene, *"Fall on us and hide us from the face of him who sits on the throne and from the wrath of the Lamb! For the great day of their wrath has come, and who can withstand it?"* (Rev. 6:16). Indeed. Notice, it is not the Lion who roars here, but the Lamb, the slain Lamb, the crucified Christ. He is the rejected king, the Creator, who came to the earth armed with only love and mercy in his hands, and yet, he was crucified. Now he roars. He will be reckoned with – and no one can stand

> In both the presence of evil and the eventual triumph over evil the sweep is cosmic. It embraces the éntire universe, what to man is both seen and unseen. The victory is to be accomplished through Christ.[5]

before him. He was crucified, dead, laid in a sealed tomb guarded by Roman soldiers. Nevertheless, the slain lamb stands. The kings and mighty men who killed him, and would do so again, cannot stand.

Here are all the exploiters, all the oppressors of the poor, all the godless who have mocked heaven and dared it with their arrogance and pride – kings of the earth, rulers, generals, the wealthy, the powerful – all hiding in caves and mountainous rocks, all contemptuous, resisting arrest, supposing that they can escape in some way from his gaze, from his reach and from justice. They bid the mountains to conspire with them against God, to *"hide us from the face of the one who sits on the throne and from the wrath of the Lamb"* (Rev. 6:16). They cry, they lament, but not with any sincere repentance, not due to any genuine sorrow over their exploitation of those on the earth and their tyranny against righteousness. *"The great day of their wrath has come, and they will not survive."*

In Revelation 18, the end finally comes. Babylon, the global system, with its roots in Babel itself, finally collapses. A mighty angel makes the announcement: *"Fallen! Fallen is Babylon the Great! She has become a dwelling for demons and a haunt for every impure spirit, a haunt for every unclean bird, a haunt for every unclean and detestable animal"* (v. 2 NIV).

The NLT says, *"that great city is fallen!"* Unlike Jerusalem, redeemed to be a home for the holy God of Israel, Babylon became *"a home for demons…a hideout for every foul spirit, a hideout for every foul vulture and every foul and dreadful animal."* It was a haunted place, *"a haunt for every unclean spirit"* (ESV). The Berean Study Bible said it had *"become a lair of demons."* As

> I don't measure a man's success by how high he climbs but how high he bounces when he hits bottom.[6]

you read the various translations, you notice all the attributes of the creatures who found a home in Babylon – *"demons...every impure spirit...every unclean bird...every unclean and detestable animal...every foul spirit...every foul vulture...every foul and dreadful animal... the unclean, the detestable, the beastly, the hated, the hateful."* All were at home in Babylon. O, how far we have fallen.

Now, this center of moral and spiritual resistance to the reign of God collapses. The godless vacuum, where Yahweh was a visitor who "went down" to explore the attempt of humanity to build community without Him, the great experiment of humanism, has ended in a baptism of paganism, and it has collapsed. Clothed in purple and scarlet, adorned with gold and precious stones, with a golden cup in her hand, a record of corruption by sexual immorality, had shared her wine with *"kings...and those who live on the earth"* until all were intoxicated and brought under her power (17:2). Vile and impure, unrepentant to the end, defiant, she is *"the mother of prostitutes"* guilty of *"the blood of the saints"* and the *"martyrs of Jesus."* John called her appearance mesmerizing – *thaumazó:* to marvel, wonder, to admire. She is repulsive and simultaneously seductive. The word can mean "astonished out of one's senses, awestruck."

Even under judgement, she herself, is blinded by her arrogance: *"I set as queen, and am no widow and will not see sorrow"* (18:7). She is delusional and unrepentant. She is a prostitute, but she is not unmarried – she is *"no widow."* Her consort is not human; it is unspeakably evil and beastly. She has married the darkness. Her judgement will be swift, *"...in one day"* (v. 8).

She is a part of a coalition that will not yield the earth to its rightful owner, Creator and Redeemer, God in Christ. She is, perhaps, the critical heart of that resistance movement. *"These will make war with the Lamb; and the Lamb will overcome them, for He is Lord of lords and King of kings: and those who are with Him are called, chosen, and faithful"* (17:14, NKJ).

"They will wage war against the Lamb, but the Lamb will triumph" (NIV). *"Together they will go to war against the Lamb, but the Lamb will defeat them"* (NLT), *"...the Lamb will conquer them"* (ESV). Babylon will finally be judged. The lament of the faithful will one day be over. Revelation 18 is the answer to the lament of the martyrs in chapter 6:10, *"How long?"* In Revelation 21, John *"saw a new heaven and a new earth"* and *"the holy city, the new Jerusalem,"* the alternative to Babel, *"coming down from God out of heaven like a bride beautifully dressed for her husband."* A voice cries,

> Look, God's home is now among his people! He will live with them, and they will be his people. God himself will be with them. He will wipe every tear from their eyes, and there will be no more death or sorrow or crying or pain. All these things are gone forever (Rev. 21:3, NLT).

Now, lament is no more! Tears are wiped away. The *"fountain of the water of life"* is opened to the former lamenters (v. 6). The *"gates into the city,"* the New Jerusalem, are opened to the faithful, as is *"the right to the tree of life."* That lost tree, from the first garden, life itself,

In 1 Thessalonians 4:13, Paul comforts those who have lost loved ones to death. *"We do not want you to be uninformed about those who sleep in death, so that you do not grieve like the rest of mankind, who have no hope."* The NLT says, *"we want you to know what will happen to the believers who have died so you will not grieve like people who have no hope."* We are in between the times, so the grief at the loss of a loved one remains, but even now, it lacks the biting force of those without faith - it is lament in the face of resurrection hope. We grieve, but not as others. We taste sorrow, but it is tempered. Weymouth uses the term "mourn." The Greek term is *lupeó*, to distress, to grieve, to be vexed and in deep, emotional pain, in severe sorrow as intense as childbearing pain. Some losses are costly. But our lament is only the foretaste of the world the come.

is now accessible. *"Come...let him who thirsts come. Whoever desires, let him take the water of life freely"* (v. 17).

Discussion Guide

1. Review the three resurrections by Jesus.
2. Jesus wept. Discuss the idea. He knew he would raise Lazarus from the dead – still he wept. Why?
3. If resurrection can interrupt lament – why not opt for resurrection and completely dismiss lament?
4. Christ lamented in the garden. He really lamented. Do you agree?
5. Why should we lament?
6. Why does John lament, 60 years after the resurrection?
7. What is the ultimate resolve of lament in heaven?

10

Modern Western Resistance to Lament

Have you ever viewed the news on television, reviewed the headlines of a major newspaper, clipped open a handful of newsy emails and followed their links, read their articles and watched their videos – and found yourself emotionally drained from the brief exposure to exploitation, human and sexual trafficking, global famine, ongoing war, the threat of pandemics, terrorism, not to mention that the family next door, whose children play with your children, are selling their house and getting a divorce? Or worse! Click on a few select websites and you can discover the recently released child molester now back in your neighborhood or a drug user down the street now out on parole. The problems of sin and self-indulgence are unavoidable, and they are not in the big city, far away, but in your small town and neighborhood.

You can't hide from life, so you gather yourself together, take a few deep breaths, and venture to the mall to engage a sea of happy faces, buying wares from stores with almost every conceivable commodity. Restaurants are full of smiling people with tables loaded with discarded leftovers. The relative peace is like another world. The profuse plenty is such a contradiction to the images of starving children and the scenes of deprivation and poverty around the world to which you were privately exposed. The ordered stop-and-go traffic on the cues of red and green are incongruent with the bombed-out buildings on the television and internet screens.

With such comfort, with such insulation from pain, with such plenty – we cannot bring ourselves to lament. In truth, disorder and deprivation are not a continent away. They are often a few miles away – on the other side of town, across the tracks, in sections of the city we, the privileged, avoid. We once worshipped in church buildings near those locations, but when the demographics shifted, we moved. And now we avoid not only the place, but the people who live there in pain.

Their reality is not our reality. We are not 'touched with the feelings of their infirmities.' We do not allow ourselves to weep with them, and we fail to appreciate the legitimacy of their lament. They are the oppressed, who like Israel in Egypt, cried out to God – and in whose behalf God acted, in judgement, against their oppressors. Jesus forever took a stand with the poor and the oppressed, the needy, and the imprisoned. He came to walk among them and deliver them; and to follow him is to follow him to places that we now prefer to avoid, and to engage people that we prefer not to engage.

> Our only hope is to march ourselves to the throne of God and in loud lament cry out the pain that lives in our souls.
> ~ Ann Weems

How can we see the pain of our world, and in many cases, our own cities – and so easily compartmentalize our lives to allow ourselves to continue to move through life without tears? We must face the obvious – our hearts have grown hard. It has become too easy to pass the sign-holder whose cardboard placard reads, "Hungry. Will work for food"..."Homeless father with children." We rationalize at such moments. We have seen the reports of scam artists doing the same thing on television, making more money in their deceit than honest people. "If he wanted to, he could find a job," we muse. "I've got some work he could do, ah – but the liability issue." Rationalizations. No tears. No lament, not in the richest nation on the face of the earth, not for the hungry and homeless, the disenfranchised, the displaced. Our sensitivities are dulled.

In part, the deadening is due to too much information, sensory overload – another lonely face, albeit from the real world and not a television drama – doesn't move us. Even if it is in our world, in our city, not on the news, not a world far away, we are calloused. It is just another face, lost in the mental images that dance in our heads and get resolved in a 60-minute television drama. We seem to be living prophylactically. What are the consequences to faith when we can no longer feel the pain of others? When we structure worship to screen out the negative? When we want only happy music and positive sermons? We are already experiencing what one writer called "...diminished theological anthropology."[1] God became flesh – in Christ. He lived here, walked and talked here, he touched people here, including the untouchable lepers, he wept here – he was homeless here (Mt. 8:20). He wants to be flesh again – in and through his body, the church! That requires a church that is not guarded, one that is compassionate, fully human but animated by the Spirit, incarnational and empowered.

Lament Avoidance in the Church

Sadly, lament is not even on the radar screen of today's celebration churches. In some places, it would be considered an affront to faith. A church that celebrates and never weeps inhibits itself from the whole blessing of God. *"Blessed are they that weep!"* (Mt. 5:4). The church is to be an intercessory community, empathizing with the oppressed, bearing the burdens not only of one another, but also of those outside – the poor and the oppressed. The anointing comes to empower us to proclaim a gospel of hope to the poor, healing to the brokenhearted, giving the promise of liberty to captives and the release of those in prison (Isa. 61:1-2). And the day of anointing for such a mission is the *"day of vengeance of our God,"* the day He acts. And He acts *"to comfort all who mourn,"* whose lives are marked by needless loss, whose garments are ashen and whose spirits are heavy (v. 3). Tears, more than talk, shout that we care for others and that we are anointed change agents.

Glenn Pemberton, in his book, *Hurting with God,* claims that laments constitute 40 percent of the Psalms. The more conservative number is 30 percent, but some suggest that twice that number have lament elements. Pemberton also notes that songs in our modern hymnals do not even approach that number. The percentage of lament songs or lyrics is a great deal less than in the psalms – 13 percent for the Churches of Christ and the Baptists; 19 percent in the Presbyterian hymnal.[2] In triumphalistic, celebrative Pentecostal-Charismatic churches, the number is probably, much, much lower.

Don Saliers quoting Roger Van Harn and Brent Strawn in *Psalms for Preaching and Worship,* contends that:

> ...it is both wonder and scandal that the modern church in the West has largely lost touch with the Psalter...The reason for such neglect, articulated by Claus Westermann, is related to the very reason that [the Psalms] must be recovered among us, namely, that they are *direct speech about a realistic faith* that traffics in the extremities of human life and human experience.[3]

In the days of the charismatic renewal, several decades ago, in Evangelical-Pentecostal churches across the denominational spectrum, there were attempts at setting the psalms to music, of singing directly from Scripture. You would hear the instruction, "Open your Bible to Psalm 42 [One of the favorite psalm tunes], and let's sing." What a great idea. For the most part, now, psalm and hymn singing have vanished.

Today's Evangelical-Pentecostal congregations have moved to choruses. Christian Copyright Licensing International (CCLI) provides clearance for the use of those choruses and the projection of the lyrics. And they not only license the worship music of congregations, but they track the songs utilized. The top 100 songs contain only five that could be identified as laments – five percent.[4] We are actually singing fewer laments than a few years ago. Celebratory praise dominates the songs of evangelical churches – "Here I Am to Worship," "Happy Day," "Indescribable," "Friend of God," "Glorious Day," "Marvelous Light," and "Victory in Jesus."[5]

Don E. Saliers observed:

At the very time when the media are saturated by news of human carnage, enmity, and suffering, Christian liturgies have largely avoided or simply neglected lamentation and complaint. I speak not only of phenomena such as the 'prosperity Gospel' or what can be called 'ultra-bright' forms of Christian worship, but also of more 'liturgical' traditions that follow the lectionary with its appointed psalms.[6]

Samuel Ballentine recalled,

The church taught me how to pray and, more subtly, how not to pray. One was to praise God, but not to protest; to petition God, but not interrogate; and in all things to accept and submit to the sometimes incomprehensible will of God, never to challenge or rebel. Yet when life's circumstances would not permit either such passivity or such piety, this advocacy of a rather monotonic relation to God seemed destined to silence if not exclude me. 'You must not question God.' If one cannot question God, then to whom does one direct the questions?[7]

165

American evangelicals seem stuck in a praise-only mode of worship.

Our pseudo, victorious, triumphal worship narrative avoids lament, but it doesn't change reality, personally or in our world. It encourages us to hide the pain, to paste on the smile, to stuff personal and family pain – such worship is feigned, it is not real. Proverbs 25:20 reminds us, *"He who sings to a heavy heart is like one who takes off a garment on a cold day, and like vinegar on a wound."* People need warmth, a comforter, and care for their wounds – and the church is failing at that task.

In our worship gatherings, there is little time for prayer, real prayer, in the context of the Sunday service, prayer in its varied forms, including lament. There is no allowance of any downer in the service, everything is positive and polished. We are in denial – and that can only last for a season. It is a far too narrow corporate worship experience, wrenched free from the reality of most worshipper's life experiences. When worship and walk are not corrected and congruent, worship is hypocritical, and it produces duplicitous Christians, and that invites the judgement of God.

> ...our family became a place where you screamed for help but no one heard, not ever.[33]

How can we come to church, have a 90-minute worship experience – and not even talk to God? Not get real? Directly? In prayer? Not shed a tear for the lost? For failing families? For the hundreds, if not thousands, of fellow Christians persecuted and martyred each week? How can we legitimately call what we do worship – if someone is singing to us, praying for us, and preaching to us, telling us what God told them, but never moving us to hear from God or talk to God directly, personally or congregationally? We have Christian 'show-time,' not New Testament worship. What we need are more opportunities for prayer engagement; moments in which the congregation itself is praying, preserving the glorious Protestant tradition of the priesthood of all believers. And in a balanced worship experience, could there be any time for public lament? Isn't it time to weep over the lostness, the backsliding of the nation, the heightened peril in our world?

The absence of lament testifies to self-absorbed Christians...

Christians who do not weep over injustice, over oppression and hunger, over the atrocities perpetrated on brothers and sisters living in totalitarian cultures. It is a narcissistic form of apathy. Unhealthy and relationally disconnected from others, we worship on an existential island designed to create a form of unrealistic bliss. That might make our worship, despite our Christianese language, more Buddhist than Christian.

What Lament Free Zones Say

Lament engages reality. It acknowledges pain, not only personally and corporately, but also of others. In the New Testament, lament emerges as intercessory in nature. It challenges the status quo, demanding tearfully and respectfully before the throne in heaven, that God act out of His own nature, that He intervene in behalf of His own purposes. We insist, in the courtroom of heaven, that justice and right are not being done here and they will not be done without His intervention. So we pray, we lament, before heaven's throne, in behalf of others, that the Kingdom come, that God's will be done.

167

Walter Brueggemann asks:

What happens when appreciation of the lament as a form of speech and faith is lost, as I think it is largely lost in contemporary usage? What happens when the speech forms that redress power distribution have been silenced and eliminated? The answer, I believe, is that a theological monopoly is reinforced, docility and submissiveness are engendered, and the outcome in terms of social practice is to reinforce and consolidate the political economic monopoly of the status quo.[8]

When there is no room for lament, when celebration worship reigns with forced smiling and amid clapping hands, it means, as Brueggemann charges above, that a "theological monopoly is re-enforced." That produces a passive, submissive people; at times a passive-aggressive people. Passion is misplaced, redirected or suppressed. The status quo is then exalted as the entrenched mode of operation, silencing dissent, even in prayer; short-circuiting passionate reform.

The Western church is so enculturated into the idolatrous world of pleasure and entertainment that it has no place for lament. It has domesticated the prophet. It has silenced the sound of wailing intercession. Lament is the voice of an alternative consciousness that liberates people from a blinding, limiting paradigm. Brueggemann observes, "As long as the empire can keep the pretense alive that things are all right, there will be no real grieving and no serious criticism."[9] Confronted with harsh realities, we are often numbed. We can neither understand our inner emotions or give them voice – and that is the power of lament. It is anguish, inarticulate confusion and pain poured out to God.

We are, in our ordered churches and prayer meetings, embarrassed by laments.

Not only by their raw energy, their seemingly unrestrained and unpredictable nature, but also with their focus – the impartiality, cruelty, and exploitation in the world around us. We are too often like Job's friends. When he lamented, his friends attempted to stifle his lament. It was, in their view, inappropriate. Job's lament not only expressed his personal pain and loss, it also challenged their settled theological assumptions that woe came only on the wicked, and therefore, his only appropriate response was repentance (Job 4:78; 8:20; 11:14-15). They were inside the old paradigm. Bad things happened to bad people; each got what he deserved. Job was, they believed, wicked in some unperceived way. Otherwise, such tragedies would not have befallen him.

Today, we struggle with that same theological assumption. We have also reshaped the gospel we prefer – a message of God's love with less or no truth. And we have refashioned God into a deity among other gods. Salvation is by human goodness, universalism, all religions lead to the same place. We use different names and read different books but it is, the culture now maintains, the same God. And like Job's friends, we create communities that marginalize the tearful, superficially categorize and label them, suppressing their lament. When we silence lament, especially as people of privilege, we become the oppressors against whom the prophets railed.

Without realizing how far we have digressed, we seem to have developed a programmed approach to faith, driven by our pragmatism. Sadly, it misses real life. It is void of authentic confession and emotion. It has no place for doubt, for the open struggle with faith. It is a reflection of our superficial culture and a form of worldliness. The modern faith and confession movement is in part responsible for silencing lament. That movement has impacted Pentecostal churches more than those in the Evangelical stream. A person of faith, who walks with God, hears and obeys, the 'faith movement' asserts, would have no need to lament. They live in iron-clad victory, speak the positive language of faith, deny aches and pains, sniffles and profound sadness, never allowing sickness or deprivation to affect them. Their world is one in which legalism has married faith. In such a world, everyone conforms. Happiness matters most. Positivity and optimism are ordered. Needs are whisked away by declarative prophecy. Faith triumphs over love, since believing is the ultimate state and that is urged on all, and is substituted for bearing one another's burdens. The result is inauthenticity. A fundamental dishonesty is encouraged – the true self is hidden in order to join the celebration of faith with a feigned face.

Living Lament

In the corner of Copenhagen's cathedral is a mark left by Soren Kierkegaard – *Vor Frue Kirke* — dedicated to Job and to all lamenters. The creedal statement reads, "We believe that God is great enough to harbour our little lives with all their grievances, and that he can lead us from darkness through to the other side."[10] God can handle tears in our worship – we are the ones who have become hardened and tearless. When we ourselves lose the capacity to weep, we are changed. We do not want to hear the sobs of others or be forced to see their tears. Happy music, please? A positive message! The result is "diminished theological anthropology."[11] This completely sets aside the power of the incarnation. It disconnects faith from real life. It is numb and heartless.

> We whine about things we have little control over; we lament what we believe ought to be changed.[34]

Don Saliers says "that many worshipers do not *know how* to conjoin their real experiences in life with the poetic and rhetorical style of the psalms of lament." We have a fundamental disconnect with the Bible as it meets life, especially contemporary life.[12] This points to another problem in the contemporary church, our lack of Bible-engagement, personally, and, our lack of worship that is guided by, informed by, and offered to God on the track of Scripture. We have not only isolated our worship from contemporary pain, but also from ancient Scripture. That strips it both of its missional nature and its theological moorings. It makes worship about affectation, happy feelings, a mood, inspiration for the moment. As someone has said succinctly, "To reduce spirituality, simply close the Bible."[13]

Our worship then, needs a fundamental overhauling. We dare not misinterpret the call to lament as a mere mood alteration – much more is at stake here. Liturgists speak of "living liturgy." Liturgy is ancient, reaching back to the synagogue, to temple and tabernacle roots, as well as the models that survive from apostolic and early church practices. It is theological; it must reflect on God, from His own word, and not merely our ideas about Him. It is missional; it must move us to act in accord with His purposes, to fulfill His will and further His kingdom. It is transformational; it must change us – our attitudes and actions, conforming us to His image. And yet, it must also be relevant; speaking to us in our times, about our lives. It is timeless and pertinent, simultaneously. It demands truthfulness. Saliers says, "The issue here is one of 'truth-telling' and the capacity to hear the truth about the lamentability of the world in which we find ourselves."[14]

Broadening Prayer

The ancient perspective persists – "Lex orandi, lex credenda," meaning, "The pattern of prayer is the basis for the pattern of belief."

Stated simply: How we pray will determine how we live. And personal prayer practices are borrowed from corporate prayer models. When the church has little room for corporate prayer, its members find their own prayer life diminished. "The *lex orandi* that neglects the psalms of lament forfeits something necessary to a more faithful and authentic *lex credendi.* "[15] Superficiality in worship is reflected in life; authentic, Christ-engagement in worship moves more personally to engage him in daily life. "Wrestling with God is intrinsic to the ongoing divine–human exchange that constitutes the heart of Christian liturgies."[16] Richard Watson noted, "Lifeless prayer is no more prayer than a picture of a man is a man."[17]

There is a difference between wanting to know God, and wanting to be known by God. The latter, being known by God, requires one to be present with God, before God, and before Him as He chooses to be – in His sovereignty and holiness. It is about accountability and transparency.[18] Only then do you move beyond knowing about God, to truly knowing God. And the reason is this – knowing God is not bound up in facts about him. To know God requires His self-disclosure.

Israel knew the *acts* of God, and they stubbornly followed, resisted, complained, and finally defected from their relationship with God. Moses knew the *ways* of God (Psalm 103:7) – that is fundamentally different. It is not a superficial knowing. It is a transforming knowing. "Prayer," Richard Foster asserts, "involves transformed passions. In prayer, real prayer, we begin to think God's thoughts after Him, to desire the things He desires, to love the things He loves, to will the things He wills." Being known of God means "living before his face."[19] It is an invitation for God's intrusiveness – you know as you are known (1 Cor. 13:12). And that is a life lived before God, and lived out of love for God and others, centered in His love. "Underlying almost all these issues is the matter of desire for God. Unless a passion is awakened that leads us into deeper self-understanding *coram deo* (living before the face of the divine),"[20] there is only superficial, inauthentic Christianity.

> Prayer must be aflame. Its ardor must consume. Prayer without fervor is as a sun without light or heat, or as a flower without beauty or fragrance. A soul devoted to God is a fervent soul, and prayer is the creature of that flame. He only can truly pray who is all aglow for holiness, for God, and for heaven.[21]

There is a Church in Durham, North Carolina that incorporates laments into their worship. Each service begins with a psalm of lament. It is form of worship designed for "the public processing of pain." They not only weep before God, imploring His action in prayerful lament, they also take their prayer and felt pain to the streets. They hold a prayer vigil at each site in Durham where a violent death has occurred.[22] They do not begin community change with a moral lecture, but with lament – and yet, with a lament out of scripture, over scripture, making use of scripture.

Weep with God.

The Consequences of Ignoring Lament

There is a short story written by Carmen Corde that describes a woman who gave birth to a child that was blind. She promptly announced to her family and friends that she didn't want her son to know he was blind. Therefore, she forbade the use of terms like light, color or sight. She wanted him to think that all others were like him, that blindness was normal. The boy grew up unaware of his disability, unaware of a seen world – he lived in darkness through the senses of taste, smell, touch and sound. Then one day, a neighborhood girl jumped the fence and came alongside his dark world and used the taboo words his family had forbidden. She shattered the limited construct of the blind boy and opened a whole new avenue for his imagination. Her language and insights revealed to him the prison in which he lived, but in yet another sense, she liberated him. Yes, that liberation was possible, if only he could and would accept the eyes of another; if he would dare to perceive beyond his physical realities.[23]

Lament rises out of scripture. It is the world that could be, that should be – and it contrasts those godly principles with the world that is. It offers vision. It refuses to be blindfolded, to move through life ignoring pain and moral incongruence, accepting oppression and slavery by poverty and ignorance. It is enlightening, even if for a moment it is also overwhelming and incalculable.

Simone Weil observed, "Imaginary evil is romantic and varied; real evil is gloomy, monotonous, barren, boring. Imaginary good is boring; real good is always new, marvelous, intoxicating."[24] Prophylactic Christianity fails to experience God and simultaneously fails to encounter the pain and very real horrors of the world around it. It ignores such atrocities, denying them, excusing itself, without bearing such things to God in prayer and acting as the intercessory community it is called to be. Such a disengaged church becomes bored and is easily seduced by wicked imaginations. Imaginations we can manipulate: reality is fixed, cold, and hard.

> *'Avoid reality,' is the motto and aim of our age. Sedate yourself on pleasure, trinkets, food and drink, escape vacations.*

Live in the imaginary world of television and movies, one that can easily be turned off and on. In that world, death and pain, crime and sabotage, murder and evil, all surrogates for the real world can be managed since it is only imaginary. It is a daily dose of proxy living substantiated for real life encounters. The substitution works until something horrific, something real that can't be dismissed, crashes through the gates of our illusory lives. A.W. Tozer observed:

In the average church we hear the same prayers repeated each Sunday year in and out with, one would suspect, not the remotest expectation that they will be answered. It is enough, it seems, that they have been uttered. The familiar phrase, the religious tone, the emotionally loaded words have their superficial and temporary effect, but the worshipper is no nearer to God, no better morally and no surer of heaven than he was before.[25]

Again, he asserts:

Between the scribe who has read and the prophet who has seen there is a difference as wide as the sea. We are today overrun by orthodox scribes, but the prophets, where are they? The hard voice of the scribe sounds over evangelicalism, but the church waits for the tender voice of the saint who has penetrated the veil and has gazed with inward eye upon the Wonder that is God.[26]

Prophets have the eye of an eagle – they can gaze at God and look down at minute movements on the desert floor. Their view is omni-directional, seeing the problem and source simultaneously, the holy and the unholy, the whole and the broken – and they weep over what could be, what should be. "*Scholars* can interpret the past; it takes prophets to interpret the present," Tozer observes.[27] Lament is a prophetic prayer – it interprets, it intercedes, it calls out sin as a consequence, it fingers the wrongdoers and asks the court of heaven to prosecute them; it is priestly, it weeps as if it were the victim, for victims.

Vaclav Havel, the former leader of the atheistic, communistic Czech Republic observed of the failed experiment of atheistic communism:

I believe that with the loss of God, man has lost a kind of absolute and universal system of coordinates, to which he could always relate everything, chiefly himself. His world and his personality began to break up into separate, incoherent fragments corresponding to different, relative, coordinates.

Havel mournfully described his country as one "where the forests are dying, where the rivers look like sewers" and citizens cannot open their windows to find fresh air, and he placed the blamed on the "arrogance of new age human beings who enthroned themselves as lords of all nature and of all the world." The arrogance of atheism had led to absence of humility – and that affected all of life.[28] In the vortex of swirling godless ideas steering nations, including our own, we are to offer our lament in heaven's courtroom. We have little voice here, so, as did the founding fathers, we "appeal to heaven."

The doorway between the world as we have accepted it and the world as God intended it to be is found in lament. Brueggemann warned us twenty years ago that while the "recovery of personal lament is a great gain," if the communal laments are not "set along side, the record of personal religion can serve only privatistic concerns – and that is no doubt a betrayal of biblical faith."[29] Without faithful communal lament, the church continues the dominant privatization of faith and fails to "think *theologically* about public issues and public problems."[30] And, "Without faithful communal lament, private hurts live in tension with public joy."[31]

Back to Lament

Fireweed, a plant species of the Northern Hemisphere, is the first vegetation to appear after a forest fire or other ground disturbance. Fireweed was the first new growth to appear on Mount St. Helens after the volcano erupted there almost forty years ago. A few days after a forest floor is made barren by fire, the green foliage of fireweed breaks through the charred or disturbed earth. Soon pinkish blossoms adorn the austere and inhospitable landscape. Fireweed grows and flowers as long as there is open space and direct light. As other, larger vegetation re-appears, the fireweed plants die out. The seeds remain in the soil for many years. When the land is ravaged again, the seeds germinate anew. Fireweed is a metaphor for *theologia crucis,* the theology of the cross. The theology of the cross is the foundation upon which lament is constructed.[32] It is a picture of grace - of life after death, of hope and new vitality. Like fire-weed, the cross is not the end - it opens to new life. Triumph follows tragedy.

No visit to Jerusalem is complete without stopping at the Western Wall, the remaining stones from the days of the Second Temple. Jewish people gather there to lament. The place is popularly called the "Wailing Wall." It is Israel's way of institutionalizing lament, in the absence of a temple, in the face of a divided Jerusalem and a war-torn nation, in the face of nations who stand against them, as is demonstrated so frequently by the actions of the United Nations.

Day after day, Jews not only from Israel, but from around the world, stream there to pray. They stuff bits of paper, prayer requests in the cracks between the stones. They turn their face to the wall – some sit, some stand, some lean, some rock, all pray. They lament.

Discussion Guide

1. Why are we so resistant to lament in America?

2. If there is a blessing to those that lament, why are so few believers lamenting?

3. Discuss our choice of psalms for devotion and worship, our choice of music. What does that say about our worship? Our churches? The lack of balance in our lives?

4. Is our worship genuine? Authentic? Balanced? This is not an easy question.

5. Do you live in a 'lament free' zone? What does that mean? What does it say about us?

6. When there is no lament permitted, only celebration worship and faith language, what does that say about us?

7. What are the consequences of ignoring lament?

11

Intercessory Lament - God's Call Upon the Church Today

There are two broad categories in the Old Testament for Lament Psalms[1] – personal/individual[2] and communal.[3] A communal lament typically involved:

1. Invoking Yahweh

2. A complaint over some misfortune, almost always of a political/nation-state nature

3. A supplication/petition to Yahweh to intervene, to reverse the misfortune

4. An affirmation of confidence in Yahweh, designed to inspire corporate faith, and to move God to action for His own honor or the sake of His name

5. A declaration of faith, that the prayer was heard[4]

The *individual* lament is basically the same, but more personal and specific. Communal lament psalms were used on national days of fasting following a calamity – drought and famine, war and exile, pestilence and plagues. Hermann Gunkel saw Lament Psalms as a subcategory in the corporate hymnbook of Israel, and subsequently, also for the church. They were always there to be sung when appropriate. In such moments, corporate grieving was given status. Tears were acceptable worship, not merely in devotion, but also in doubt.

And though there was sadness, even tragedy, laments were sung – they took place against the backdrop of music, offered to God as music. The song of the believer did not die even with doubt or in the face of death. Lament was a melody, a hymn. It was at times personal, and at other times public and communal. It was singing though one's tears.

Today, intercessors must find a back corner, a basement room to pray and lament. Intercessory lament has no place in the gathering of the church corporate – grieving is taboo, eclipsed by pseudo, syrupy victory songs, mouthed by a church living less than stellar and authentic Christian lives, but nevertheless satisfied.

> *The suppression of lament is itself a sign of the superficiality; evidence of the plastic worship in today's church.*

Lament should be mainstreamed, but even intercessors don't understand it, its role and place, its power, especially from a unique New Testament perspective.

Lament allows us to express anguish and pain, disappointment and confusion to God. It is not merely emotional; it is raw life at prayer. Lament gives us permission to grieve, with the Holy Spirit, who must be deeply grieved, not only over the lack of righteousness and resistance to truth in society, but also with the church that has lost or suspended its convictions. No one it seems, in culture or Christendom, is being 'arrested' anymore, 'convicted' of wrong by the Holy Spirit. We should lament over a runaway culture, steeped in sin and increasingly a candidate for judgement. Laments give us language to express angst, from our own inner turmoil and that around us. They give dignity to authentic but struggling faith. They let us cry out to God.

Giving Voice to the Groans of Victims

As Gunkel pointed out, there are personal laments and communal laments. But, in the New Testament, what emerges is the church as an intercessory community, praying in the place of others, giving voice to a lost world, pleading as if we were the lost soul.

In Psalm 12, we meet pervasive, global wickedness. It sounds so contemporary. At the end of the psalm, *"the wicked"* are said to *"freely strut about"* and *"what is vile is honored by the human race"* (vv. 7b-8). We could be reading from our own newspaper. The psalmist laments, *"Help, Lord, for no one is faithful anymore...[the] loyal have vanished from the human race"* (v. 1). This is a lament of deep despair, bordering on hopelessness. Wickedness is so pervasive, it is normalized, *"Everyone lies to their neighbor"* (v. 2). Speaking pleasantries to one another, remaining superficially civil, offering compliments – *"they flatter with their lips."* But their real intent is hidden, they *"harbor deception in their hearts"* (v. 2). The sincerity of the culture is diluted with disingenu-

What a lamentable thing it is that men should blame the gods and regard us as the source of their troubles, when it is their own wickedness that brings them sufferings worse than any which destiny allots them.[11]

ousness, deceit, hypocrisy, and duplicitousness. Relationships are artificial, at best. The wicked are convinced that they can 'talk their way out of any dilemma' – as if their words were divine: *"By our tongues we will prevail; our own lips will defend us – who is lord over us?"* (v. 4). Individualism, arrogance as narcissism, reigns. 'No one will stop us, not even God!' Such arrogance demands that a lamenter plead for God to intervene. *"Because the poor are plundered and the needy groan, I will now arise,' says the Lord. 'I will protect them from those who malign them'"* (v. 5).

This is the role of intercessory lament – to step into some disputed middle, between good and evil, right and wrong, peace and war, the powerful and the oppressed – to weep and pray, and identify with the powerless, and plead with God for intervention. It is for this reason that Christ came to the earth – to pray, from the middle, between earth and heaven, lost humanity and eternity.

When evil triumphs, the righteous are to lament, to intercede with tears. Such intercession, coupled with the 'groans' of the victims, reaches God and He acts. Yet the groans of the victims are not enough. It is the lament of the righteous that gives them voice. It is the legal standing of the redeemed before the throne of God that is the catalyst for God to act. A groan is a groan, but a lament is a prayer – and when the righteous, in prayer, interpret and give voice to the pain in culture, in an intercessory manner – God arises. He acts. The problem is that we continue to lament over narrow slices of our own pain. The church has not embraced its role as an intercessory community, bearing the pain of a dying world to the throne of grace and pleading for intervention from heaven.

A church in a nation, any nation, might find it appropriate to lament over an abusive leader who had not acted responsibly or had created a context of oppression that resulted in the abuse of the people (Ps. 58). African nations have a long history of such abuse, as do countries in eastern Europe, from its century of totalitarian socialism. In such situations, the people take their case directly to God. This was also the case in the founding of the United States. The founding fathers, not reaching a reasonable agreement with England, not being allowed representation in the House of Commons or the Parliament of England, and still being taxed, without representation, being forced to buy only English goods, at inflated prices, felt unjustly treated, and so they made their appeal to heaven. The first flag of the colonies was not the familiar red, white, and blue flag with stars and stripes. It was a prayer flag with a lone pine tree against a simple white background. The tree stood, as if it were pointing to heaven, and it carried the words, "An Appeal to Heaven." The American Revolution started as a prayer movement, a protest before God, for justice. The chances of their winning independence in a war with England, the world's superpower, were non-existent, in the natural. But the colonialists prayed, and God intervened and gave them a nation.

An intercessor, or the church as an intercessory community, offers a petition in the courtroom of heaven, in behalf of another. This is a kind of 'friend of the court' brief, filed in behalf of another whose faith may be frazzled, who is perhaps suffering, maybe ill and unable to adequately pray. It may be for someone without standing in heaven's courtroom – the unsaved. The intercessor asks God, "Why? How long?" Intercessory lament may also advocate for justice, pleading for God's direct intervention in some matter. In such cases, it often weeps as if it were the sufferer. It finds a reference in God's promises or His history of dealings with His people and it appeals on that basis. Such an appeal is made from inside the covenant. It glances back for perspective, but its major focus is the present need and the desire for the immediate intervention of God. The appeal is personal. It is not made to a stranger or to a distant God, but to the God who is known, with whom we have a relationship and history. That is what makes the lament so pregnant – it is full of passion about some personal sense of disappointment, confusion, an unfulfilled expectation or hope. This is an exchange with the God who is known – a friend, a supposed protector and provider in the face of some poignant need or disappointment. It is no wonder the lament psalms are charged with emotion.

Intercessory Laments

We individualize prayer. And further, we see it as a narrow personal privilege. Prayer requests are spouted out in some congregations, so fast and furiously, that no one remembers, and even then – the call to pray is only for friends and acquaintances, and at that, for the narrow needs in one another's personal lives: sickness, decisions, provision, protection, direction – all valid, all important to someone, but all falling short of the noble use of prayer in its missional, intercessory function or that of the church, as an intercessory community for the lost.

Israel, as a nation, was constituted, to serve God to and before the other nations of the earth. They were not simply given a land, a new place to live and build a home and raise a family. The nation was charged with a mission. Israel's corporate responsibility was legalized in a covenant at the base of Mt. Sinai. The priests, and later, as in other monarchies, the king, became the custodian and guardian of the nation's constitution. Israel's law laid claim to the conscience, not only of the nation, but also of each individual.[5] Beyond the king, in Israel's theology was the Creator, the giver of life (Creation Psalms: 8, 19, 29, 104, 135, and 147). They were a nation tightly bound to their unique God. The earthly king was only His surrogate, the throne in front of His Throne (Isa. 6:1-3). Yahweh was Israel's king twice – as creator and redeemer-liberator. He gave life in creation, and then he had given them liberty in life in the miraculous exodus from slave status in Egypt. There, He triumphed over the gods of Egypt. He had heard their lament (Ex. 2:24), their groans under slavery and He acted to redeem them. At Sinai, He entered into covenant with Israel. They were to be His representative nation to the nations, living among them, on the land-bridge connecting three of the continents of the earth.

When the people sinned or felt abandoned by God, there were provisions in the covenant, which were the means by which God renewed the relationship. When they discovered themselves in sin, they rightly lamented and repented, usually in a solemn assembly. More often, when they felt that God had failed them, when enemies were overpowering them, when nature had given them drought and famine, or when pestilence threatened – they lamented, offering God their complaints, charging Him with not keeping the covenant, asking Him to fulfill his covenant promises, and often in the end, repenting. The relationship was dynamic, authentic and often raw. At times, the whole nation charged God with not appropriately blessing them or protecting them. At times, the prophets charged the people with unrighteousness, as the root and cause of some calamity. It was in the midst of such messiness, confusion and accusation, of anger and disappointment, of searching for right and wrong, that tearful lament occurred. These were corporate arguments with God and one another about critical life and death issues.

In the New Testament, a major shift takes place, away from lament as a complaint before God about some lack of provision or breach in covenant. The shift is toward intercessory lament. Sadly, like Israel, we continue to use prayer almost exclusively for ourselves or those we know and love, asking God to take away personal pain and deprivation. God invites us to come – that is not the question. Jesus instructs us to pray "for daily bread," and about stuck relationships, about evil, direction in decisions, temptations and trials

(Mt. 6:11-13). All of that is both permitted and invited. But prayer also has a noble, selfless use, that of the church as an intercessory community, pleading with God, to end the tyranny of Lucifer's reign and that of his earthly co-conspirators. The church as an intercessory community prayerfully stands against oppressive kings and governments that are aligned with evil, imploring God to deal with wicked men and intimidators, to put away, finally and forever, sin and death.

The church is called to be an intercessory mediator, as Jesus taught us, praying for the *"name"* of God to be glorified, the *"kingdom"* of God to come, and the *"will"* of God to be done (Mt. 6:9-10). We rarely pray like this. When we do, it is usually rote, a liturgy, a recitation without tears. We do not present a forceful protest before God in behalf of broken families, orphans and widows, sex and drug trafficking, gangs and cartels, crooked cops and jaded judges, compromised clergy and congregations. We do not weep over senseless murders, abortions of the innocent, abandonment, euthanasia, corporate exploitation or despotic banks – the system of tyranny and coercion, repression and domination. We no longer weep over extra-marital affairs – too common among us, even by pastors and leaders; homosexuality or gender disorientation. Lying and cheating are now normal in the culture. Sin is accepted as entertainment. War and international conflict

> We live in a world that is beyond our control, and life is in a constant flux of change. So we have a decision to make: keep trying to control a storm that is not going to go away or start learning how to live within the rain.[12]

are everyday news. Pestilence and pandemics threaten us. Drought is common and famine may not be far behind – they all have become acceptably common, and there are no tears, no lament. Such things should require us to consult with God as a city or a nation. They should move us to brokenness and repentance.

Do you not think that Jesus expects us to lament over the common blasphemy of his name? Is it not to be treated as holy, as sacred speech – *"hallowed be thy name?"* (Mt. 6:9). The name of God and Jesus are now common swear words and they are offered as such, so frequently, that no one is any longer shocked. No one objects. Do you not think it was the intent of Jesus, when he gave us the model prayer, that we would pray daily, about the rebellion against his rule, his lordship – *"thy kingdom come?"* (Mt. 6:10). Should we not lament over the wholesale rejection of His will and way, not only by friends and family, but by nations – *"thy will be done?"* (Mt. 6:10). Blasphemy, rebellion, defiant independence – should grieve us as genuine Christians. The legitimate expression of such grief is in prayerful lament. In that way, we join the grieving Holy Spirit, sent to *"convict the world of its sin, and of God's righteousness, and of the coming judgement"* (John 16:8 NLT). The NIV says, *"he will prove the world to be in the wrong about sin and righteousness and judgement."* The KJV, *"... he will reprove the world of sin."* The Aramaic Bible in Plain English, *"...he will correct the world concerning sin and concerning righteousness and concerning judgement."*

If the mission of the Holy Spirit, in part, is to convict – to arrest men and women, and to convince of righteousness and reveal possible judgement, we must ask – what is the progress in the mission? We seem to be going in the opposite direction. Paul warned in Ephesians 4:20 against grieving the Holy Spirit. In Romans, the Spirit is not merely *grieved*, but *groaning* (Rom. 8:26). Charles Finney noted that where force stopped, no longer being necessary, moral agency began; and where moral agency stopped, force became necessary.[6] The man who polices himself needs no coercion to behave; and a culture that is guided by a biblically informed conscience is by definition, self-governed. This was the vision for America owned by the founding fathers. A people who lived moral lives tethered to Scripture. Where moral agency, a grace-empowered respect for the conviction of the Holy Spirit, is in place, force is not necessary. Judgement is stayed. But, where there is no respect for the conviction of the Holy Spirit, for Biblical values, no acceptance of grace-based discipline, God may choose to resort to force!

Is it possible that we are to be partners with the Holy Spirit and his missionary work in our world, as we grieve with him? What is a role of the church, as an intercessory community? Is it not to join the Holy Spirit in lamenting over the injustice and oppression around us? What if our role is to give him voice in grieving over lostness and cultural fragmentation, broken relationships and the lack of peace? If that is true, then we are indeed grieving the Holy Spirit. And if the convicting work of the Spirit is tied to our giving voice in lament over the degree of sin in the culture, then is the restraint he would offer subdued by our tearless, incense-free churches? In intercession the church is called to act as an agent of reconciliation, preaching a gospel of reconciliation (2 Cor. 5:11-21), praying for God to move in hearts and heads, so that gospel work can be done – reconciling men to God, and then, one to another – sharing in the gospel of peace. Reconciliation happens in an environment of love, but on the track of truth.

The peace offering was the crowning offering of the five basic sacrifices (Leviticus 3), and it is still God's goal – inner peace, peace with God, the peace of God, feet shod with the preparation of the gospel of peace (Eph. 6:15), peacemaking (Mt. 5:9), and therefore, peace with one another (Psa. 34:14; 1 Peter 3:11; Rom. 12:18;

14:19;2 Cor. 13:11; 1 Thess. 5:13; Heb. 12:14). Peace is the crowning proof of salvation. Peace is made and celebrated at the altar. So prayer altars should be built by the church everywhere, invisible altars, established by the intercessory agents of reconciliation. They should be established at places of disunity and anger, in the midst of unforgiving divides, all over a city. Such an altar is not built with natural materials; it is created by the act of sincere prayer.

Tears and Triumph

In the gospels, we find several stories about lament over personal loss, specifically in the face of death. As we noted earlier, in each case, the response of Jesus was resurrection power – pointing forward to his own lament and resurrection, to Gethsemane and Golgotha, and the empty tomb. He met lament at the gates of the village of Nain in the form of a funeral procession. A widow's only son had died, and she was crying. He was moved. He stopped the procession, urged her out of lament and raised the young man from the dead (Luke 7:1-17). He found lament at the home of Jairus over the untimely death of the synagogue ruler's daughter. He cleared the room of the lamenters, momentarily displacing it, and he raised the girl from the dead (Mark 5:21-43). And of course, there is the case of Lazarus, where Jesus wept, and then raised his friend from the dead (John 11:38-44).

Each case meets desperation, tears – the symbol of lament. And each time Jesus called for the cessation of tears and performed a power miracle which pointed to the resurrection. What does this say to us? Is lament then being silenced by Jesus? The New Testament does not nullify laments[7] – it changes their character, lacing them with hope, based on the resurrection. It energizes them by the praying help of the Holy Spirit. It redirects and repurposes lament as an intercessory function. To lament in behalf of another requires us to stand with them, in an incarnational manner.

There is also the story of the Canaanite woman, crying, arguably lamenting. Seeing Jesus, she *"began to cry out, saying, 'Have mercy on me, Lord, Son of David; my daughter is cruelly demon-possessed'"* (Mt. 15:22). Here Jesus grows silent, not answering or responding. She is using covenant language, but she is Canaanite, outside the covenant. She does not have the legal right to appeal to the covenant. Lament is from inside the covenant, an appeal to the court of heaven by those who are its blood-bought citizens. *"I was sent only to the lost sheep of the house of Israel"* (v. 24), Jesus tells her. This is when her whole demeanor changes. She becomes authentic, no longer faking covenant status. She worshipfully bows and pleads, *"Lord, help me!"* (v. 25). He presses the matter of the covenant, telling her that he cannot give *"the children's bread"* to Gentiles (v. 26). She persists, intensifying her dependence, deepening her humility, evidencing faith. *"Yes, Lord; but even the dogs (Jewish vernacular, slang, for Gentiles) feed on the crumbs which fall from their masters' table"* (v. 27). She does not wrangle with Jesus about Jewish prejudice against Gentiles, about Jewish arrogance – she brushes the degrading language aside, using it to her advantage. 'Okay, call me a dog, but give me what beloved house dogs get – they too feed from the covenant table.' Jesus commends her faith, *"it shall be done for you as you wish,"* and her daughter was healed at once.

The story was instructive precisely because it reaches to a Gentile, outside the covenant. Standing inside the covenant as intercessors, we are to respond to the needs, the hunger for God's help, the faith of those outside. Here we are presented with a child in distress, and a mother in crisis. No cure exists. No doctor can fix the problem. The tormenter is destroying the child's life. There is no solution to the cruelty of a demon's torture except by the hand of God.

Here, Jesus models the role he desires for the church to assume as a compassionate, intercessory community, offering deliverance and reconciliation. The cross, the new covenant is not exclusive, it stands open to *"whosoever will."* Jew and Gentile may come and enter the covenant written in the blood of Jesus.

In the chapter in this volume, entitled, "Lament in the New Testament – Answered with Resurrection," the string of stories above is expanded, and they climax with the scenes of Christ in the Garden of Gethsemane, Golgotha, and the empty tomb – resurrection. Paul's theology picks up this theme of living out of the resurrection. It is the resurrection that Peter preaches so powerfully in Acts 2:24-33, at Pentecost. It was resurrection power that raised up the lame man at the gate called Beautiful (Acts 3:6-8). Peter explained the miracle by saying, *"You denied the Holy One and the Just...[you] killed the Prince of life, whom God raised from the dead, of which we are witnesses. And his name, through faith in His name, has made this man strong"* (3:14-16). It is the concern about resurrection preaching that moves the temple authorities to "lay hands" on Peter and John, and arrest them (4:1-3).

When the church gathered only days after the ascension of Christ, they faced the possibility of death (Acts 4). The apostles were in jail with an order to silence and gag their witness. All the authority of Jerusalem had lined up against them. Their response was corporate prayer. And they prayed from Psalm 2, *"Why do the nations rage?"* They found correspondence to their situation in scripture and prayed from its pages. Amazingly, their prayer does not narrow to personal concerns, to pleas for their own deliverance, for safety and a reduction of the pressure on them. Rather, they prayed for boldness. *"The kings of the earth prepared for battle"* – they recognized that the arrest of Peter and John meant that the war against Christ would now continue, but it would be focused on them. They were tasting the cross, the cross Christ told them they must carry in order to follow him.

"The rulers" had *"gathered together against the Lord! And against his Messiah."* How could they fight against God and win? The battle ultimately turned back to Jesus. The church was merely caught in the middle. And they would choose, in face of their own possible death, to not back down. In the prayers of the church, they named their adversaries – *"this city," "Herod Antipas," "Pontius Pilate the governor," "the Gentiles,"* and the *"people of Israel,"* all *"united against Jesus, your holy servant, whom you anointed."* They assert the sovereignty of God in prayer: this did not take God by surprise. Neither the crucifixion or the current persecution were revelations to God, everything *"was determined beforehand according to your will"* (Acts 4:24-27).

Pointing out, naming their enemies in an imprecatory manner, they out them before God. They entered the record of their obstinacy before the court of heaven. And then they did a remarkable thing. In the typical Old Testament lament, the plea would have been for intervention, for relief, for God to crush their enemies or some similar imprecation. Not here. Not now. *"O Lord, hear their threats, and give us, your servants, great boldness in preaching your word."* It is not for extrication from the crisis that they pray. They are not leaving town. They will not be silenced. They will not be intimidated. They call for God's intervention, not in saving them, but in proving Christ to be alive. *"Stretch out your hand with healing power; may miraculous signs and wonders be done through the name of your holy servant Jesus."* Let miracles happen, not for us, not to us, but in relationship to the name of Jesus.

In the face of evil and brazen bullying, they pray to be bolder. In the face of tyrannical authority, they pray for power! They don't ask for the comfort of the Holy Spirit, but for his commanding dominance. *"Stretch out your hand, God"* – ekteinō, meaning to extend, to lay hands on, by inference – to touch. 'Hands', the hands of power had been laid on Peter and John, now, though the Greek uses a different term here, they pray that God will extend his "hand" and touch. They pray that there will be signs, wonders and healing associated with the name of Jesus. It is not a miracle show for them, focused on them or their needs for which the pray. They are asking for a demonstration of the resurrection. 'He is not dead,' these actions will shout. Surprisingly, it is not the church that is in trouble, up against fleshly authorities. The opposite is true – the worldly authorities are fighting God Himself. They are in trouble. *"After this prayer, the meeting place shook, and they were all filled with the Holy Spirit. Then they preached the word of God with boldness"* (4:31 NIV). This is lament and resurrection coupled together. It admits pain and displeasure – they had been arrested, but rebounded with resurrection hope. It is part human – tears; it is part divine – buoyant faith.

Being Silenced

The early church refused to be silenced. Sadly, we have succumbed to a number of legal rulings and threats. We subordinate the practices of our faith to whatever the law of the land dictates, no matter how frivolous. Faith practices are subordinated to company policies and culture or even to the preferences of a club to which we belong, or yet, to the faithless choices of our circle of friends. This includes practices such as prayer, wearing Christian symbols or jewelry, specifically crosses, hiding a Bible, and working on Sunday, when asked. All these are indicators of our being conditioned and silenced by the culture. Our churches and pulpits have been muzzled by an obscure congressional ruling dating to the era of the 1950s, silenced by the IRS, silenced by popular opinion, silenced by the fear of man. Faith sounds are rarely heard in the dominant culture. Prayer has been pushed to margins, even in the church. The name of Jesus has been virtually outlawed, except as a curse word. When silence has been demanded, by anyone, anywhere, we have accommodated them. Where such duplicity is found, its partner is the condition of apostasy.

In Habakkuk, you find the command, *"Let all the earth be silent"* (2:20b). There, silence is finally imposed by God on the raging nations as predicted in Psalm 2. Though the rulers of this world have ignored Him, killed his prophets, persecuted His disciples and crucified His Son; they have oppressed the poor and opposed the righteous – soon, they will have to listen. In Habakkuk, God proves Himself the more powerful. He asserts His Sovereignty over those who have resisted Him, if for no other reason, to make clear His justification for their coming judgement.

Brueggeman points to a larger picture here. Silence, he argues, is imposed by a coercive agent, one who is more powerful. It is an unequal transaction – the powerful say to the weak, "Be silent!"[8] When speech is taken away, it disarms. When the one who is silenced is silent – the silencer has prevailed. He is free then to do as he wants – the silence is the cue to domestication, to submission. The most powerful tool of any human is their capacity for speech. Ultimately, God alone has the right to demand silence! And one day, He will silence both the earth and hell.

Elaine Scarry argues that when rogue governments torture people, the goal is rarely information. The goal is to silence them, and by silencing them, to dehumanize them, to "unmake" them as persons, to chip away at their identity, to break them down. The only counter, she argues, to such a tactic, is speech.[9] The imposed silence does not dispense with the tension that speech normally both releases and reasonably resolves. The tension only goes underground, or arguably inside. At some point, the tension will break forth into aggression, perhaps violence, or the individual will collapse inwardly, onto themselves, in despair and depression or self-destruction. The best resolution is speech – not violence. Rather, it is prayerful speech to God, against the powerful silencing party. The only rational choice in the face of totalitarianism – whether it is government induced or cultural, as in the USA, is to the break the silence.[10] Pray. Lament. Protest in the courtroom of heaven.

In granting mankind the power of speech, God puts humanity on a different plane. The creatures in heaven are endowed with the power of speech, while creatures on the earth are only given the capacity for sound. Humans, made in the image of God, are granted a heavenly ability, speech. We live on the earth, but we belong to heaven – formed in the image of God, given dominion, the power of procreation, the promise of eternity, and the capacity for speech.

Having words for things presupposes some level of control. Have you noticed how the medical community, physicians and psychologists, quickly apply labels to new illnesses and phobias? The naming of it assumes power over the thing – it can be managed or dominated. Science and technology do similar things. In intercession, the Spirit helps us give language to things that seem out of control to the senses. We don't have the power to cure, but God does. In the naming of the disorder, we identify it. We lament over it. And we engage God as healer.

The structural components of communal laments are identified by Paul Ferris in the following way:

1. Invocation — or direct address to God, calling him by his name (Yahweh) or identifying a relationship with God ("my" or "our God").

2. Hymn of Praise — usually addresses God in the second person and recounts past acts.

3. Expression of Confidence and Trust — prior to the complaint, e.g., that God is able and willing to hear; a trusting confidence that God is listening and will respond.

4. Lament — description of lamentable circumstances along with an expression of the anxiety, fear and hurt that accompanies those circumstances as well as the questions and doubts which arise within the believer.

5. Appeal and Motivation for Response.

   a. for deliverance — or, redemption; seeks to move God to act on the ground of God's mercy, faithfulness and/or love.

   b. for cursing — or, imprecation; seeks to move God to avenge his people on the ground of God's justice and righteousness.

6. Protestation of Innocence — though rarely explicit, the laments often reflect bewilderment and perplexity over the cause of their lamentable circumstance

7. Expression of Confidence and Hope — expresses the expectation that God will deliver and act on behalf of his people.

8. Vow of Praise—when the day of deliverance comes they will praise God for his redemptive act.

According to Ferris, "invocation, the lament proper, and the appeal are the elements found in all communal laments."[13]

Discussion Guide

1. Have you ever lamented – personally, before God? Can you recall the dynamics of that experience?

2. Have you ever been in a group where lament was experienced corporately? Describe the moment? What was the impact?

3. Do you think we displace intercessory lament? If so, how do we change that?

4. What is the role of intercessory lament?

5. Discuss the idea that intercessory lament is a kind of 'friend of the court' brief filed to the courtroom of heaven.

6. Have we allowed ourselves to be silenced, in offering a prayerful protest in heaven against the way things are on the earth?

7. Review Paul Ferris' structural elements in a communal lament.

12

Breaking the Silence

The lament psalms reveal a people often oppressed. They are depicted as up against some wicked, overpowering force that has been legitimized in a corrupt government running rogue, one described as 'wicked, vile, unrestrained' (Psalm 12:8). In intercessory lament, the silence against such tyranny is broken as the only way to unstick the logjam of injustice and domination. By prayer, God is summoned. At times, intercessory lament breaks the silence against God Himself. The lament becomes the "voice from underneath,"[1] the one, as it were, "crying in the wilderness," a revolutionary voice, not advocating for a geo-political revolution, but one of the heart, a spiritual-moral revolution that produces a more compassionate and just world. The prayer is for a government that is godlier, fair to all, calling people to righteousness and mercy.

Refusing to be Victims

Today Christians, as did the Jewish voices we find in the psalms, often see themselves as powerless victims. In the New Testament, believers are never described as victims. The posture of the New Testament believer is that of an overcomer. We are *"seated with Christ in heavenly places"* (Eph. 2:6), *"standing,"* staying on our feet even in the face of spiritual warfare (6:14), *"...hard pressed, but not crushed…perplexed, but not in despair…persecuted, but not forsaken… struck down, but not destroyed…knowing that he who raised up the Lord Jesus will also raise us up…"* (2 Cor. 4:8-9, 14).

The language that describes us is positive, as privileged, empowered *saints*. We are called *saints*, no longer captive to the grip of sin or condemned by its guilt. 'Saints' describes the moral and ethical distinctive of the redeemed (used 67 times in the New Testament).[2] We are *overcomers* – not victims (found 28 times in 24 verses in the New Testament). We are also called an *heir[s] of God* (Rom. 8:17), *chosen* (Col. 3:12; Rev. 17:14; 1 Peter 2:9; cf. Isa 45:4), *royal* (1 Peter 2:5, 9), the *called* (Rev 17:14), and the *elect* (Mk. 13:20, 22, 27; Titus 1:1; 1 Peter 1:1). These are not terms that denote victims. These are terms of lavish grace, of strategic positioning, of heaven's imprimatur and an elevated status. These are terms that reveal heaven's notice and appraisal of us, despite the dismissive and repressive posture of the world toward believers and their faith.

> The time comes when silence is betrayal. That time has come for us today…some of us who have already begun to break the silence of the night have found that the calling to speak is often a vocation of agony, but we must speak.
> ~ Martin Luther King, Jr.

We must decide who we are – a narrow-minded group of people committed to a 'book' and its out-of-date values as the culture suggests? Or the *royalty* of a rising kingdom, *heirs of God, chosen* and *called?* Sadly, our identity, our sense of self, is being molded by the cultural rejection of Christianity – and we are acting as the apostles initially did when Christ was arrested and led to the cross. Once open about our faith, we are now in hiding, denying our association with him, as did Peter (Mark 14:50; Matthew 26:56; John 18:15-27). We are in danger of betraying Christ for our 'thirty-pieces of silver' (Mt. 26:15) – to keep our job, to hold onto our retirement, to not lose our entitlement, to be in the running for the new position. Christians are now running scared. The scandalizing of Christianity in America is new to our history; but, in truth, this is the meaning of the cross – we are now back to the new normal.

Whose identity will we accept? We are Christians. We believe and live as if Jesus is truly the Son of God, the Savior, the King of kings, the Messiah, the lamb of God, and the lion of the tribe of Judah. He is, all of this. But there has always been another narrative, and in truth, it is the dominant cultural narrative globally – it names Jesus as scandalous, divisive, irreverent (of other faiths), blasphemous, disrespectful, worthy of dying as a criminal next to and between other notorious criminals, worthy of the worst kind of death: death on a cross. Not only was it a cruel means of death, but it was meant to deleteriously brand the dying person, tainting their reputation forever. In this worldly narrative, Jesus is not a good man. This is the now the dominate narrative of our time. Jesus is again being crucified, and Christians are silent, fleeing, for various reasons. Jesus, we are told, might be acceptable, standing in the pantheon of the gods, no better or no worse than the others. His uniqueness is denied and we are silent. His historicity is doubted and we say nothing. His words are questioned – as real, as his own, as authentic, as the word of God. Silence. Over such convenient capitulation to mainstream culture, we must lament.

The Choice: Jesus or Jesus

The trial of Jesus took place during the Passover Festival. A tradition had been established in commemoration of the Jewish liberation from Egypt, to release a prisoner, a Jew, held captive by Rome. Pilate presented two men, almost certain, given their profiles, that they would release Jesus of Nazareth, the teacher and miracle worker. He was shocked when they chose to have Barabbas released over Jesus of Nazareth. He was a ruthless criminal who would probably rob and kill again.

The actual name of Barabbas, the man chosen by the crowd to be set free over Jesus of Nazareth, was *Jesus* Barabbas, *Joshua* Barabbas, *Savior-Deliverer* Barabbas. The name ironically means, 'Jesus, son of the father.'[3] *Bar* – means *son;* and *abbas, abba,* from Aramaic, means *father,* thus son of the father.

This is not widely known – that the crowd was given the choice of Jesus or Jesus. Since Origen, one of the early church fathers, the other name of Barabbas, 'Jesus,' Joshua, Savior, has been suppressed. Origen saw the name of Jesus as so precious that he fought to erase from history the fact that the other name of Barabbas was also Jesus. It was a noble thing he attempted; but also flawed. The world is forever presented with two choices, two saviors, two named 'Jesus.' Two very different movements. Two very different spirits. Two agendas. Two visions for change. Two methods – one by surrender and service, the other by the sword and superiority. One merciful, the other ruthless. One principled, the other poison.

> When the Nazis came for the communists, I did not speak out; I remained silent. I was not a communist. When they locked up the socialists, I remained silent; I was not a socialist. When they came for the trade unionists, I did not speak out; I was not a trade unionist. When they came for the Jews, I remained silent; I wasn't a Jew. When they came for me, there was no one left to speak out.
> – Pastor Martin Niemöller

At the Passover, given the choice offered by Pilate, the crowd preferred Barabbas (Matthew 27:15; Mark 15:6; Luke 23:17; John 18:39). So insistent were they that Barabbas be released, and Jesus of Nazareth be crucified, and so reluctant was Pilate, that he did not relent until the crowd declared with fervor, *"Let his [Jesus of Nazareth] blood be upon us and upon our children"* (Matthew 27:25). The "notorious prisoner," Jesus Barabbas, was set free, noted as the preference of the crowd – the one who had been involved in a revolt (Mark 15:7; Luke 23:19) and was called a bandit (John 18:40), a term also employed to indicate a political revolutionary.[4]

We face the same choice today. Who do you choose? For whom will you speak up? Whose 'spirit' do you want released, openly into the culture? Jesus of Nazareth; or, Jesus Barabbas? In what revolution are you participating? The outer political revolution; or, the inner revolution of the heart. These are two different ways to relate to the world. Israel was looking for another Joshua, a leader, and they were given two choices – and they chose wrong. So now, the world is again looking for another Joshua, a Savior, and the choices are the same – Jesus of Nazareth and Jesus Barabbas: Christ or anti-Christ.

Their choices on that momentous day are also our choices today – Jesus of Nazareth; or Jesus Barabbas. Both – sons of a different father. One advocated a revolution of the heart; the other was an insurrectionist who had led a riot. One turned the cheek, the other struck with the sword. One healed, the other harmed. One advocated peace, the other practiced violence. One called for repentance, citing Israel's wrong; the other justified any means to accomplish a political, revolutionary agenda that would free Israel and reestablish her independence.

A nation is changed, one heart at a time, by examining its own immorality and advocating for a revolution of righteousness. Without that, no other revolution can succeed. The other choice is an agenda of change without a moral script, 'the end justifies the means,' power over principle. Such a revolution is established on a flawed foundation, like the beast of Daniel with feet of baked clay mixed with iron, it can never stand (Daniel 2:43).

On the Day of Pentecost, after days of prayer, days of sorting through the facts, 120 believers were empowered by the Holy Spirit. And they broke their silence. Roaring into the streets, speaking languages they had never learned, they crossed ethnic and linguistic lines. They united a significant representative portion of the world to hear a searing and yet hopeful word. At the recent Passover, they had chosen wrong. They had killed the Messiah. But there was also good news. Jesus, the one crucified, was not dead. Not only was he risen, but he had reclaimed David's throne. The revolution was on – but not in the way in which Israel had anticipated or wished.

The empowering of the Spirit confirmed the status of Christ-followers as the true sons of the Father. Such undeserved blessing and divinely given standing demands that we not be silent, and that we not be selfish. We are to share our victory. Having been set free, liberated, pulled from the fire (Jude 1:23), we now give voice, first in prayer, then in evangelism, to the others still trapped in Adam's fallen and condemned house.

Our victory declaration is not an egotistical boast of power. It is quite contradictory. It is strength in weakness. Power in meekness. Exaltation in humility. It is gentleness and boldness tethered together. It is God, nailed to a tree; God, in Christ, *"delivered over by the predetermined plan and foreknowledge of God…nailed to a cross by the hands of godless men…"* (Acts 2:23), *"and put Him to death"* (v. 24). But this slain lamb has roared. *"God raised Him up again, putting an end to the agony of death, since it was impossible for Him to be held in its power"* (v. 24). He, the weak one, the helpless man who needed assistance in bearing his cross, is now at the right hand of God, the

Father, in heaven (v. 25). Neither he nor his kingdom, nor yet his followers, can *"be shaken"* (v. 25). This is confidence. This emboldens. It lifts up: *"Therefore my heart was glad and my tongue exulted; Moreover my flesh also will live in hope"* (v. 26). Christ has risen from the dead. He was not abandoned in the grave. His flesh did not suffer decay (v. 30-31). He has been *"exalted to the right hand of God,"* (v. 33), and the *"promise of the Holy Spirit...[God] has poured forth..."* which can be seen and heard in demonstrable ways.

> Now when they heard this, they were pierced to the heart, and said to Peter and the rest of the apostles, "Brethren, what shall we do?" Peter said to them, 'Repent, and each of you be baptized in the name of Jesus Christ for the forgiveness of your sins; and you will receive the gift of the Holy Spirit.' And with many other words he solemnly testified and kept on exhorting them, saying, 'Be saved from this perverse generation!' (Acts 2: 37-38, 40).

This is no time for culturally induced humiliation and silence – Christ is exalted. Heaven sees him as the true heir of David's throne. He has been recognized as the rightful king, though he must for some season reign in exile. The question Peter set forth was, "will you now switch sides?" It is the question we face, as a church, in reverse. With the crucifixion of Christ happening in our culture – will we switch sides? Will you be saved from this *"perverse generation"* (v. 40)? Will we succumb to peer pressure and be silenced? Will we continue to live as otherwise normal humans, whose secondary identity is that of Christians? As neighbors, who are differentiated only by a Sunday trip to church? As fellow-workers whose witness fails to adequately differentiate us from our peers, rendering us as selfless and lightless? As citizens who are far too silent when Jesus is again being crucified? Powerful things happen when the powerless find their voice – and that begins in prayer. We lament. We first protest, at the throne.

> Listen, my friend! Your helplessness is your best prayer. It calls from your heart to the heart of God with greater effect than all your

uttered pleas. He hears it from the very moment that you are seized with helplessness, and He becomes actively engaged at once in hearing and answering the prayer of your helplessness.[5]

The Time for Silence is Over

The silence must be broken for God's intervention into our world. God acts, by His own Sovereign design, in connection with prayer. *"We have not, because we ask not"* – we don't pray! That means, first, a rising tide of intercessory prayer must fill heaven's temple from the earth. The cries of intercessors are far too weak, too few, too scattered at this point. We need an army of intercessors. The church itself must become an intercessory community.

We face a formidable sociological stronghold of and by this world. That stronghold is only a front, itself under the influence of the god of this age. Kings and governments are in active alignment or passive complicity with this malignant evil. That further victimizes the "deformed ego-structure" of humans who are living in and under the oppression, in silence, having accepted a less than God-desired existence. These "are all one piece," so argues Brueggeman.[6] The social structures, the cultural threads, the geo-political trends, the elite power structures – are components of one whole. The key to breaking free and becoming necessitates speaking out, first prayerfully, then prophetically, and that is also the key to God's intervention. The forces we face require supernatural opposition – we cannot do this alone, by ourselves, with mere human resources – God must act. Jeremiah's prophetic voice was partnered with his lamenting intercession. We must have both – intercessory lament, pleas for God's intervention; and prophetic clarity. These are bound together.

This is a prayerful movement, starting in one soul who will no longer be silenced. It is prayer as protest, prayer as quiet – but catalytic change, prayer for the kingdom of God to come. It is prayer as the backbone of a spiritual awakening, an inside-out social movement for change. In such a movement of passionate prayer before God, people will not be silenced until He hears and acts.

Finally, there is the intervention of God in behalf of people, who are acting together out of prayer, in faith and trust, with no other option but His intervention. They pray – and obey, and yet realize, that noble efforts alone will not result in social-cultural transformation. That requires the finger of God.

Perhaps, the reverse is true as well – God begins to intervene in people and their consciousness, simultaneously. One person boldly acts, one person breaks through in prayer by grace and is changed – then others are similarly moved to boldly pray, then to speak out and to act. More people are then aligned to act with God. A movement is born and sustained out of prayer. The lament psalms are a script, first for prayer, but also for the "subversive activity of finding voice."[7]

We will not be silent – in prayer, privately or publicly. We will not be silenced – our voice must be heard in heaven, at the throne: tyranny reigns here, someone must tell God, and invite His intervention. We will not be silenced before the intimidating culture – we are *"not ashamed of the gospel"* (Rom. 1:16). We will not be silent before the authorities – God is the Creator, the *"earth is the Lord's,"* it is twice His, by creation and redemption.

> We pray aloud, out loud, and yet alone with God, as a means of finding our voice. Private lament gives birth to public witness.

Walter Brueggemann says, first, you must voice the rage. That is, according to Brueggemann, a therapeutic standard. However, expressing mere rage, indeed, the unrestrained and repeated expression of anger only grows rage. We also know that denial of inner turmoil is not an option, nor is repression, or yet 'acting-out' in angry episodes. Second, Brueggemann says, you must submit it to God, prayerfully, authentically. Expression articulates it and prayer presents it to God as a complaint. Finally, you must relinquish it, saying to God, "I entrust my rage to you."[8] You lay your frustration and confusion on the altar. You dare not attempt to control only what God, the Sovereign, has the power to control. This is the point, in the lament psalms…you reach resolve – the case is now with the judge and He will decide and act, choosing if and who to prosecute. Vindication is His job; worship is yours – and a toxic state of internal anger makes you and I poor and hypocritical worshippers of a forgiving God. Here, imprecations (the plea for judgement) and lament (the tears that tell the story of pain) are joined.

Imprecatory prayers without tears reveal a hardness, a lack of balance.

On the other hand, lament, without the right to plea for justice and the intervention of God, even if that means judgement, absorbs too much pain. That pain is what Christ alone can carry, indeed, what he did carry to the cross.

Refusing Silence

Psalm 39 is where the church seems to be today in the United States. In this psalm, we find a righteous people tempted to succumb to silence as a means of coping with cultural wickedness. *"I will guard my ways…I will guard my mouth as with a muzzle while the wicked are in my presence"* (v. 1). It seems reasonable. In fact, it has become the new standard for American Christians: "Don't ask, don't tell."

In the psalm, the person of faith chooses silence, *"I was mute and silent."* Even identifying acts that might reveal faith were withheld, *"I refrained even from good"* (v. 2). Here is a stealth believer, hiding their light, not willing to be open about their faith for fear of conflict with the wicked. The tactic is flawed. Silence is not a solution. When true believers attempt to be silent, another problem emerges, notice, *"… my sorrow grew worse. My heart was hot within me"* (vv. 2b-3). The more he sought to avoid external conflict by the repression of faith, the greater the inner tension grew. He lost his joy. Within, *"the fire burned."* The inner fire of faith and love for God either burns openly or goes out – the latter being the worst of the options. His fire is still burning, but it lacks oxygen. He is smothering his own candle.

The choice is clear and compelling – be silenced by the wicked, conform to worldly culture and either hide or douse the flame of faith within. Or, honor that flame and confront wickedness. Allow your light to stand out against the darkness, your salt to burn out immorality. *"Then I spoke with my tongue,"* first prayerfully – that is always the initial act. *"Lord, make me to know my end…the extent of my days… how transient I am"* (v. 4). The prayer is for assistance to live in view of eternity, not this moment, not in fear of the consequences of being a person of bold faith discovered by wicked men.

The second prayer step is a view of God as Creator, as Sovereign, *"You have made my days…Surely every man at his best is a mere breath"* (v. 5). Before God, the wicked, all men, are *"mere breath,"* hot-air. *"Surely every man walks about as a phantom"* (v. 6). He is reassessing his fear of men in light of human frailty and eternity, in view of God's Sovereignty and man's mortality. The wicked, loud and clamorous, proud and

> In the end, we will remember not the words of our enemies, but the silence of our friends.[9]
> ~ Martin Luther King, Jr.

intimidating, *"...they make an uproar for nothing; he amasses riches and does not know who will gather them"* (v. 6). The righteous man, with faith-fire in his bones, eternity in view and a recognition of God's sovereignty, now downsizes the intimidating giant-like scale of the wicked which he had wrongly allowed to silence him. He is mortal, mere breath, a phantom, frail and flawed. Now, with a new perspective, he is ready to break his silence. *"Lord, for what do I wait? My hope is in You"* (v. 7). He asks for forgiveness for his transgression of silence (v. 8). He is moving toward witness, regaining his voice.

Suddenly, he encounters another problem, one not anticipated – it is the strange absence and silence of God. In his hushed-up state before the wicked, he did not notice that God had grown silent. When he kept silent, God kept silent. He had so focused on men hostile to faith that he no longer saw and felt God's presence. The fear of these men had grown greater than his own inner fear of God. By fearing such men more than God, he dismissed God from his life. Suddenly, he realized that his deference to the world was an offense to God. He had momentarily preferred the favor of men more than the favor of God, and the result, now clear, was costly – the silence of heaven.

God's silence is not related to the almost deafening sounds of an unbelieving world, but to our silence, in prayer, and as witnesses of Christ. We give up on prayer – and God becomes silent. We fail to lament, to offer a protest in the courtroom of heaven, asking for intervention here, so no intervention comes. We withdraw over cultural witness to Christ, and God no longer boldly acts in ways that silence unbelief. On our silence, first in prayer, is related to His silence.

The psalmist prayed again, *"Hear my prayer, O Lord, and give ear to my cry; do not be silent at my tears; for I am a stranger with You"* (v. 12). He had cozied to the world and had become *"a stranger"* to God. When he prayed, almost immediately, God was back, but there was another problem. He now found himself uncomfortable in God's presence. He felt the piercing stare of God. *"Turn Your gaze away from me, that I may smile again…"* (v. 13), he pleaded. The eyes of God were so woefully lethal that they drained his life. 'Stop staring at me,' he might have said, *"…before I depart and am no more."* God was not merely looking at him, but through him. There was divine disfavor.

Though God is full of grace, He cannot be so easily set aside and then expected to fall back in line on our command, doing as we anticipate. Not wanting to offend the world, the psalmist had offended God. He had taken God for granted. That is never permissible in a love relationship. He had presumed on God's mercy without sensitivity to the relationship.

E. M. Bounds notes, "Heaven is too busy to listen to half-hearted prayers or respond to pop-calls." Isaiah had declared (62:1), *"For Zion's sake I will not keep silent, and for Jerusalem's sake I will not keep quiet, until her righteousness goes forth like brightness, and her salvation like a torch that is burning."* Earlier, he confessed, *"I have kept silent for a long time, I have kept still and restrained myself. Now like a woman in labor I will groan, I will both gasp and pant"* (Isaiah 42:14).

> These are the signs and sounds of birthing - intercessory travail gives birth. Silence is not an option in prayer or witness.

These are the signs and sounds of birthing – intercessory travail gives birth. Silence is not an option in prayer or witness.

These are powerful principles in Psalm 39. Let's review them.

1. We dare not muzzle ourselves as a means of coping with the wicked or wickedness – <u>silence is not an option</u>.

2. We must not *"refrain even from good,"* hiding Christian behavior patterns, working to keep our association with Christ and faith hidden.

3. Such action will multiply sorrow. It will douse our joy. It will threaten the flame of faith (vv. 2b-3).

4. The choice is clear and compelling – be silenced by the wicked and conform to the worldly culture, hide or douse the flame of faith within; or, speak out. Live out the gospel, publicly. Not ostentatiously, not in a tasteless manner, not with brash speech, but deliberately and gently.

5. The first act, always the initial act, is prayer.

6. Our perspective must change, viewing the world, not in a temporal, but an eternal manner, *"Lord, make me to know my end...the extent of my days...how transient I am"* (v. 4). This is a plea for grace and insight to live in view of eternity.

7. The second prayer surrenders to God as Creator, *"You have made my days..."* He is the beginning and end of life. Our days belong to Him.

8. He then affirms the sovereignty of God. The wicked, he determines, are not independent rogue agents, acting apart from God, *"Surely every man at his best is a mere breath"* (v. 5). In light of who God is, he reassesses his view of the powerful wicked who had intimidated him. They are *"mere breath,"* hot-air, phantoms – *"Surely every man walks about as a phantom"* (v. 6).

9. Having downsized the intimidating giant-like scale of the wicked, he is ready to break his silence. *"Lord, for what do I wait? My hope is in You"* (v. 7). He asks for forgiveness for his transgression of silence (v. 8). He is moving toward witness.

10. Suddenly, he encounters the silence of God – a problem he had not anticipated. He had kept silent; and God had grown silent without his notice. He had assumed, that his silence, his lack of faithfulness, would not affect his standing with God. He was wrong. He had treated God presumptuously.

He prays again, *"Hear my prayer, O Lord, and give ear to my cry; do not be silent at my tears; for I am a stranger with You"* (v. 12).

11. When he prayed, almost immediately, God was back, but there was yet another problem. He was now uncomfortable with God. <u>It was now clear to him that he could not so easily move from a cozy-with-the-world posture, back to a cozy-with-God status without consequences</u>. *"Turn Your gaze away from me, that I may smile again..."* (v. 13), he pleaded. He felt that he might die. He had offended God. It was worse than the disapproval of the wicked that he had sought to avoid.

12. The psalm does not resolve itself well. Before, when he was silent, it was due to the pressure, the fear of the wicked. His great concern was to avoid personal suffering due to their discovery of his faith and values. So, he was superficially identified with them, and without realizing it, he had profoundly differentiated himself from God. Now, he felt that God was a "stranger," foreign and distant. *"Do not be silent at my tears"* (39:12). A great shift has taken place. His tears are no longer about the rejection of this world. They are about the distance he feels from God. That's progress. His values have changed. He is weeping not over temporal pain from the world's rejection, but from the wound he has given to God by his betrayal. His joy, his smile, will return, when the relationship is fully healed. And that means – he must be public about his faith. Not hiding. Not silent. <u>He has accepted his role as a sojourner, a pilgrim, an alien of this present world</u> (v. 12).

Discussion Guide

1. We are not victims and yet we lament. How is that possible?

2. Discuss the terms that describe our standing before God – saints, heirs, chosen, regal, overcomers – how do they relate to lament?

3. Isn't it interesting that we are presented with Jesus Barabbas and Jesus of Nazareth? Who is the world choosing today?

4. How can we be empowered lamenters? What does that mean? How is strength found in weakness?

5. Review the idea of silence, especially Brueggemann's ideas? Do you understand? Do you agree?

6. Work through the ideas in Psalm 39. Is God silent because we are too often silent before the world?

7. Review the principles in Psalm 39 at the end of the chapter. Which three stand out most to you?

13

Grounding Lament in God's Sovereignty

U nder King Jehoiakim, the son of the righteous Josiah, the nation of Judah had hurried into backsliding. The impact of the revival led by Josiah quickly disappeared. Injustice became the norm. Morality as a public standard disappeared. The people reverted to idolatry, quickly, precipitously. Jehoiakim, to pay tribute due to the Egyptians and avert war, taxed the poor into oppression (2 Kings 23:33-36). Jeremiah, a contemporary of Habakkuk, spoke out against the king's use of forced labor in building himself a new palace (Jeremiah 22:13-14) while the nation itself was in peril.

The king was blind. He could not see Babylon as an international threat to Judah. Nor could he see how quickly national morale had sagged on his watch. He was blinded by the power and privilege of being king, busy building his own palace. He paid tribute from the temple treasury, surrendered temple artifacts, and handed over members of his own family and nobility as hostages to Babylon. But he did not pray; he did not call upon Yahweh. Then, almost overnight, he switched sides, aligning with Egypt for security. Rabbinical sources describe him as godless, guilty of incest and murder. Under his royal robes, his tattooed body testified of his paganism.

During Babylonia's second siege of Jerusalem, Jehoiakim died. According to Jeremiah, the king was not even given a decent burial, his body was merely tossed over the wall of the city. He was respected by few (Jeremiah 22:18–19; Jeremiah 36:30). Josephus confirmed the death of the king at the order of Nebuchadnezzar. Judah's world was crumbling.

As the culture deteriorated, Habakkuk lamented,

> *"How long, Lord, must I call for help and You do not listen or cry out to You about violence and You do not save?"* (HCSB). *"Must I forever see these evil deeds? Why must I watch all this misery? Wherever I look, I see destruction and violence. I am surrounded by people who love to argue and fight"* (v. 2, NLT).

Judah, like the United States at this writing, was falling apart. The Holman Christian Standard Bible is more forceful, *"Why [God] do You tolerate wrongdoing?"* The International Standard Version: *"Social havoc and oppression are all around me; there are legal conflicts, and disputes abound."* The judiciary was no help, *"the law is paralyzed, and justice never prevails. The wicked hem in the righteous, so that justice is perverted"* (v. 4 NIV). The NLT says, *"there is no justice in the courts. The wicked far outnumber the righteous"* and the effect is that *"justice has become perverted,"* it *"never goes forth. For the wicked surround the righteous"* intimidating them (ESV). In such an environment, *"the law is slacked,"* and that results in *"wrong judgement."* (KJV). The *"wicked restrict the righteous"* (HCSB), and *"the law is torn to pieces"* (Douay-Rheims Bible), *"powerless"* (Darby Bible Translation).

This sounds so like our times.

> All that is necessary for the triumph of evil is for good men to do nothing.
> ~ Edmund Burke

It was also a time of international moral decay, of spiritual apostasy, of commercial greed and failing international businesses whose economies threatened the multi-national economic stability of the Middle East. As today, with corporations whose wealth exceeds that of nations, their business tycoons were protecting their assets in the face of the collapse of the nation itself. Habakkuk cites examples of these enterprising rich, who were busy solidifying personal power, seeking a kind of personal invincibility (2:5, 8-9). Their cities were bloody and lawless (2:12) – and that was accepted as normal; at least, no one had a satisfying solution. Behind the scenes, the treatment of one neighbor to another was manipulative and scandalous – a culture of alcoholism and sexual exploitation and abuse emerged (2:15, 17). The ultimate snapshot of national chaos was the wholesale abandonment of Yahweh in favor of idolatry. The children of Abraham had chosen to fashion their own gods (2:18-19). The children of the generation that experienced revival under Josiah had now switched gods. In one generation, the nation took a radical turn to godlessness. Imagine the shock of godly prophets – this is the dilemma of Jeremiah, the 'weeping' prophet and of Habakkuk's lament.

We could be reading the news or watching television – the parallels are stunning.

Habakkuk's Lament – A Shift

Standing behind the book of Romans, and Paul's theology of "the just living by faith," and not by sight, not by demanding proofs, is the book and prophet Habakkuk (2:4; Romans 1:17). In an era in which national sins were destroying the social fabric of Judah, Babylon had been tasked by God to destroy the city of Jerusalem and the nation, to scatter the people, to lead away exiles, and destroy the beautiful temple of Solomon. They would snuff out the light

217

LAMENT: WHEN PRAYER BECOMES TEARS

of Israel's international witness. Sadly, it had already been virtually extinguished due to their own sin (1:6). It was, as far as Habakkuk could see, the end of it all. A terrible ending for the nation and for Jerusalem.

It was a time to lament – and that is what Habakkuk did. Paul, reaching back to the ancient prophet, writes the book of Romans, around 56 A.D. Jerusalem is only a decade away from being destroyed again and of having the Second Temple dismantled, and seeing the nation re-scattered, this time, by Rome. The whole world, Paul declares, is facing the wrath of God (Rom. 1:18). Creation and the Spirit are already groaning, lamenting (8:22, 26) over what is coming. We, Paul argues, should join them in tearful prayer – in lament. We should do this as a priestly-prophetic-intercessory community representing Jesus in the earth. That was true then, and it is true now. Where is the sound of lament that discerns the times?

One generation after Jesus, after the resurrection, after Pentecost, after the whole city had seemed to embrace faith in Christ, the religious machine that had called for the crucifixion of Christ, had managed to survive. It had increasingly hardened itself against Christ and his church. It had decidedly rejected faith in Jesus as Messiah. To turn the tide against defections to faith, it had martyred James, the brother of Jesus and Bishop of the Jerusalem church. The apostles were gone from the city, and Paul's appearance, a few years before the martyrdom of James, created a riot. Forty years after

> Those who would give up essential liberty to purchase a little temporary safety deserve neither liberty nor safety.
> ~ Benjamin Franklin

Jesus had predicted it (Luke 21:5-38), the temple and the city were sadly destroyed. For 40 years, the city and its religious ceremonies lived on, as if Christ had never come. He was dead; they were alive. His followers were few and dying at the hands of Rome, and they were an established protected, global faith enterprise. This Rome came with force and leveled both the temple and the city as Jesus had predicted.

The church continued – it flourished, but in new centers, reaching both Jews and Gentiles. And so, the faith would survive after Babylon's invasion, as it did, after Rome's destruction of Jerusalem. In both cases, it would be a hardy faith that survived.

This is the theme of Romans – that *"tribulation, or distress, or persecution, or famine, or nakedness, or peril, or sword"* cannot separate us from God's love, that, *"We are more than conquerors through Him who loved us"* – *"neither death nor life, nor angels nor principalities nor powers, nor things present nor things to come, nor height nor depth, nor any other created thing, shall be able to separate us from..."* God, in Christ Jesus our Lord. This is a vibrant faith. It is a praying faith. *"Groans in the Spirit"* should be common. This includes the groans of the Spirit, Creation's groans, and our own – thus lament, in the midst of triumph, the cross and the resurrection conjoined forever. It is not a faith trapped in this world – it can see the consummation of all things. It is not a faith given to flippant challenges of God, taunting Him to act. Lament is now on a wholly different plain. Gone are the superficial, self-interested laments that characterized many of the psalms.

Protesting God's Silence

In Habakkuk, lament begins as a protest against God's silence in the face of national collapse, Babylonian aggression, and royal treachery. The prophet is conflicted – sin is raging. It is destroying the society. God decides to act, but Habakkuk objects to the instrument God chooses to use – the pagan nation of Babylon. While Judah's condition is despicable, God's use of Babylon to judge Judah is unthinkable to the prophet (1:12-13, 5-6). Babylon is the ultimate icon for sin and idolatry! How can God choose Babylon? *"You, O LORD, have appointed them to judge; And You, O Rock, have established them to correct"* (1:12) – it's a question God must answer! It's inconceivable that a more wicked nation than Judah, known for its idolatry, should be the instrument of righteous judgement.

In Habakkuk's world, the neat categories are gone (Psalm 1). As an idealist, he longed for the simple formula – righteousness = blessing; and wickedness = judgement/correction. However, things were complicated. The little nation of Judah was entangled in a complex international crisis. Nations were raging (Psalm 2). Indeed, the kings son, Josiah's son, Jehoiakim, had gone to war against the faith of his father's house in favor of idolatry (Psalm 3).[1] The removal of the moral lines: the good-get-blessed and the bad-get-what's-coming to them mystified Habakkuk, leaving him confused. God's use of Babylon as an instrument, one of the ungodly raging nations, broke apart his simple world view (Psalm 1-2 paradigm). He complained, *"Your eyes are too pure to approve evil, And You cannot look on wickedness with favor"* (v. 13). The proposition was inconceivable.

As in every lament – the prophet demanded an answer from God. He called God into account. He questioned and quarreled with Him. Here is a short list of his complaints. It isn't difficult to hear the echo of our own sentiments in the prophet's questions.

Habakkuk: *Why do You look with favor on those who deal treacherously?*

Paraphrase: How could you choose, favor, allow a nation more wicked, more treacherous than Judah, a nation like Babylon to triumph over us? How could you use them as an instrument of correction? It is not right. It doesn't make sense. It seems inconsistent with your own nature.

Habakkuk: *Why are You silent when the wicked swallow up those more righteous than they?*

Paraphrase: Why are you silent? Why don't you speak? Why don't you object to Babylon – they are going to swallow up Judah. We have sinned, but we are not the sinners they are. God, we're talking Babel here – Babylon, the ultimate symbol of evil. How? Why?

Habakkuk: *Why have You made men like the fish of the sea, like creeping things without a ruler over them?*

Paraphrase: The NLT says, *"Are we only fish to be caught and killed? Are we only sea creatures that have no leader?"* But that translation misses the point. It is not the assertion that the prophet is making. His charge is the most toxic component of a lament – God is the Sovereign, the Creator, and it is his fault that things are the way they are. Yahweh is "the author of all this inhuman violence." It is the same charge made by Job (9:24), *"...if not He, who then is it?"* God did this!

The second charge implied here is that the distinction between "creeping things," the lowest creatures and humanity, is now erased. The prophet is not merely pointing out the 'low-down' nature of humanity, that they are a nation of snakes, as Jesus called the self-righteous Pharisees. In fact, even without a king, the 'creeping creatures' may survive better than Judah. Or, the text may mean, "When this is all over, we will be no better than a mere swarming disorder, reduced to such by our conquerors." So – God, why did you not take better care of us? Give us a better ruler? Make us men and not minnows? It's your fault (Proverbs 6:7; 30:27).[2]

In the chaos caused by sin, it becomes difficult to see the distinction between men and animals. Left to ourselves, without godly leaders, we sink to act out of base instincts. The vacuum created by Adam's fall from godly dominion is like a black-hole that now threatens all of creation.

Why? Why? Why? – so much confusion is found when exasperation pushes us to lament. It is important to notice where lament stands here – it stands in front of, just before wrath. In fact, lament always stands with, in front of, and around judgement. Christians, led by the Spirit, should be on-the-alert, when the person, place or thing, assigned to their intercessory watch-duty is in danger. In such times, we must double down on the watch. As Paul warned us, "... *the wrath of God is revealed from heaven against all ungodliness and unrighteousness of men, who suppress the truth in unrighteousness..."* (Romans 1:18). We are living on a ticking time bomb. The globe is under judgement.

Shifting the Prophetic Intercessory Paradigm

There are five 'woe' oracles in the book of Habakkuk, all about to be announced. Judgement is looming and rightly so, due to the nation's sin. Prophetic lament stands, appropriately, in that intersection, then and now, between judgement and the people. The prophet seeks clarity from God – he is a 'seer' and hearer of God. This is a primary function of a prophet. First, to plead for mercy – to lament (in a priestly posture). Second, in the tradition of the Old Testament, the prophet may confront God and accuse Him of being culpable for some part of the dilemma, as Habakkuk does. We do this – we innocently cannot see the whole picture from the earth's perspective. We offer pieces of insight that imply God's culpability – and He gives us a more complete perspective. Then, lament wants an answer to the "How long?" and "Why" questions. It needs to deliver a reasonable explanation of God's impending action to the people (prophetic posture).

This is the reason the ignored book of Habakkuk is so important. It plays such a significant role as a root system for the book of Romans. In Habakkuk, we see a shift; a shift in theology and prayer that Paul made prominent in Romans. The prophet begins with the typical, *"How long!"* And with that, he complains that 'God does not listen, He doesn't pay attention to prayer!' (1:2). He also has his list of "why?" questions (vv. 3, 13-14).

Paul, from the New Testament perspective, understands that assigning the blame to God, after the cross and its ultimate display of God's mercy and vulnerability, is not acceptable. This

> Never doubt that a small group of thoughtful, committed, citizens can change the world. Indeed, it is the only thing that ever has.
> ~ Margaret Mead

is the essence of Paul's view of faith. It is not merely about the ability of God, but about His character. After the incarnation, God's coming to earth and humanity's complicity in the crucifixion of God, after the resurrection and God's grace – how can we any longer accuse God? This is Paul's point, his great crescendo:

> *What then shall we say to these things? If God is for us, who can be against us? He who did not spare His own Son, but delivered Him up for us all, how shall He not with Him also freely give us all things? Who shall bring a charge against God's elect? It is God who justifies. Who is he who condemns? It is Christ who died, and furthermore is also risen, who is even at the right hand of God, who also makes intercession for us. Who shall separate us from the love of Christ?* (Romans 8:31-35).

Paul declares – God is for us; He has forgiven and justified us; and He loves us! These are the principles that Habakkuk only begins to sense – God is not the problem. He is not the one to be put on trial. He does not yet see what Paul saw, but he is beginning to understand the futility of charging God lightly.

In the short book, God quickly answers Habakkuk, both speaking to him and acting. Less than halfway through, and certainly, by its end, the prophet's position completely reverses itself. He will no longer demand an answer from God. He will no longer demand proof of God's intervention. He *"will live by faith"* (2:4). All the things that triggered past laments – a failed harvest, empty barns, dying cattle, personal loss – are now set aside. Unlike previous prophets who, when such famine came or personal reversals were encountered, demanded action by God to care for his end of the covenant – that changes in Habakkuk (3:17-18).

This is the background of Romans 8, Paul's 'why?' – *"What shall we say to these things?"* (Romans 8:31). Even now, *"we do not know what we ought to pray for,"* arguably, how to pray, *"but the Spirit himself intercedes for us through wordless groans...he...knows!"* There is more, *"And we know,"* Paul declared, that *"God foreknew"* and *"predestined...those he called..."* Here is certainty – the new ground on which intercessory lament is to stand. We join our "groans" to those of Creation and the Spirit (8:22, 23, 26). We 'don't know, but he knows, and we do know.' This is not a left-brain knowing, it is a knowing in and by the Spirit. It is knowing without knowing. 'We don't know, but He knows, therefore we know!' It is the call to a new level of faith – in God, through a new level of dependence on God in the Spirit. *"We do not know...the mind of the Spirit..."* but, we can pray effectively, nevertheless, *"because the Spirit intercedes for God's people in accordance with the will of God"* (8:26-27).

Lament shifts from demanding answers to 'why?' questions, to grounded faith to God's sovereignty, to His omniscience, to His action in history, in Christ. *"He justified...glorified..."* Indeed, *"God is for us...* "He loves us. To the kind of things that created the 'whys?' of lament in the Old Testament, Paul declared a giant, *"No!"* – death and life, angels and demons, the present and the future, powers high or deep – nothing should be allowed to contest God's love. *"I am convinced..."* He places his faith, not in God's response to some narrow, albeit painful crisis, but in the larger sweep of God's action in history, His character, in the example of the cross – the love of God in Christ (Romans 8:28-39). And of course, on the resurrection. Paul *"will live by faith,"* not sight.

In Habakkuk, we find these roots of prayer's larger role. Lament, petition and intercession, will now, going forward, have a grander function. The prophet stands as a priestly advocate for the nation in the face of God's wrath, and simultaneously, he weeps over a nation's baptism in immorality and idolatry. This is the precarious place of the believer in intercession – between Jesus, heaven's intercessor and the people; between the way things are and the way they should be; between – judgement for sin and the hopeful salvation of the nation; between – an unrighteous nation and an even more unrighteous instrument of judgement, Babylon.

Habakkuk's Dilemma

It is easy to identify with Habakkuk and his initial logic. So much of our current Christian petition and intercession is rested here, in his rationale, in his unchallenged prayer theology. The book begins where we begin, with the classic lament inquiry, *"How long shall I cry?"* (1:2) He immediately charges God with inactivity, *"I cry, and you will not hear!"* I *"even cry out to You, 'Violence!' and You will not save"* (v. 2b). He accuses God of exposing him, as a prophet, to iniquity and trouble, opening his eyes to see it, and pray about it, all to no end. This is fascinating. In a sense, Habakkuk seems to wish that God had left him alone, in ignorance and bliss. Instead, God awakened awareness in him. His concern for the nation and its impending doom led him to discover a level of sin he had not imagined; to which he had not been previously exposed. He is no longer wonderfully naïve. He has become informed in order to intercede more effectively. His heart is torn, disturbed by such explicit images of a sinful nation. He has cried out about the violence and iniquity, but he does not feel that his prayers have been heard, and he knows they have not been answered – this is so typical of our intercession today.

We have prayed, virtually from coast to coast. Prayer drives have taken place along the eastern and southern borders, and marches up the west coast have occurred, following the old mission trail. There have been prayer fly-overs of every state capitol. Shofars have sounded on the steps of every state capitol, and in the halls of congress. Identificational repentance has addressed major national sins – abortion, euthanasia, national pride, divorce, sexual perversion, oppression, slavery and Indian treaty violations. Solemn Assemblies have taken place. All of this, but no national revival has come forth. We, like Habakkuk, are experiencing the silence of heaven.

Habakkuk despairs, as we do, over a government that no longer efficiently functions, *"The law is powerless, justice never goes forth"* (v. 4). The immorality of the culture now sits on the bench of the judiciary – and the society is coming unglued.

God challenges him, as He does us, to broaden his vision, to *"look among the nations and watch – be utterly astonished, for I will work a work in your days, which you would not believe though it were told you"* (v. 5). Suddenly, God shows Himself active, but not in and through Judah, rather, in the instrumentation of Babylon. That is, God is active in the most unlikely place, the seat of godlessness. *"I am raising up the Chaldeans, a bitter and hasty nation which marches through the breadth of the earth"* (v. 6). Yahweh is not a local god, not a god among the gods. He is not the God of America or the European white man. He is not the God of the governments of one people over others. He is the Sovereign, God over all nations, even if they do not acknowledge Him, including Babylon – and China and Russia, India and Pakistan, North Korea and Cuba, Saudi Arabia and Israel, and also of America. He is, of course, Israel's God, and the God of any and every nation that acknowledges Him, but He is also God – to all, over all. And His purposes are larger than any nation.

Still, the notion that Babylon could be an instrument of righteousness was untenable, unthinkable for Habakkuk. *"Are you not from everlasting…my Holy One?"* And *"You have appointed them for judgement…for correction?"* (v. 12). Babylon? An instrument of the Holy One? *"Your eyes are too pure to behold evil…and cannot look on wickedness,"* so *"why do You look on those who deal treacherously?"* (v. 13). Judah was indeed wicked, sinful, deserving of judgement, but Babylon was even more decadent and ungodly (v. 13). Habakkuk demanded an answer: *"I will stand on my watch…to see what He will say to me"* (2:1). Immediately, the Lord answered, instructing him to *"write the vision, make it plain, that he may run who reads it. The vision is for an appointed time; at the end it will speak, and it will not lie"* (vv. 2-3).

It is, perhaps unthinkable to us, that Russia or China, with their communist history – or nations steeped in Islamic or Hindu traditions, might be used to discipline so-called "Christian" America. This was Habakkuk's thesis. Babylon as God's instrument? Babylon invading and dominating Judah? Impossible. Heresy!

God in Action – Against Pride

Then, God urged him, *"Behold, the proud!"* He turns his attention not to Babylon or even to Judah, per se, but to the condition of arrogant hearts and self-sufficient people all around him. The problem, the narrative suggests, is not nations – Judah or Babylon, it is pride – in the hearts of singular men. Pride, infecting relationships, threatening families, driving poisonous business dealings. The soul of the proud is the root of the evil against which all of the woe oracles are directed. In contrast, *"…the just shall live by his faith."* The just must learn God-dependence, not self-sufficiency, especially in such uncertain times. Faith, not sight, must sustain us. Faith in God, not in governments must emerge. Faith in the character of God must grow – He will do the right thing, even if we do not understand His actions or inaction. The just are not proud; they are humble. The proud resist God; the humble run to Him. When they do, He draws near to them.

At times, the Bible pictures God as 'arising.' Habakkuk sees the coming intervention of God in His action: *"Now I will arise,"* (Isa. 33:10-13; also, Psalm 12:5). *"I will lift up my hand to the nations and raise my signal to the peoples"* (Isa. 49:22). In Isa. 59:15b, it is said, *"his own arm brought him victory."* Habakkuk 3:3-15, finds God on the march, coming *"from Teman…He stood and measured the earth… You did bestride the earth in fury…You went forth for the salvation of your people."*

We may lament, protest, charge God with inaction, question and express our confusion, demanding an answer from heaven. But God answers, we discover in Habakkuk, on the basis of divine prerogative.

There is a tension here, a contradiction. God acts in the midst, in behalf of a praying people. This is, of course, true – but it is not the whole truth. *"If my people, called by my name, will…"* How often do we quote the familiar passage from 2 Chronicles 7:14, that admonishes our repentance, humility, and our prayerful dependence and desire to see His face. *"Then…"* the scripture thunders, heaven will hear and we will hear from heaven, forgiveness will come, with healing for the land. It is true; it is not the whole truth.

Habakkuk reminds us, that it is God who chooses when, and if He will answer, and in what manner. He chooses His answer as well, both the content and the form. Prayer is not sovereign, God is sovereign. In one sense, we must repeatedly insist, God does not answer prayers – He answers people. He hears – He always hears. He knows – He is not uninformed. He invites our petitions and pleas, but He is not bound to them, as some cosmic vending machine, or even as 'our' God. He answers freely, not always providing the answer we prefer.[3] Prayer, no matter how passionate, must respect His deity. And yet, this is no call to passiveness. This is not an exercise for silence.

Woe Oracles

As a prelude to God's action, he discloses the 'why' behind his judgements. These insights come as five woe oracles. In a sense, they are all directed to the proud man:

1. The first woe is toward the unbridled international expansion of business enterprise (2:6-8) – increase and expansion with prolific debt. This proud traveler cannot be satisfied (v. 5). His practices are unethical, exploitive – "he plunders nations," skimming profits. He is guilty of bloodshed and violence, directly or indirectly (v. 8), all neatly covered. He is endangering the economic stability of his own nation, Judah, as well as other nations – out of his own pride and greed.

2. The second woe is the man who covets gain, and does so without conscience, without moral values – his gain is by evil means (v. 9). He is unprincipled. He justifies his actions as for the benefit of his house. His goal is to make himself and his personal dynasty invincible, beyond the power of disaster. In truth, he is setting a corrupt example, offering

by his actions, "shameful counsel" to his children (v. 10). He is mentoring the next generation in valueless insensitivity and selfishness – 'woe' to him. The inanimate stones and timbers in his house are watching, listening, remembering – and they will testify against him (v. 11). All of this is not occurring in a human courtroom, but before the Throne of God, where the proud man faces eternity unprepared.

3. The third woe is the man who is building a town, but on the back of violence and bloodshed (v. 12). He has come to rule the town with a disregard for law – he considers himself the law. He has reversed Lex Rex (the law is king), to Rex Lex (the king makes up his own law). This is always, in the end, despotism. It always leads to anarchy.

   Verse 13 is difficult to understand. The NLT offers the clearest idea: Has not the Lord of Heaven's Armies promised that the wealth of nations will turn to ashes? They work so hard, but all in vain! The ESV says, *"that peoples labor merely for fire, and nations weary themselves for nothing?"* The NASB, *"that peoples toil for fire,"* and the KJB, *"that the people shall labor in the very fire, and the people shall weary themselves for very vanity."* The HCSB, offers another slightly different idea, *"the peoples labor only to fuel the fire and countries exhaust themselves for nothing?"* The ISV, *"people grow tired putting out fires."* The NET says simply, the Lord has decreed that *"the nations' efforts will go up in smoke; their exhausting work will be for nothing."*

   A tiresome and non-productive cycle has been created. A culture of aggressive labor feeds of insatiable fire' to which there is no end and there will be no reward. A society established on materialism with a culture of iniquity and violence can never endure. The Lord of Heaven's Armies will fight against such a nation and its cities. The tiresome efforts to make the city, Jerusalem, a hub of international business and wealth will end in ashes. The problem is not in the goal alone. Rather, the goal became the god. And in pursuing the goal, they compromised all godly values.

A life whose only focus is the accumulation of riches is a dead-end street. It means nothing in view of eternity. God measures true value on a different scale.

4. <u>The fourth woe is against the man who drives his neighbor to drink in order that he might exploit him</u> (2:15). This is the shame of drunkenness and the unseemliness that accompanies it. These values rise out of and dance with the acquisition of power and health. This is the underbelly of unbridled lust and fleshly behavior. It is the nightlife of the city, up close, and ugly. It is the corollary to addiction – to both power and pleasure. The problem is not alcohol or drugs, it is the shortcut, they seem to offer to pleasure. Notice – the position and the accomplishments were not enough to satisfy the inner man. There is still a hole in the heart of this man. But he now has power and position, enough wealth to seize and possess pleasure. It is an illusion – a trap, there is no true pleasure apart from discipline and self-government. We are forever at the tree of good and evil, tasting stolen fruit, looking for the magic that makes us 'gods.' Satan's exploitation of man (Adam and Eve), has now become our temptation for behavior. What gets us a quick fix? The consequences to the 'other' are not considered. Love of self has displaced love of neighbor. "Woe," God says to such a culture – and to such a person.

5. <u>The fifth woe is against idolatry</u>. Here, a man fashions an image of wood or stone, and prays to it, attempting to 'awaken' it, to move it to 'arise and talk to him, teaching' (2:18-19). He overlays it with gold or silver, investing in it, but *"in it there is no breath at all"* (v. 19). This is a pitiful picture of a society that creates its own gods. Their idols are dazzling and sparkling works of shimmering art. But, they are dead, lifeless and silent. Here, man talks to transformed trees and rocks, overlaid with gold, recrafted into some shape or image – and he expects the tree and the rock to speak back to him. He is delusional. His idol is only a symbol of his own ideas about deity. He has rejected God's self-disclosure. He has closed the book of the law and revelation. He is, in fact,

intoxicated on himself. Idolatry is only the projection of self onto an object. It imagines God and re-images him, shaping, fashioning, forming him, but in actuality the idolater is only projecting his own imagination. He is only hearing his own echo. His god is no god at all. It is simply a symbol of his own pride.

Watch the progression. First, there is self-centered greed and a lust for power and money. Second, the conscience is muted. Ethics and morals are cast aside. Third, violence and bloodshed are employed to consolidate power over a city. They create a sense of invincibility. Fourth, drugs are introduced. Debilitating habits and addictive substances create a vulnerable sub-population, at the mercy of the power broker. Fifth, the end is idolatry. This is the man-made construct of values that drive the new culture. It is also the gateway through which demonic disorder comes.

Here is unbridled and insatiable empire building. It is the international good-life of the global traveler. It is a life that increasingly casts away moral restraint. All in an attempt to empower a personal catastrophe-free existence, a "nest on high." And that in or near a city without God, where bloodshed and violence are common, The chaos is exploited for a profit. A frenzied work ethic keeps a population enslaved for nothing, except shameful living and neighbor exploitation – all ending in idolatry. Pride, greed, violence, bloodshed, lust – all roads lead to deeper idolatry; and yet, all are at the same time manifestations of idolatry. They are the consequences of a nation that forgot God.

The Resolve of Habakkuk

Finally, Habakkuk prays, *"O Lord, I have heard Your speech, and was afraid…revive your work in the midst of the years…and in wrath, remember mercy"* (3:2). God answered him with the coming woes of anticipated judgement. God revealed to him reasons – the obvious and unseen sin of the powerful and wealthy, driven by pride. The answer overwhelmed Habakkuk. What follows is breathtaking. He had complained about God's silence and inaction – now, in the remainder of the book, he sees God acting – *"God came... "* (3:3), *"He stood and measured the earth"* (v. 6), and *"He looked and startled the nations"* (v. 6). He is no longer hidden. Just his gaze is paralyzing.

In verses 6-15, there is devastation everywhere following the movement of God – on mountains and hills (v. 6), in the tents of Cush and the curtains of Midian (v. 7), with the rivers and the sea and the earth itself (vv. 8-9). Mountains tremble (v. 10), floods follow, the deep utters its voice, the sun and moon stand still (vv. 10-11). Why such cosmic disorder? God marched through the land – mad! He trampled the nations, and did so, for the salvation of His people (vv. 12-13). He decapitated the head from the house of the wicked (v. 13). Was this what Habakkuk had longed for? Is it what we long for when we call God to action? When we pray, *"How long?"*

The news of such judgement, such raw energy, such cosmic devastation is not what Habakkuk had longed to see at all. *"When I heard, my body trembled; My lips quivered at the voice; Rottenness entered my bones; and I trembled in myself... "* (v. 16). He cannot sleep after hearing such news. This is exactly how it should be with all of us – we may pray for God's judgement, but, when it comes, we will no doubt lack the capacity to welcome it, celebrate it, or be glad when we see it unwrap. To enjoy judgement is to testify against godly hearts.

Remember the principle, *"For it is time for judgement to begin, starting with the house of God. And if it starts with us, what will be the fate of those who are disobedient to the gospel of God?"* (1 Peter 4:17 NET). God will deal with the nations, yes, but Judah, for a season, will be in exile. The city of Jerusalem will be destroyed. The temple will be no more. The light of their witness will be darkened. To his people, God makes a promise: *"He will invade them"* as well, not just the enemy. And to the prophet Habakkuk, engaged in prophetic intercession, he promises, He will make the prophet's feet "like those of the deer" for stability, so that he can walk on high hills.

The Final Declarations

The high point of the book of Habakkuk comes in the declaration at the end of the 'woe' oracles. Immediately following the woe pronounced against idolatry, we have this declaration, *"The Lord is in His holy temple, let all the earth keep silent before Him"* (2:20). Idolatry, as prolific as it had become, could not displace Yahweh. Nor would the coming destruction of Solomon's temple leave Him homeless. God remains unmoved – in His holy temple, not on earth, but in heaven. When idolatry rages. When proud and powerful men exploit nations. When violence seems to triumph. When addictions fuel passions. When the rich seem invincible. When the simple becomes complex, the local is subsumed by the international, covetousness reigns without conscience, communities are built on the back of bloodshed, and idolatry displaces a true and holy faith in Yahweh – the message of Habakkuk calls us to be silent! Strangely silent! The railing against God, so characteristic of the Old Testament lament, must now give way to our gathering, in silence, before God! Pray! Stand in God's courtroom. Our collective presence in God's courtroom, in the face of the increasing disorder is a plea for God to act. It is a settled confidence in God's judgement.

His purposes have not changed with Judah's apostasy and Babylon's coming seeming triumph. *"For the earth will be filled with the knowledge of the glory of the Lord, as the waters cover the sea"* (Hab. 3:14). One day, it will happen. There will be no place on the face of the earth that has not heard the story, that does not know God's love in Christ, that has not seen some measure of His glory. His purposes engage us, but they stand apart from us! He is committed to invade the earth with the knowledge of His glory. Wanna' come along? Judgement is only an instrument of righteousness – the goal is the knowledge of the glory of God.

Meanwhile, while this all plays out, as Judah packs its bags to be carried away, *"the just shall live by faith"* (2:4). This is, of course, Paul's taproot for the book of Romans (1:17). And when the Romans destroy Jerusalem and its second temple, the 'whys' of Old Testament lament are not the primers for the answers we need. We have learned, *"the just shall live by faith."*

In the end, the prophet has learned that it is not wise to attempt to press God into action, to demand answers of Him. It is better to simply trust Him, to *"live by faith,"* and not sight or sound.

> *Even though the fig trees have no blossoms, and there are no grapes on the vines; even though the olive crop fails, and the fields lie empty and barren; even though the flocks die in the fields, and the cattle barns are empty, yet I will rejoice in the LORD! I will be joyful in the God of my salvation! The Sovereign LORD is my strength!* (3:17-19).

He will no longer demand proof of God! He does not have to see the harvest to believe. His barns do not have to be full for him to trust. His flocks may die, and his stalls be empty – but outer circumstances will no longer affect his joy. He has shifted his faith from answers, to the One who answers: the "Sovereign Lord" will be his strength. The answer is not a solution to a problem. The answer, the solution, is a person – God Himself.

This is quite a seismic shift.

Habakkuk is centuries ahead of his time, a pioneer among the prophets. He grasps what Paul will later more fully articulate. He moves from lament to joy; from petition, questioning, as Westermann describes it, to praise. He is already on the New Testament side of the change in lament. So many today are still on the back side of the mountain. Their laments are over personal losses. They are consumed with "why" and "how long" questions – focused on their narrow slice of pain. They are still at Sinai, at a mountain that can be touched, burning with fire, full of both promise and peril tied to behavior; and not at Mt. Zion, *"the city of the living God, the heavenly Jerusalem"* with *"thousands upon thousands of angels in joyful assembly,"* a part of *"the church of the firstborn, whose names are written in heaven."* Here is *"Jesus the mediator of a new covenant…"* (Hebrews 12:18-24). Sinai is the orientation of the law; Zion, of grace and glory. Sinai is earthly; Zion is heavenly. Sinai is centered in the covenant given by Moses; Zion, in the covenant given by Christ. Sinai engenders fear; Zion faith. At Sinai, one dances with death; at Mt. Zion, the firstborn (life) are *"registered in heaven"* and *"the spirits of just men are made perfect."*

Lament! But do so, from Mt. Zion, out of heaven, as it were, not from Mt. Sinai, and surprisingly, not from Mt. Calvary. Join the 'lion,' around the throne in lament. Weep; be tender. Rejoice; be tough. Doubt. Wonder, "see through a glass darkly," be authentic; be confident – the lamb is roaring. Join lament to the empty tomb. We may not know, but He knows. All is well. God is on His throne. Christ reigns, through yet for a season, in exile. We weep now, with those that weep, but soon, our tears will be wiped away.

Discussion Guide

1. Jehoiakim was the son of Josiah, his antithesis. How could such a reversal come in one generation?

2. Jeremiah is the prophet that is so dominant in this era. What is he known for? In a sense, he embodies lament for the nation and what it is about to experience. Discuss that idea.

3. Habakkuk is also a prophet in this era. In the beginning, he is frustrated with God for not interfering. How does that change?

4. How is the book of Romans connected to Habakkuk?

5. How do you handle God's silence?

6. Review the 'woe' oracles. Can you see their connection? An escalation of compounding wickedness?

7. How is the book of Habakkuk resolved? How do we resolve lament?

APPENDIX

APPENDIX 1

Examples of Lament in Scripture

Gunkel: Individual Laments

Psalms 3; 5; 6; 7; 13; 17; 22; 25; 26; 27:7-14; 28; 31; 35; 38; 39; 42-43; 54-57; 59; 61; 63; 64; 69; 70; 71; 86; 88; 120; 130; 140; 141; 142; 143.

Gunkel: Communal/Corporate Laments

Psalms 44; 58; 60; 74; 79; 80; 83; 106; 125.

Paul Wayne Ferris: Communal Laments

Psalms 31, 35, 42-44, 56, 59, 60, 69, 74, 77, 79-80, 83, 85, 89, 94, 102, 109, 137, 142.

Bernhard W. Anderson: Communal Laments

Psalms 12, 14, 58, 60, 74, 79-80, 83, 85, 90, 94, 123, 126, 129.

The "Why?" Psalms

Psalms 5, 7, 17, and 26.

Additional Laments

- Confessional: Psalms 51; 130.
- National Penitence: Psalms 78, 81, and 106. (Also see Ezra 9:9-15; Nehemiah 9:9-38; Daniel 9:4-19).
- Edgy Laments with curses and requests for God's retribution on enemies: Psalm 109.
- Laments that resolve in trust and faith: Psalms 4, 11, 16, 23, 27:1-6, 62, and 131.
- John Calvin asserted, "...the Psalms are the mirror of the soul." He classified 42 psalms as individual laments, and sixteen as corporate laments.
- R. W. L. Moberly: Ten Lament psalms echo wisdom literature, with their roots in the Torah.
- National Song of Trust: Psalm 125.

The Psalms and their Relationship to Other Books

Pentateuch	Psalm	Magillot	Feast
Genesis	Book 1	Song of Song	Passover
Exodus	Book 2	Ruth	Pentecost
Leviticus	Book 3	Lamentations	Trumpets
Numbers	Book 4	Ecclesiastes	Tabernacles
Deuteronomy	Book 5	Esther	Purim

Physical-Emotional Affect and Lament Psalms

- Lament Images: helpless, outstretched arms, kneeling in humility, abandonment and loneliness, lying helpless and hopeless on the ground. The body acting with the soul and spirit are praying. The grief has become public.
- Physical affects in the Laments: Psalms 22:14-15, 17; 38:3, 7-8, 10, 17; 55:17; 69:3; 77:4-10; 88:4; 137:1.

- Social stressors and disengagement, confusion and relational disruption: Psalms 22:6, 11; 38:9, 11; 41:9; 66:10; 88:8, 18.

- Emotional raggedness: Psalms 13:2; 22:1-2, 6; 38:4, 6, 9; 42:3, 5; 55:4, 5; 56:8; 69:1-2, 20, 29; 73:21; 77:2, 4; 80:4-5; 88:4; 137:9; 143:4.

- Cognitive dissonance and spiritual disorientation: Psalms 13:2; 22:1; 42:11; 43:5; 55:2; 60:1, 3; 69:21-22; 77:3, 7-9; 88:5, 14.

- Behavioral acting out: Psalms 39:12; 55:7-8; 77:4; 88:13; 126:5-6.

The Psalms and their Relationship with the Lord's Prayer:

Michael Matlock, in "Praying the Psalms," drawing from an earlier work by Dietrich Bonhoeffer, *Life Together and the Prayerbook of the Bible*, proposes that in the Lord's Prayer are cues to various psalms, each line, a thread that reaches back to a larger narrative.

- *"Our Father:"* Psalm 23; also, 2:7; 68:5; 89:26; 103:12

- *"Hallowed be Thy name:"* Psalm 8

- *"Thy kingdom come:"* Psalm 110

- *"Thy will be done, on earth as in heaven:"* Psalm 119

- *"Give us this day our daily bread:"* Psalm 136, see the refrain, *"His mercy endures forever,"* and the note, *"God gives food to every creature;"* see also, Psalm 104:14-15, 27-28; 145:15-16; 146:7; 147:9); and,

- *"Forgive us our debts, as we also have forgiven our debtors:"* Psalm 51

- *"Lead us not into temptation:"* Psalm 91

- *"But deliver us from the evil one:"* Psalm 25, especially v. 15

- *"For Thine is the kingdom and the power and the glory forever and ever:"* Psalm 22.

In the psalms, lament occurs:

1. When God seems hidden (Psalm 13, 22, 44).

2. When God is silent. God seems disengaged and inactive (44). He seems to have cast off Israel, dumped them – being the unfaithful party to the covenant. The result is that they are shamed, without a god among the nations with their visible and multiple gods.

3. When God seems inattentive. He is at times accused of sleeping (44:10; 78:6; 121:4).

4. When there are extraordinary external threats. Peace and safety are threatened by enemies (13, 22, 44, 58, 137). God has failed at his task in protecting the nation against their enemies. The enemy has triumphed.

5. When there is internal abuse, for example, the abuse of a leader (58).

6. When death threatens, there is a cause for lament (13).

7. When anxieties are heightened. Apprehension and unrest, a state of misery, may provoke a lament (13), emotions become raw in times of stress.

8. When sin is uncovered. David's great personal lament, laced with repentance, is found in Psalm 51.

9. When there is confusion and disappointment. In Psalm 42, we meet confusion that comes in a time of disappointment and depression, *"My tears have been my food day and night, while people say to me all day long, 'Where is your God?' These things I remember as I pour out my soul: how I used to go to the house of God under the protection of the Mighty One with shouts of joy and praise among the festive throng"* (vv. 3-4).

John Calvin asserted "...the Psalms are the mirror of the soul." At least 42 psalms are individual laments, and another 16 are corporate laments.[10] Ten echo wisdom literature, with roots in the Torah. R. W. L. Moberly argues,

...the predominance of laments at the very heart of Israel's prayers means that the problems that give rise to lament are not something marginal or unusual but rather are central to the life of faith...Moreover they show that the experience of anguish and puzzlement in the life of faith is not a sign of deficient faith, something to be outgrown or put behind one, but rather is intrinsic to the very nature of faith.[11]

10. When there is an abundance of wickedness. Psalm 58 is a striking imprecatory psalm that stands against wicked men who have rebelled against God's kingdom and are intoxicated with abusive self-interests resulting in brutality and injustice.

APPENDIX 2

A Caution Against Mysticism

Mysticism sees prayer as contemplative and meditative. Contemporary Christianity also sees prayer as reflective and meditative – focused on Scripture. But Biblical prayer is more – it is fruitful,[4] it moves to action, it aligns with God, it seeks to do His will, advance His kingdom, and glorify His name. Mysticism jettisons petition, seeing it as a lower form of prayer; as does much of liberal Christianity. Mysticism does so because it is not about promoting a connection with an objective God, the differentiated 'Other,' but about one's own inner strength to do, to become. For mysticism, the god is within. Similarly in liberal Christianity, prayer primarily strengthens one to do, to become, not to plead with God for intervention, into a time-space world.

In Biblical prayer, God is seen as separate, as listening, speaking, and acting, at times in us and through us, yet, at other times, separately, quite apart from us. Somehow prayer connects with His entrance into time-space-history. Prayer is a mystery and God is the greater mystery. Mystery, we embrace; mysticism, we reject. Petition and intercession, appealing to God for action and intervention, we affirm; but self-interested petition and intercession that bends prayer with a focus back on the praying community itself should not be affirmed. It is too narrow, too narcissistic. It fails to see prayer as the forerunner to God's advancing kingdom. Petition, our appearance in the courtroom of heaven is a noble thing, especially if we have come to enter a protest against a world that is resistant to the gospel. Too much of our prayer is in the small claims court of heaven, not in the Supreme Court where we are arguing God's case, "that the earth is the Lord's," and He should immediately claim it.

Christian prayer is at times and in some places, and among certain groups skewed, off-center and theologically warped - and that is a concern. However, mysticism and New Age religions have not skewed prayer - they are wrecked it, with self-interest, man-as-god motifs, prayer as manipulation, prayer as self-gratification, and more. We dare not be influenced by them. We need a profound recovery of bible-informed prayer. Far from confusing ourselves with God, as mysticism and New Age religions do, laments make a clear separation between humanity and God, especially in view of some overwhelming challenge. *"But You, O Lord…"* (Psa. 3:3; 6:3; 22:19; 55:23; 59:5; 86:15; 102:12).

It may seem, in charging God with inaction or a lack of care, that such prayers are disrespectful. Quite the contrary. They have a high view of God, and it is to that view that they appeal – His holiness, His mercy, His benevolence, His power. In these engagements, God may seem to be distant, waiting, charged with sleeping, recognized as enthroned but unengaged. The petitioner petitions, knowing, in contrast, he is human and he is not God. At times, the petitioner feels like a deaf man, unable to hear (Psa. 38:13), poor (70:5), or an innocent victim (26:11). God, however, is powerful. In the moment, the petitioner may feel overwhelmed by circumstances or some evil. So in the prayer, he engages God by faith – *"I have trusted in your steadfast love"* (Psa. 13:5; 31:14; 52:8), and in the unbroken fellowship with God (73:23). Because of God, despite some challenge, his *"head will be lifted up"* (27:6), he will believe (27:13), *"rejoice in the Lord"* (35:9), and hope (71:4) and be glad (109:28).

FOOTNOTES

Chapter 1

1   W. Blaine-Wallace, *A Pastoral Psychology of Lament*, (Robbins; 1993, 2009), 39.

2   Ron Guengerich, *Laments – Misunderstood, Truncated, Exiled, Silenced* (Vision: Fall, 2006), 48.

3   Hermann Gunkel, "A Form-Critical Classification of the Psalms," < biblical-studies.ca/pdfs/Gunkel_Classification_of_the_Psalms.pdf. Accessed 9/24/2016>.

4   Gunkel includes Psalms 3; 5; 6; 7; 13; 17; 22; 25; 26; 27:7-14; 28; 31; 35; 38; 39; 42-43; 54-57; 59; 61; 63; 64; 69; 70; 71; 86; 88; 102; 109; 120; 130; 140; 141; 142; 143 as individual laments.

5   Gunkel classified Psalms 44; (58); (60); 74; 79; 80; 83; (106); (125), as communal laments.

6   Guengerich, Ibid.

7   Leonard P Maré, *A Pentecostal Perspective on the Use of Psalms of Lament in Worship* (Ph. D. Thesis: University of South Africa, 1988). <www.academia.edu/6233171/A_Pentecostal_perspective_on_the_use_of_Psalms_of_Lament_in_worship>.

8   Ibid.

9   Guengerich.

10   Bernhard W. Anderson, *Out of the Depth: The Psalms Speak for Us Today* (Philadelphia, PA: The Westminster Press, 1983), 66; Quoted by Jason Jackson, "A Prayer of the Afflicted: A Study of Psalm 102." <www.christiancourier.com/articles/1154-prayer-of-the- afflicted-a-study-of-psalm-102-a>.

11   Anderson, 76-77. The elements – address to God, complaint, confession of trust, petition or request of God, words of assurance, and vow of praise, very similar to Ferris, Gunkel and others.

12   Donald G. Bloesch, *Spirituality Old and New: Recovering Authentic Spiritual Life* (IVP Academic: Downers Grove, IL; 2007), 31.

13   Dietrich Bonhoeffer, *Life Together: Prayerbook of the Bible*; G. B. Kelly, ed. (DBW), 5.

14   Charles Spurgeon, *The Complete Works of C. H. Spurgeon*, Volume 36:

Sermons 2121-2181.

15 R. Mark Shipp; Editors: Michael R. Weed and M. Todd Hall, *Christian Studies: Scholarship for the Church,* "Psalm 22 – The Prayer of the Righteous Sufferer" (Austin Graduate School of Theology; Volume 25; 2011-2012), 50-51.

16 Walter Brueggemann, *The Psalms: The Life of Faith, From Hurt to Joy, From Death to Life,* 67-83; *The Formfulness of Grief,* 84-97; *The Costly Loss of Lament,* 98-111.

17 Craig Broyles, *The Conflict of Faith and Experience in the Psalms: A Form-Critical and Theological Study,* (University of Pennsylvania Press), 13; Review by, Ellen F. Davis, Jewish Quarterly Review, Volume 82, No. 1/2 (July-October, 1991), 191-193. <www.jstor.org/stable/1455011?seq=1#page_scan_tab_contents>.

18 Paul Wayne Ferris, Jr., *The Genre of Communal Lament, SBL Dissertation Series,* (Atlanta, GA: Scholars Press, 1992), 7.

19 Hermann Gunkel and Joachim Begrich, *An Introduction to the Psalms* (trans. James D. Nogalski; MLBS; Macon, GA: Mercer Univer- sity Press, 1998).

20 Heath A. Thomas, *Relating Prayer and Pain: Psychological Analysis and Lamentations Research,* Bulletin 61/2 (2010), 183-208 (197-206).

21 Heath A. Thomas, *The Power of Lament Prayer: Commentary on Habakkuk.* Online book preview. Permission is given by the author. The language "God-denying/affirming" is borrowed.

22 Claus Westermann, *Praise and Lament in the Psalms* (Atlanta: John Knox Press, 1965, 1981), 52.

23 Gunkel, Ibid.

24 Quote by C. S. Lewis, *Christian Clippings* (New Port Richey, FL; January-March, 2014), 16. See also: www.ChristianClippings.com.

25 Tennessee Williams. Quoted by W. Blaine-Wallace, *A Pastoral Psychology of Lament,* (Robbins; 1993, 2009), 175.

26 Ibid.

27 Donald G. Bloesch, *Spirituality Old and New: Recovering Authentic Spiritual Life* (IVP Academic: Downers Grove, IL; 2007), 133.

Chapter 2

1   In the KJV, the structure of the five books of psalms was not preserved in the translation, but it can be seen in the original Hebrew texts.

2   Dr. Ernest Martin, Restoring the Original Bible, "Preliminary Suggestions on the Structure of the Book of Psalms," 474-482. Online resource: "The Structure of the Book of Psalms," <afaithfulversion. org/appendices-b>.

3   James L. Mays, *The Lord Reigns – A Theological Handbook to the Psalms*

(Westminster John Knox Press; November, 1994), 12-22.

4   Seumas Macdonald, <thepatrologist.com>. This site is a blog, by Dr. Macdonald, who studies patrology, or patristics, the study of early Christian writers and theologians between the 1st and around the 7th century. The blog has a number of blog posts and additional resources, some related to Greek and Latin language studies, as well as the Classics, Patristics, and Theology. Macdonald holds a BA in Philosophy and a PhD in Ancient History. He is an Anglican, and a retired seminary professor, who taught Greek, Hebrew, New Testament, and Church History in Mongolia. At present, he works as a freelance academic, translator, and language instructor.

5   Ibid.

6   Charles Spurgeon quoted by James Nicodem, *Prayer Coach* (Wheaton, IL: Crossway Books, 2008), 87. Source: Charles Spurgeon, *Morning and Evening.*

7   Macdonald.

8   Walter Brueggemann, *The Message of the Psalms* (Minneapolis, MN: Augsburg, 1984), 167. Reference by Seumas Macdonald.

9   Glenn Pemberton, *Hurting with God* (Abilene, TX: Abilene Christian University Press, 2012).

10   Charles Spurgeon, <www. brainyquote.com/quotes/keywords/lament. html>.

11   Philip Yancey, *The Bible Jesus Read,* (Grand Rapids, MI: Zondervan, 2002).

Chapter 3

1   Bryant McGill, *Simple Reminders: Inspiration for Living Your Best Life.* Goodreads Quote: <www.goodreads.com/quotes/tag/emotional-pain>.

2   Westermann, *Praise and Lament in the Psalms,* 169.

3   Bruce Waltke, quoted by G. K. Beale and D. A. Carson, eds., *Commentary of the New Testament on the Old Testament,* (Grand Rapids: Baker Academic, 2007), 638.

4   Walter Brueggemann, *The Psalms and the Life of Faith,* Fortress Press, 1995.

5   Paul Wayne Ferris, *Lament,* 14.

6   B. W. Anderson, *Out of the Depths* (Philadelphia: Westmin- ster, 1983), 242.

7   W. H. Bellinger, Jr., *Psalms: Reading and Studying the Book of Psalms* (Peabody, MA: Hendrickson, 1990), 45.

8   Bouzard, *We Have Heard,* 113.

Chapter 4

1   Bruce K. Waltke and Charles Yu, *An Old Testament Theology* (Grand Rapids: Zondervan, 2005), 10-12, 875-80.

2   St. Basil the Great, "A Lament for Sin." An online resource.

3   Ibid.

4   C. A. Vos, *Theopoetry of the Psalms* (London: T & T Clark International, 2005), 79.

5   Vernard Eller, ed., *Thy Kingdom Come: A Blumhardt Reader* (Grand Rapids: Eerdmans, 1980), 77.

6   R. Mark Shipp; Editors: Michael R. Weed and M. Todd Hall, *Christian Studies: Scholarship for the Church*, "Psalm 22 – The Prayer of the Righteous Sufferer" (Austin Graduate School of Theology; Volume 25; 2011-2012), 58.

7   Ibid, 59.

8   Karl Rahner, "On the Theology of the Incarnation," *Theological Investigation,* Vol. 4, trans. Kevin Smyth (Baltimore: Helicon Press, 1966), 116.

9   Alan Watts, *Behold the Spirit: A Study in the Necessity of Mystical Religion* (New York: Vintage Books, 1971), 17.

10   R.W. L. Moberly, "Lament," NIDOTTE, IV, 879.

11   Ibid.

12   Claus Westermann, *Praise and Lament in the Psalms,* 15.

13   Jason Jackson, "A Prayer of the Afflicted: A Study of Psalm 102." ChristianCourier.com. Access date: July 30, 2016. <www.christiancourier.com/articles/1154-prayer-of-the-afflicted-a-study-of-psalm-102-a>. Jackson draws from a number of other sources: Allen, Leslie C. 1983. *Word Biblical Commentary. Psalms 101-150.* Waco, TX: Word; Barnes, Albert. 1950 Ed. *Notes on the Old Testament – Psalms.* Vol. 3. Grand Rapids, MI: Baker; Harrison, Everett F. ed. 1960. *Baker's Dictionary of Theology.* "Deism" by J. Oliver Buswell, Jr. Grand Rapids, MI: Baker; Maclaren, Alexander. nd, *The Psalms.* Vol. 3. New York: George H. Doran Co.; Spurgeon, Charles. nd, *The Treasury of David.*

14   Ibid.

15   Othmar Keel, *The Symbolism of the Biblical World: Ancient Near Eastern Iconography and the Book of Psalms,* trans. Timothy J. Hallett (Winona Lake, IN: Eisenbrauns, 1997), 318-23.

16   Walter Brueggemann, *Voice as Counter to Violence* (A lecture delivered at Calvin Theological Seminary; April 22, 1993).

17   Shipp, 54.

18   Ibid.

19   Brueggemann, *Voice as Counter to Violence.*

Chapter 5

1 Andrew Williams, "Biblical Lament and Political Protest" – an online resource.

2 Bruce K. Waltke, James M. Houston, Erika Moore, *The Psalms as Christian Lament* (Wm. B. Eerdmans Publishing, 2014), 1.

3 Keel, *Symbolism,* 318-19.

4 There is a place for intercessory laments, but the power of the lament is that it is offered by the person or people in pain. They appear before God and lament. They offer their complaint. They detail the problems, in some cases, charge God. They plead for his intervention – this is not a job for a surrogate. Once the plea has been entered, God enlists intercessory voices to join the plea.

5 R. Mark Shipp; Editors: Michael R. Weed and M. Todd Hall, *Christian Studies: Scholarship for the Church,* "Psalm 22 – The Prayer of the Righteous Sufferer (Austin Graduate School of Theology; Volume 25; 2011-2012), 48.

6 "The Psalms as Christian Lament," 7-14.

7 Erich Zengar, *A God of Vengeance? Understanding the Psalms of Divine Wrath,* trans. by Linda M. Maloney (Louisville: Westminster/John Knox Press, 1996), 38.

8 Martin Luther, *Word and Sacrament, Luther's Works,* vol. 1, ed. E. T. Bachmann (Philadelphia:Fortress, 1960), 255-56.

9 Brueggemann, *The Costly Loss of Lament,* 64.

10 Quoted by Teresa S. Johnson, *Treasures of Hope: Testimonies of Hope* (Author House: Bloomington, IN, 2010), 20.

11 Brueggemann, "Models and Authorizations: An Interview with Walter Brueggemann." Interview by Micky Jones, Online Resource.

12 John Mark Hicks, *Preaching Community Laments: Responding to Disillusionment with God and Injustice in the World.*

13 <www.negrospirituals.com/news-song/sometimes_i_fell.htm>.

14 Dave Bland and David Fleer, eds., *Performing the Psalms* (Chalice Press: St. Louis, MO, 2005), 79. See also, John Mark Hicks, referencing, Daniel L. Migliore and Kathleen D. Billman. *Rachel's Cry: Prayer of Lament and Rebirth of Hope* (Cleveland, Ohio: United Church Press, 1999).

15 W.E.B. Du Bois, *The Souls of Black Folk,* 1903. Portions of the work can be found online at: <www.bartleby.com/114/14.html>.

16 A spiritual that is believed to have organized in the Appalachian mountains, author unknown.

17 <www.negrospirituals.com/news-song/trouble_done_bore_me_down. htm>.

18 Ron Guengerich is a pastor at Zion Mennonite Church in Archbold, Ohio. Before pastoring, he taught at Hesston College (Hesston, Kansas) and Eastern Mennonite Seminary (Harrisonburg, Virginia), following doctoral studies in Old Testament at the University of Michigan.

Chapter 6

1 Dietrich Bonhoeffer, "A Bonhoeffer Sermon," trans. by Donald Bloesch, *Theology Today* 38 (1982), 465-71, available at <theologyto-day.ptsem.edu/jan1982/v38-4-article3.htm>.
2 Ibid, 469.
3 Zengar, *God of Vengeance*, 85.
4 Quoted by Donald G. Bloesch, *Spirituality Old and New: Recovering Authentic Spiritual Life* (IVP Academic: Downers Grove, IL; 2007), 57.
5 Walter Brueggemann, "Models and Authorizations: An Interview with Walter Brueggemann." Interview by Micky Jones, Online Resource.
6 Bloesch, 94.
7 Ibid, 95.
8 Ibid.
9 Martin Luther, quoted by Michael Parsons, David J. Cohen, *On Eagles' Wings: An Exploration of Strength in the Midst of Weakness* (Cambridge, United Kingdom: The Lutterworth Press, 2008), 100.
10 Cf. Paul Wayne Ferris, Jr., *The Genre of Communal Lament in the Bible and the Ancient Near East*, SBL Dissertation Series 127 (Atlanta, GA: Scholars Press, 1992), 107-108.

Chapter 7

1 Maria Boulding, *Gateway to Hope: An Exploration of Failure* (Petersham, MA: St. Bede's, 1985), 37-38.
2 John Koessler, "Theology Matters: God, Emotion and Suffering" (Moody Institute of the Bible; Online Resource, Devotional: Job 42:7-12, "The False Comfort of Easy Answers," Friday, October 24; from 'Today in the Word'), 31.
3 Lawrence A. Hoffman, *Beyond the Text: A Holistic Approach to Liturgy* (Bloomington: Indiana University Press, 1987).
4 There is almost a sense here of Genesis 2:19-20, when Adam is presented a parade of God's creation, the animals brought to pass before him, and his naming of them. The wisdom he failed to extract from that moment, Job now perceives. For him, the sovereignty of God is settled, his questions are answered, but for Adam, the sovereignty of God has been

left open to a challenge. When the questions came, from the serpent at the tree, Adam did not have the right answers. In reaching the last few chapters of Job, one has to be struck with wonder. It is a stunning mental safari of nature, leading to the obvious – we live in the midst of mystery. We cannot understand God's ways with the wind and water, or yet, the animals, so how can we fully grasp his ways with us? We are left to trust. We must live within our limitations as do the animals is the lesson from Job. And it is precisely the opposite that Lucifer's formula suggested in the garden, namely, the throwing off of limitations, the rejection of God's sovereignty for the reach of our own – an illusion. Limitation, in the garden, demanded dependency on God; in our world, we are offered the fruit of the same poisonous tree – a life of independence from God and anyone or anything else. Hyper-individualism, it is both old and new.

Chapter 8

1 P. Douglas Small, *The Praying Church Handbook, Volume III*, "In Search of a Pentecostal Liturgy," (Kannapolis, NC: Alive Publications, 2015), 316.

2 Of course, writings attributed to the Apostles were collected and circulated early, as were Pauline epistles. By the end of the first century AD, they were probably being read alongside Old Testament readings in Christian gatherings. Justin Martyr mentions the "memoirs of the apostles" being read on Sunday alongside the "writings of the prophets." By 180 AD, Irenaeus had collected the four gospels and asserted their usage. In the early 3rd century, Origen is said to have collected the same 27 books that comprise our New Testament. For the next 200 years, however, some leaders and churches disputed the credibility of such books as Hebrews, James, 2 Peter, 2 and 3 John, as well as Jude and the Revelation. By the middle of the 3rd Century, most Christians accepted the list of books we read in our NT. In 367, Athanasius, Bishop of Alexandria, used the term "canonized" in reference to the list of the 27 books. Church councils subsequently ratified that idea, and soon the books as a whole collection began to be circulated.

3 Bulletin for Biblical Research, 21.2 (2011) 213-226; "NT Scholars' Use of OT Lament Terminology and Its Theological and Interdisciplinary Implications," Keith Campbell: International Institute for Christian Studies. (Paper presented at the annual meeting of the Evangelical Theological Society, New Orleans, LA, November 19, 2009).

4 Keith Campbell, 761.

5 Ibid, 759.

6   Matthew 15:8-9; 26:26-27; Mark 14:22-23; John 4; Luke 4:16; 22:19-20; Acts 2:42; 5:42; 15:21; 20:7; 1 Corinthians 11:23-26; 14; 2 Corinthians 3:15; 1 Thess. 5:12-21, 27; Col. 4:6; Heb. 10:24-25.

7   Michael Matlock, "Praying the Psalms" (with Assistance from the Lord's Prayer,) Biblical Studies, Christian Formation and Discipleship; On- line Resource. Matlock, citing an earlier work by Dietrich Bonhoeffer, Life Together and the Prayerbook of the Bible, proposes that in the Lord's Prayer are cues to various psalms, each line, a thread that reaches back to a larger narrative. Our Father (Psalm 23; also, 2:7; 68:5; 89:26; 103:12); Hallowed be Thy name (Psalm 8); Thy kingdom come (Psalm 110); Thy will be done, on earth as in heaven (Psalm 119); Give us this day our daily bread (Psalm 136, see the refrain, *"His mercy endures forever,"* and the note, *"God gives food to every creature;"* see also, Psalm 104:14-15, 27-28; 145:15-16; 146:7; 147:9); and forgive us our debts, as we also have forgiven our debtors (Psalm 51); and lead us not into temptation (Psalm 91), but deliver us from the evil one (Psalm 25, especially v. 15); for Thine is the kingdom and the power and the glory forever and ever (Psalm 22). Date of this posting: 4/9/2014.

8   Keith Campbell, *NT Lament in Current Research and Its Implications for American Evangelicals* (JETS 57/4, 2014), 757-72.

9   R. Mark Shipp; Editors: Michael R. Weed and M. Todd Hall, *Christian Studies: Scholarship for the Church*, "Psalm 22 – The Prayer of the Righteous Sufferer" (Austin Graduate School of Theology; Volume 25; 2011-2012), 58.

10 Campell.

11 Campbell, 764. 12 Ibid, 764.

12 Ibid, 764.

13 Quote by O. Hallesby.

14 Quote from Charles Spurgeon.

15 Patrick D. Miller, "Trouble and Woe: Interpreting the Biblical Laments," Interpretation 37 (1983): 34-35. Gerald T. Sheppard, "Enemies and the Politics of Prayer in the Book of Psalms," in The Bible and the Politics of Exegesis, ed. David Jobling, Peggy I. Day, and Gerald T. Sheppard (Cleveland: Pilgrim, 1991), 70.

16 Francis Bacon, "Essays or Counsels Civil and Moral," Essay V, in Harvard Classics, vol. 3, ed. Charles W. Eliot (New York: P. F. Collier & Son, 1937), 16.

17 Quote by Charles E. Cowman.

Chapter 9

1   Keith Campbell. See also: Gail O'Day, "Surprised by Faith: Jesus and the Canaanite Woman," Listening 24 (1989), 290-301; Martin Ebner, "Klage und Auferweckungshoffnung im Neuen Testament"; and Matthew Boulton, "Forsaking God: A Theological Argument for Christian Lamentation," SJT 55 (2002), 58-78.

2   Keith Campbell, reflecting on Stephen Ahearne-Kroll, "The Psalms of Lament in Mark's Passion: Jesus' Davidic Suffering (SNTSMS 142; Cambridge: Cambridge University Press, 2007).

3   <biblehub.com/greek/4036.htm, Strongs #4036>.

4   Mary Todd Lincoln, <www. brainyquote.com/quotes/authors/b/basil_hume.htmlcom/quotes/authors/b/basil_hume.html>.

5   Kenneth Scott Latourette, historian, <www. brainyquote.com/ quotes/ keywords/ triumph_3.html>.

6   George S. Patton, Jr., <www.goodreads. com/quotes/tag/triumph?page=3html>.

7   Basil Hume, English Clergyman, <www.brainyquote.com/ quotes/authors/b/basil_hume.html>.

Chapter 10

1   Saliers, Don (2015) "Psalms in Our Lamentable World," Yale Journal of Music & Religion: Vol. 1: Iss. 1, Article 7. DOI: dx.doi. org/10.17132/2377-231X.1013.

2   Glenn Pemberton, Hurting with God (Abilene, TX: Abilene Christian University Press, 2012).

3   Roger E. Van Harn and Brent A. Strawn, eds., Psalms for Preaching and Worship: A Lectionary Commentary (Grand Rapids, Mich.: Eerdmans, 2009), xv–xvi.

4   Soong-Chan Rah, "The American Church's Absence of Lament," 10-24-2013; Movie: "12 Years a Slave."

5   Ibid.

6   Saliers.

7   Samuel Ballentine. Quoted by Ruth Haley Barton, "The Prayer of Lament: What To Do When We Don't Know What To Do"; Online Resource: Transforming Center (209 S. Naperville Rd.; Wheaton, IL 60187).

8   Walter Brueggemann, 'The Costly Loss of Lament', Journal of Studies of Old Testament, 1986, 60, 59.

9   Walter Brueggemann, The Prophetic Imagination, 2nd edn, Fortress Press, 2001, 11.

10 Bruce K. Waltke, James M. Houston, and Erika Moore, *The Psalms as Christian Lament* (Wm. B. Eerdmans Publishing, 2014), 5.

11 Saliers, Don (2015) "Psalms in Our Lamentable World," *Yale Jour- nal of Music & Religion: Vol. 1: Iss. 1,* Article 7. DOI: dx.doi. org/10.17132/2377-231X.1013.

12 Ibid.

13 Unidentified quote, *Christian Clippings* (New Port Richey, FL; July-September, 2014), 46.

14 Saliers, Ibid.

15 Ibid.

16 Ibid.

17 J. P. Millar, Ed., *The Preacher's Complete Homiletical Commentary:* (on an Original Plan), Volume 6; Chapter IV, Homiletical Commentary: Judges, (New York: Funk and Wagnalls, 1896), 207.

18 Bruce Waltke, Ibid.

19 Richard Foster, *Celebration of Discipline,* 33.

20 Salier. Ibid.

21 Quote from E. M. Bounds.

22 W. Blaine-Wallace, *A Pastoral Psychology of Lament,* 67.

23 Phillip Yancey, *Rumors of Another World: What on earth are we missing?* (Grand Rapids, MI: Zondervan, 2003), 43.

24 Ibid, 99.

25 A. W. Tozer, *The Quotable Tozer I,* Harry Verploegh, compiler (Camp Hill, PA: Christian Publications, 1984), 112. Source: *Born After Midnight,* 1959, 100.

26 Ibid, 43.

27 Ibid, 100.

28 Yancey, 25.

29 Walter Brueggemann, *The Message of the Psalms,* 68.

30 Ibid, 67.

31 John Mark Hicks, *Preaching Community Laments: Responding to Disillusionment with God and Injustice in the World.*

32 Blaine-Wallace, 37.

33 Marceline Loridan-Ivens, *But You Did Not Come Back.* Goodreads Quote: <www.goodreads.com/quotes/tag/emotional-pain?page=2>.

34 Philip Yancey, *The Bible Jesus Read,* <www.goodreads.com/quotes/tag/lament>.

Chapter 11

1 Hermann Gunkel, "A Form-Critical Classification of the Psalms," Online Resource: biblical-studies.ca/pdfs/Gunkel_Classification_of_the_

Psalms.pdf. Accessed 9/24/2016.

2   Gunkel includes Psalms 3; 5; 6; 7; 13; 17; 22; 25; 26; 27:7-14; 28; 31; 35; 38; 39; 42-43; 54-57; 59; 61; 63; 64; 69; 70; 71; 86; 88; 102; 109; 120; 130; 140; 141; 142; 143 as individual laments.

3   Gunkel classified Psalms 44; (58); (60); 74; 79; 80; 83; (106); (125), as communal laments.

4   Gunkel.

5   Ibid.

6   Charles Finney, "The GOSPEL TRUTH: The Oberlin Evangelist," Professor Finney's Lectures: "Grieving the Holy Spirit (Lecture XXI, December 4, 1839). Source: <www.gospeltruth.net/1839OE/391204_grieving_hs1.htm>.

7   Keith Campbell, reflecting on Rosann M. Catalono, "How Long, O Lord? A Systematic Study of the Theology and Practice of the Biblical Lament" (Ph. D. diss., University of St. Michael's College, 1988).

8   Walter Brueggemann, *Voice as Counter to Violence* (A lecture delivered at Calvin Theological Seminary; April 22, 1993). Online resource: <www.google.com/search?q=voice+as+counter+to+vio - lence&oq=voice+as+counter+&aqs=chrome.1.69i57j0l5.6544j0j8&-sourceid=chrome&ie=UTF-8>.

9   Elaine Scarry, *The Body in Pain: The Making and Unmaking of the World* (New York: Oxford University Press, 1987). See also: William T. Cavanaugh, *Torture and Eucharist: Theology, Politics, and the Body of Christ* (Oxford: Blackwell, 1998). Cited by Brueggemann.

10   Ibid.

11   Homer, *The Odyssey;* <www.goodreads.com/quotes/tag/lament>.

12   Glenn Pemberton, *Hurting with God;* <www.goodreads. com/quotes/tag/lament>.

13   Paul Wayne Ferris, *Lament,* 89-100.

Chapter 12

1   Walter Brueggemann, *Voice as Counter to Violence* (A lecture delivered at Calvin Theological Seminary; April 22, 1993).

2   'Saints' is typically plural in form. Only once is it used in the singular. Solitary saints are not a common biblical notion. We need community to keep us holy.

3   From the Aramaic, Barabbâ, "son of the father." Some ancient manuscripts of Matthew 27:16-17 have the full, "Jesus Barabbas," as it was originally written in the text (See: Craig A. Evans, Matthew, New Cambridge Bible Commentary, published by Cambridge University

Press, 2012, 453. See also: William Warren, "Who Changed the Text and Why? Probable, Possible, and Unlikely Explanations," *The Reliability of the New Testament,* Fortress Press. 118. Origen was troubled by the fact that the earliest copies of the gospels gave the full name of Barabbas – "Jesus Barabbas." And he declared that it was impossible that such a despicable character should have such a holy name, "Jesus." He supposed the name had been added, as a kind of insult, by some heretic. And therefore, the appellation "Jesus" should be removed from the text in reference to Barabbas. It dishonored the Messiah.

4   Jesus Barabbas may have had connections with the sicarii, a radical, militant group of Jews who sought the overthrow of the Roman occupation by insurrection, murder, or any other means. Political independence, at any cost, was their goal. Their ethics were unscrupulous, but their goals were consistent with the Jewish mainstream. Jesus Barabbas, who called for a political revolution, even if procured by immoral means, was preferable to Jesus of Nazareth, who called for a revolution of heart.

5   Ole Kristian Hallesby, *Prayer* (Minneapolis, MN: Augsburg Publishing, 1975), 17.

6   Brueggemann.

7   Ibid.

8   Ibid.

9   Martin Luther King, Jr.; Quote at: <www. brainyquote.com/ quotes/ keywords/silence. html>.

Chapter 13

1   In the chapter entitled, "The Lament Psalms – Finding a Theological Trajectory," we pointed out that Psalms 1, 2, and 3 provide a kind of trajectory for the entire book. Of course, the book of Habakkuk is not written on this specific paradigm. He does reference those psalms, and, yet, he is a kind of Psalm 1 idealist, longing for its clear, crisp theology: the righteous are blessed, they prosper; and the wicked perish, they are judged. In Psalm 2, we are immediately met with a challenge to that idea. Nations, it is said, rage against God. Righteousness is challenged, globally. The kings of the earth, rather than honor God, are aligned against Him. Historically, this references David, but eschatologically, it points to Christ, and arguably, beyond Christ, to the era of the end-times and the Anti-Christ and the coming global alliance he will forge and lead. Then, in Psalm 3, we are met with another surprise. The rebellion in David's own house, the defection of Absalom, and his treacherous reach for his father's throne, his dishonor of his father

and his failure to remain loyal. Habakkuk seems to long for the clear crisp edges of Psalm 1 – why can't righteous people be blessed, wicked people punished, and that be that? Why, Psalm 2, do the nations rage, do things seem to be upside down? Why are evil men empowered? Why do they prosper? Why does God not intervene? He is an idealist! Against the backdrop of Psalm 1's idealism, the international turmoil reflected in Psalm 2, and, the treachery of Jehoiakim, who abandons the reforms of his father – we see in the background all the dynamics of Psalm 1, 2, and 3 played out.

2   Cambridge Bible for Schools and Colleges, *Commentary on Habakkuk 1:14;* See <biblehub.com/commentaries/habakkuk/1-14.htm>.

3   Heath A. Thomas, *The Power of Lament Prayer: Commentary on Habakkuk.* Online book preview. Permission is given by the author.

4   Donald G. Bloesch, *Spirituality Old and New: Recovering Authentic Spiritual Life* (IVP Academic: Downers Grove, IL; 2007), 133.

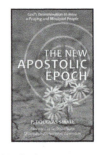

HOST A SCHOOL OF PRAYER
WWW.PROJECTPRAY.ORG

"I can't believe how this has changed my prayer life."

A School of Prayer is training focused on learning, experiencing and leading in the area of prayer. Schools of Prayer are facilitated by P. Douglas Small or through our new associate presenter program. Our glorious role is help people begin to recover a Biblical view of prayer, one that is not merely transactional and acquisitional, but also transformational.

PRAYER – THE HEART OF IT ALL
Grow deeper in your prayer life by discovering why God wants us to pray. Discover how to: develop a personal prayer life; pray together as a family; start a prayer ministry in your church; prayer missionally for others and for a Great Awakening.

THE PRAYER CLOSET: CREATING A PERSONAL PRAYER ROOM
What we seek is more than mere words or a disciplined, noble routine for prayer. Prayer is a relationship that has to be centered in the heart. Prayer is not something we do, it is someone we are with. And that needs a place!

THE GREAT EXCHANGE: WHY YOUR PRAYER REQUESTS MAY NOT BE GETTING ANSWERS
Prayer works, because God works. It is effective, because its hope is in Him and His action. But it also demands changes in us. Learn practical steps to answered pray!